ISRAEL'S COMING REVIVAL

ISRAEL'S COMING REVIVAL

THE UNTOLD STORY

Dr. Peter Wyns

$21.95

To contact the author, please write to the below postal or email address:
Great Reward Publishing – a ministry of Christian for Messiah Ministries
PO Box 36324
Rock Hill, SC 29732
www.peterwyns.org
email: ReachUs@peterwyns.com

All scriptures taken from the New International Version unless otherwise noted.
Scriptures taken from the Holy Bible, New International Version ®.

First Great Reward Publishing edition published 2010.

Cover design by: Mike Wedge

Special editing by Sarah Roach, Jesse Enns and Mary Greene

Manufactured in the United States of America.
By Books Just Books.

ISBN: 978-0-9771633-6-6

CONTENTS

Israel's National Defense 121

Israel's Revival and Beyond 179

DEDICATION

I dedicate this book to my grandmother Lydia Prince, who, before she married Derek Prince, was Lydia Christensen. She was the first one of my maternal family to answer the call for the ministry. In 1928, she took a step of faith, left Demark and became a missionary in Jerusalem. Soon after, she was caring for children in the city of Ramalah. It was there in 1933 that she recieved my Jewish mother, Miryim Magdelene Katz, who at the time was five days old.

In 1943 a young soldier named Derek Prince visited her. She introduced him to the importance of God's chosen people, the Jews. Soon after, they married and adopted nine girls as their own.

Grandma Lydia was the pioneer who followed the Lord, rescued my mother, connected Derek Prince to his Israel-focused ministry, and stood by his side as a powerful minister of the gospel for more than thirty-two years.

Grandma Lydia, we owe so much to you. Thank you for being a great example. Thank you for your compassion for children, your love for Israel, and your amazing faith for the work of the ministry.

INTRODUCTION

I come by it honestly; God prepared me for the message of Israel and put me in the ministry. I can see His fingerprints on my life as I look back. I was unaware of it at the time, but He ordered my steps, gave me revelation and commissioned me to teach His Church about His love for Israel.

My mother was a Jewish baby from the tribe of Levi when she was adopted by Grandma Lydia and then by Derek Prince, after he married Grandma. My father, Irvine Wyns, was a Pentecostal preacher, but he married one of Derek's daughters, so from the days of my youth I learned about God's chosen people.

In 1943 Grandpa Derek visited Lydia in Jerusalem, and God began to teach him about His plans for Israel. Later, he became a well-known international Bible teacher, and God used him to restore the message of Israel to the Church. He became my mentor, and the revelation and spiritual anointing that I received from him has formed the focus of my ministry.

For more than forty years, I have studied my Jewish roots and taught on God's special call to the Jewish people. I am amazed at the constant flow of new revelation that comes from the Scriptures on this theme. In years past, I have preached hundreds of sermons, written many articles and composed a four-part booklet of notes about Israel. Since I was a young preacher, I have known that I was to write this book. The timing of the Lord for Israel has come, and I have been called to play a small part in the unveiling of her blessings.

The Lord said to Daniel that His revelation about the last days would be sealed and hidden from view until the end times (see Daniel 12:9-10). The end times have begun, and revelation about Israel that has not been known is now coming to light. God has turned His search light on the Scriptures, and many people are discovering the depth of His love and the power of His plans for Israel.

The story of Israel's future is largely an untold story. In this book I share dozens of truths of which most Christians are not aware. Due to a lack of knowledge, many good people are in the dark regarding this subject. That means they minimize Israel's importance and fail to focus on the issues of the day that God is focusing on. Because of this lack of understanding, many who want to be in the center of God's will, at this time in history, are actually on the periphery. The following list reveals some of the details that I focus on in this book. I trust the book will be a tool that will help train and equip you for the call of God on your life and your partnership with Him for these last days.

I have written this book because so many do not know.

1. Many Christians have erroneously viewed Israel as insignificant and unimportant in the end-time purposes of God.
2. Most Christians have never heard that God Almighty is planning to move His thone room to planet Earth and set up His new headquarters in Jerusalem.
3. Some Christians have no understanding of Israel's coming revival.
4. Some Christians have no idea that Israel will be honored as chief among the nations.
5. Some Christians do not grasp the details of Israel's promised inheritance.
6. Some Christians have no idea of the one-new-man anointing that is coming for Israel and the Church.
7. Many Christians do not understand that the Church cannot reach her potential until Israel is restored and partners with her.
8. Many Christians fail to understand Israel's special identity and her amazing role in the eternal purposes of God.

These, and many other truths, are uncovered in the writing of this book. I trust that it will be an amazing blessing to you, that your faith will be greatly increased and that your focus on the purposes of God will be sharpened.

PART ONE

THE RESTORATION
OF ISRAEL

CHAPTER ONE

ISRAEL IS SPECIAL

ISRAEL - A BIBLE THEME

EXCEPT for the first eleven chapters of Genesis, almost all of the Old Testament is about the Jews. I am amazed at how much the Bible speaks of them. I am taken aback when I think of the intensity of God's focus on this small group of people called Israel.

Even in the New Testament, we find undeniable attention given to the Jews. More than seven hundred verses in the New Testament address the subject of the Jews or one of their twelve tribes.

It seems that God is staring at the Jews with a relentless kind of passion. Throughout history, He will not take His eyes off of them. He called them His people in the distant past and will once again, in the future, embrace them and focus His love toward them.

THE JEWISH CROWN

One day, He intends to hold them in His hand like a king holds a crown. Speaking of Israel's future, the Lord says the following:

"You will be a *crown of splendor* in the Lord's hand, a royal diadem in the hand of your God" (Isa. 62:3; italics added).

The Lord says that Israel will be a crown of splendor in His hands. That means that Israel is special. Like a king's crown, Israel will become a symbol of God's glory and blessings.

This picture of God's Jewish crown can be discovered in other parts of the Bible. If we have eyes to see, we find it in Revelation 12. Here, the Lord presents to us an elaborate illustration of His human family on earth: "a woman clothed with the sun." We read:

"A great and wondrous sign appeared … *a woman clothed with the sun*, with the moon under her feet and a crown of twelve stars on her head" (Rev. 12:1; italics added).

As always, the sun is God, and the woman clothed with the sun is God's bride or family. God's people are ideally clothed with the grace and glory of the Lord. The woman represents the people of God throughout history. A few verses later, in the same chapter of Revelation, we discover that she will give birth to the powerful, prophetic, end-time Church. This is the Church that will overcome the devil by the blood of the Lamb and the word of her testimony. This is the Church whose members are not afraid to die for the cause of Christ when the Great Tribulation comes (see Revelation 12:11).

The woman clothed with the sun is defined by the crown of twelve stars on her head; these stars represent Israel. She is further defined by what she is standing on. She stands on the moon, and the moon represents the Gentile Church. The woman clothed with the sun is a picture of the people of God. The Lord has two human groups that He identifies Himself with: Israel and the Church.

ISRAEL IS LOVED

Israel is the unquestionable apple of God's eye, the sheep of His pasture; the Jews are God's chosen people. If you are a Gentile, do not despair; the Jews are not His only children. It is not that He loves Israel only; God loves the whole world. Every man and woman was made in His image. Besides the crown (the Jews), the woman clothed with the sun is defined by the moon (the Gentile Church) beneath her feet. At both ends of the woman, at her head and at her feet, we have people whom God calls His own.

A good father loves all of his children, but every child is different. A father may encourage and even designate different responsibilities to different children. He may promise something to one and not to all. Even though he sees a different gift or purpose for each child, he loves them equally, for all of them are his children.

The Jews hold a very special position in the plans and purposes of God, and He has a unique task for them and endears Himself to them for this purpose. He will never let them go.

AN EXAMPLE FOR THE WORLD

The Lord uses the Jews as an example for all of the nations to see; they are an object lesson for the world. The Lord demonstrates His intentions for humanity by showing the details of His involvement with the Jews. Watching the Jewish story of failure and restoration gives hope to every man and every nation. Many Christians (the Gentiles who serve the God of the Jews) even call themselves "spiritual Israel" (although this title is an error). They do this because they identify, to such a great extent, with the Jewish disposition.

A student of the late C. S. Lewis said, "We read to know that we are not alone." [1]

Well I say, "Then read about Israel, and you will find that you are not alone!"

ISRAEL, THE BIBLE EXAMPLE

The history of the Jewish people is God's storybook, written for the world to read. They live in a glass house, and nothing that is important about their history is hidden. When people of other nations read the Good Book, they discover the Jews, and they also see themselves reflected in the Jewish narrative. The world sees God's dealings with Israel, and every God-conscious person can relate. The Jews are examples, and the picture is not all pretty.

"God was not pleased with them ... these things occurred as *examples*" (1Co. 10:5-6; italics added).

"Make every effort ... so that no one will fall by following their *example*" (Heb. 4:11; italics added).

For thousands of years, Jewish Bible stories have been meticulously shared from pulpits and firesides, from courtrooms to classrooms. They have been shouted from the housetops and whispered in the corners of dark dungeons. God has put His spotlight on Israel. The Jewish patriarchs wandered through the wilderness and into the Holy Land. They wandered onto the pages of the Bible and into our lives. God uses them to show the world what He expects from every person. Most nations have used them to teach their children; the peoples of the world have preached the Jewish story.

In Israel, the Old Testament Bible is used as a history book in public schools. They have no better reference that describes their own history than the Bible. Oh, that all nations would use the Bible as a history book in their schools.

ISRAEL IS STILL GOD'S EXAMPLE

Since Bible days, even when the Jews were a scattered people, they still captured the eyes of the world. Today, if we fail to watch Israel, we will miss much of what God is doing on the earth. This is a most important time to get connected with God's big picture, and that means getting connected with Israel.

In times past, the Jews walked with God, but over the years many have turned away. Even with all of their failings, the Lord promises to restore them. It seems that most of them fell and suffered, but they will be redeemed one day. The restoration of Israel is an often-repeated prophecy in the Scriptures and its fulfillment has already begun.

The coming blessings for Israel are extravagant. Rejoice with me, for their gain will result in blessings that will touch the whole world and bring about a global revival. When Israel is blessed, the Church will be blessed, and when the Church is blessed, the nations will be blessed. Eventually, even the planet and the environment will be blessed (see the last chapters of my book – *Unexpected Fire*). [2]

God's promises of blessings are not just for Jews but for all humanity. Israel is God's example, and that brings hope for every person. With all of their failings, the Jews are promised a bright and glorious future. As we look to the nations, we see many people groups who have turned away from God as well, but, like Israel, the Lord is still calling them.

God loves people, and He will do whatever is necessary to bring the nations to the fountain of life. This is a book of hope; it is about Israel's coming revival and revival for the nations. With so many doom-and-gloom prophets in the Church and in the world, it is easy to lose hope. The message, however, is turned to joy when we flip the coin and look at the other side. Then we discover the prophetic words that contain the promise of God's blessings. Come with me on a journey. Come and discover God's ultimate intention. Look through the fog, and you will see Israel's renaissance, revival and resurrection. You will see that the same ultimate blessings promised to Israel also apply to the Church and to the nations. Let the adventure begin; come and discover the untold story of Israel's restoration.

CHAPTER TWO

WHY JERUSALEM?

JERUSALEM IS MARKED BY GOD

JERUSALEM is a city of amazing importance, and many people do not know why. Since King David claimed the city three thousand years ago, it has been a hot spot of international controversy. The heart of Jerusalem is located on Mount Moriah, which became significant a thousand years before David's arrival because it is the site where Abraham offered his son, Isaac, to the Lord. At that time, God tested Abraham to see if he would trust Him fully. Abraham passed the test by being obedient to the Lord; then, just before he killed his son on the altar, the Lord stopped him. He showed Abraham a ram that was caught in the thicket, and the ram became the sacrifice instead of Isaac. Two thousand years later, Jesus was crucified a few hundred yards from the exact spot, on the same mountain. Like the ram, Jesus became the sacrificial Lamb of God and died as God's substitute. He took our place and paid the price that was required for the salvation of the human race.

THE CROSSROADS OF THE WORLD

When God created the world, He made sure that Jerusalem was marked from the beginning. If you look at the city from an aerial view, you can see His name, written in Hebrew, on the typography of the land.

Jerusalem is the capital city of Israel, and for geological reasons Israel became the crossroads of the ancient world. Every carriage carrying a dignitary or a heavy cargo and every chariot army travelling east or west had to pass through Israel. The Promised Land is nestled in the four-thousand-mile-long African Rift Valley. Mountains are on both sides of the valley, so it takes the shape of a narrow trough, running north and south. Anyone travelling east or west has to cross this difficult land formation. They have to get past two mountain ranges, and it is almost impossible for a large chariot or a carriage to use footpaths to cross a mountain. For hundreds of miles, there are only footpaths over these mountains, and it is not efficient for a large army to try to negotiate them.

God designed something special for this piece of land. In Israel, there is a wide opening in the African Rift mountain range, and it runs east and west. There is a gap in the mountains where carriages, chariots and armies can easily pass. This gap is a level plain called the Jezreel Valley or the Valley of Armageddon. The plain provides a passageway that leads from the Mediterranean Sea to the Jordan River. Any western army travelling from the Mediterranean has to pass through the Valley of Armageddon to go east, and every eastern army attacking the lands of the Mediterranean has to come through this same opening from the opposite direction. Even the chariot armies of Egypt in the Southwest must travel north along the Mediterranean coast and then turn east at the Valley of Armageddon to approach or attack any eastern nation.

An army coming from Rome would sail to the eastern shores of the Mediterranean and land at the seaport of Caesarea. They would amass their army, pass though the Valley of Armageddon and come to the Jordan River. Then they would travel north along the Jordan River, inside the African Rift Valley, until they would come to the Sea of Galilee. They would continue north toward Damascus, and then turn east to the Euphrates and Tigris Rivers. This journey would ultimately open the way to the Far East. All east or west travel had to pass through the Valley of Armageddon in Israel.

RIVERS OF FRESHWATER

Besides the gap provided in the mountain, this route is the only one that provides an abundant source of drinking water and agricultural land for food supplies. This east-west passage stays close to the rivers and forms the shape of an arc, going north, then east, and then south. The arc is called the Fertile Crescent. It is contrasted by the vast, dry desert sands of any other route through the Middle East. Because of this opening in the Rift Valley and the abundant source of freshwater and food, Israel became the only passage and, therefore, the crossroads of the ancient world.

Israel's significance, among the nations, was her travel routes and her strategic battle position. The Valley of Armageddon was a bottleneck that all chariot armies had to pass through if they travelled east or west, so it became the hot spot for battles. This is where the Persians and the Assyrians set up their fortifications to protect themselves against the Egyptians and the Romans who were coming from the west, and vice versa. This was the place where east and west met. It is where armies clashed, for whoever controlled the land of Israel had the military advantage for world domination.

If Rome, for example, could rule over the land of Israel, at the end of the Mediterranean, then it had a buffer zone and could protect its entire realm from every invading army that was coming from the east.

Since Jerusalem was the capital city of Israel, it was extremely significant in the eyes of the world. It seems that Israel has always been under attack, by some army coming from the east or the west. Here is a list of the nations and people groups that have attacked Jerusalem and ruled over the land of Israel.

THE JERUSALEM TIMELINE

1. Canaanite – 3300 BC
2. Israelite (First temple Period) – 1006 BC
3. Babylonian (Exile) – 586 BC
4. Persian – 538 BC
5. Hellenistic (Greek – Alexander the Great) – 332 BC
6. Roman – 63 BC
7. Byzantine (Christian) – 324 AD
8. Early Muslim – 638 AD
9. Crusaders (European Christians) – 1099 AD
10. Mamluk – 1260 AD

11. Ottoman (Muslims) – 1517 AD

12. British – 1917 AD

13. State of Israel – 1948 AD

THE ETERNAL SIGNIFICANCE OF JERUSALEM

Jerusalem has an eternal purpose that far exceeds any earthly significance. Once we understand her spiritual significance, the biblical focus on Jerusalem becomes clear, and the question of why this city is so important is answered.

The answer is very simple: God has chosen Jerusalem for His new throne room. This is seen throughout the Scriptures, but it becomes glaringly obvious when we see God's plans for the end of the Millennium. At that time He will move His throne to the city of Jerusalem. We read about it in the last chapter of the last book in the Bible. The Scripture reads:

"No longer will there be any curse. *The throne of God* and of the Lamb *will be in the city*, [Jerusalem] and his servants will serve him. *They will see his face*, and his name will be on their foreheads" (Rev. 22:3-4; italics added).

Several monumental things happen at the end of the thousand-year reign of Christ. For the first time, since Adam walked in the Garden of Eden, we will be able to see God's face and live. Then God's name will be on our foreheads, and we will serve Him. The most important detail for our study is that His throne will be moved to Jerusalem. *For one thousand years, Jesus' throne will already be situated in Jerusalem, but at the end of His millennial reign, the Almighty will move His throne to Jerusalem as well.*

If heaven is where God's throne is, then heaven is moving to the earth because His thone will be in Jerusalem. If God rules from His throne, then God will one day rule the universe from the city of Jerusalem. In other words, God is moving His headquarters from heaven to earth. This is an amazing revelation, and it has the power to adjust our thinking about the significance of the earth, the land of Israel, and the city of Jerusalem.

Let us explore God's *plan*. It includes His *planet*, His human *population*, His *person*, His chosen *people*, His *Prince*, and His *place*.

GOD CHOSE A PLAN

I ask you to think this through with me. If, at the end of time, God's throne is in the city of Jerusalem, then many things become clear.

In eternity past, God decided that He wanted a new headquarters from which to rule the universe. He developed a plan, and since then, everything that happens is designed to eventually fit into His plan. If anyone tries to hinder God's plan, he or she will suffer great disappointment and failure.

GOD CHOSE A PLANET

Like a man going out to find a piece of land to build on, God went out and chose a planet for the fulfillment of His purpose. Of all of the planets in the universe, God chose Earth. He created it and filled it with great beauty. God is bringing His throne here, so this planet called Earth has to be an amazing place.

GOD CHOSE A POPULATION

Then, according to God's plan, He made humankind in His own image. This had never happened before. The greatest creation that ever came from God was a human baby. No planet, angel or animal has been made in the image of God, but the human population is made in God's image. That is His design and His choice. He made us and called us to come into fellowship with Himself.

A PERSON

About two thousand years after Adam left the Garden, God chose a man named Abram (Abraham). This person was so full of faith that he became the Father of all people who have faith in God and His Son, Jesus. Abraham obeyed the Lord and moved forward to set in motion the eternal plans of

God for this planet. From his lineage, the chosen people, the Jews, would come. Even Jesus would be born from Abraham's descendants.

A CHOSEN PEOPLE

God's plan is not negotiable; He chose a plan, a planet, a population and a person. He also chose a specific people group within the human race. They are called His chosen people, the Jews, the people of Israel. Many people, Christians included, do not understand that the Jews are God's chosen people, so they give no significance to them. When people realize that God has chosen the Jews for a special purpose in His eternal plan, then they will give more respect to them and they will be careful how they treat them.

THE PRINCE OF HEAVEN

From before the creation of the world, God planned to send His Son ahead of Him to the planet. Jesus would show the people how to live godly lives. He would die to pay for their sins. He would rule over them in the Millennium and be their Lord and King for all eternity. He would be fully God and fully man, and He would be born of this people called Israel. Even in heaven, Jesus is still called the King of kings, the Lion from the Tribe of Judah and the Root of David (see Revelation 5 and 19). Regarding God's plan, every lasting thing that is accomplished on the earth will come about through the life of Jesus, God's Son, the Prince of Heaven.

A PLACE

Besides the other details of God's plan, He also chose a special place on the planet. He chose the land of Israel and the city of Jerusalem, the place where His thone will be at the end of the age.

The city of Jerusalem is so significant; God chose it for Himself from the very beginning. He looked across the universe and, in His heart, He designed and chose the city of Jerusalem. That is why Jerusalem is so important, and it is why He chose Abraham and the Jewish people. They all fit into His plans to move His throne. It is why He will protect the land of Israel and the city of Jerusalem. This is why the nation of Israel must be honored.

Abraham was not perfect, and the Jews are not perfect, but God is perfect and He has chosen Jerusalem as the city to house His thone. He has chosen the people of that place, the Jewish people, for Himself. That is why Jerusalem is important.

CHAPTER THREE

DARK AGES' THEOLOGY

A MISGUIDED DOCTRINE

I am disappointed and still a little shocked as I realize that many Christian leaders give no special place to Israel in their theology. Many believe in Replacement Theology, a doctrine that purports that the Gentile Church has replaced Israel in the plans of God. They say that Jews can still be saved, but they are no more special than any other people; in fact, this theology claims that they are no longer God's chosen people.

This thinking leads many to assume that God's unique blessings and protections for Israel are off the table. They say that Israel has no God-given claim to the Holy Land and no special privileges. Many actually believe that the Jews are still being punished for killing Christ. Some Christians even have a distain for the Jews and inadvertently side with Israel's enemies.

GRANDPA DEREK PRINCE

Several years ago I sat down with my grandfather, Derek Prince, to talk about this dangerous persuasion. I told him that I did not understand how well-meaning church leaders could be so blind to Israel's importance, so indifferent to her blessings and so calloused toward her present disposition. Many are adversarial toward her as a people, and some prominent leaders have said to me, "What difference does it make, how we feel about Israel? They are just not unique or special anymore."

As I continued, I asked Grandpa Derek, "Why can they not see that Israel is God's prophetic time clock and that participating in her promised restoration will release God's blessings on the Church and on the nations?"

Grandpa looked up at me and said, "I have also been amazed at this, but I have come to the conclusion that without a direct revelation from God, they will never understand Israel's significance. God has to open their eyes."

HISTORICALLY SPEAKING

Historically speaking, anti-Semitism has infiltrated the traditional Church to such an extent that nothing less than a supernatural, Holy Spirit brainwashing is needed to shift the ideology. I am glad to report, however, that a shift toward understanding and loving Israel is coming. The change has already begun even though there will be a huge spiritual battle before it comes into its full light. Israel's most significant season is emerging, and indifferent saints must be careful not to be on the wrong side of God. Stubborn, anti-Jewish theologians need to humble themselves, for God is jealous over His inheritance and the time has come for Him to demonstrate His love for them. Long ago, nations were punished because they said that Israel was not special. Some of these stories are recorded in the Scriptures, and they stand as a warning for us today.

JUDGMENT FOR MOAB

Read what happened to Moab and the Ammonites.

> *"This is what the sovereign Lord says: "Because Moab and Seir said, 'Look, the house of Jacob has become like all the other nations,' therefore I will expose the flank of Moab, beginning at its frontier towns - Beth Jeshimoth, Baal Meon and Kiriathaim - the glory of the land. I give Moab along with the Ammonites to the people of the East as a possession, so that the Ammonites will not be remembered among the nations; and I will inflict punishment on Moab. Then they will know that I am the Lord." (Eze. 25:8-11)*

Because Moab and the Ammonites said that Israel was not special, they were rejecting God's word and therefore rejecting Him. The Lord took it personally; He judged those nations and wiped them out so that the world would know that He is the Lord and that His word is final. God exposed Moab's most glorious towns to her enemies in the East. The towns were destroyed, and their inhabitants are now a forgotten people. In Moab's case, the lie that Israel was not special to God was born out of witchcraft, and those who held to it are gone forever.

There is a great difference between the Church and Moab. The Church is the assembly of God's people, while the Moabites and the Ammonites were His enemies. We should note, however, that Moab and Ammi were fathered by Lot, who was a man of God. These people groups came from God's people; you see, Moab and Ammi were Lot's ill-conceived, incestuous children, born of his own daughters. Lot impregnated his daughters while in a drunken state, and two nations were formed from these sons. They could have been redeemed, but they chose to live under the curse that had been passed down to them because of sexual perversion. As with many who are cursed, they became a demonized people. For teachings on this subject, see my book *Blessings or Curses for the Next Generation.* [3]

In the end, God judged the Moabites and the Ammonites because they said that Israel had become like the other nations. Their story is a heavy warning. All who read it must listen to what God has to say about Israel. This is so important to Him; the Israelites are not like any other nation.

DARK AGES' THEOLOGY

A God-planned phenomenon is unfolding around the world; the Church is being taught the truths about God's heart and purpose for Israel. Although this teaching is gathering momentum, there is still an immense lack of understanding in some quarters. Many Christians are still in the dark ages of theology because they have not grasped the spiritual truth concerning God's blessings and purpose for the Jews at the end of the age. Even worse, although it is hard for me to believe, some are still wallowing in the horrors of Replacement Theology.

I do not blame the vast majority of these saints for their lack of insight on the subject; they are only living what they have been taught, and some are serving the Lord brilliantly in many other ways. You see, some were taught about God's judgment for Israel but were not taught about her restoration. They have been left with partial truth, and this is very dangerous. They learned that the kingdom of God would be removed from Israel, but they did not learn about her reinstatement in the kingdom. It is true; Jesus did pronounce devastating judgments on Israel. He said: "The kingdom of God will be taken away from you and given to a people who will produce its fruit" (Matt. 21:43).

The judgment continues. Speaking to Jerusalem, Jesus said the following: "Jerusalem, Jerusalem, you who kill the prophets and stone those sent to you … your house is left to you desolate. For I tell you, you will not see me again until you say, 'Blessed is he who comes in the name of the Lord'" (Matt. 23:37).

THE WORD UNTIL

Many fail to grasp the second half of this verse. The judgment is in effect *until* the Jews recognize Jesus as Messiah and say, "Blessed is He who comes in the name of the Lord." The word *until* is a time word. It lets us know that change will come and the judgment will be lifted.

In Romans, Paul says, "And if they do not persist in unbelief, they will be grafted in, for God is able to graft them in again" (Rom. 11:23).

GOD WILL REVEAL IT

I know that the Lord will reveal the pivotal change that is coming to Israel, and all of His Church will see it in His time. The Replacement Theology mindset will be removed, and the Church will finally understand. This revelation will take a while to reach everyone; it may even take a few generations before the entire Church is on the same page, but the Church will get there.

I thank God for the light that is growing brighter and the increased love for Israel that is emerging in the Church right now.

NOT A GUESSING GAME

The Bible speaks plainly with regard to Israel in the last days. It tells us about Israel's restoration and of her coming revival. At an appointed time, the majority of the Jews will receive Jesus as Messiah and all of Israel (though not every individual) will be saved. Later in this book we will look at Zechariah 12:10 and 13:1, Ezekiel 27, Isaiah 60, Romans 9:1-5, Romans 11:25-29, Revelation 7:4-8 and other Scriptures to discover the details of Israel's coming revival and her promised inheritance. If you want a head start, study these Scripture passages for yourself.

The truth is, we need not play a guessing game when thinking about God's plans for Israel. The details of her coming glory are given to us in the Bible. Zechariah 12 tells us about Israel's national defense and her coming revival. It starts with an amazing eye-opener:

"This is the word of the Lord concerning *Israel*. The Lord, who stretches out the heavens, who lays the foundations of the earth, and who forms the spirit of man within him, declares" (Zec. 12:1; italics added).

The Almighty emphasizes the importance of what He is about to say about Israel by introducing Himself as the one who made the universe, created the earth and put the spirit of man within him.

Many individuals, nations and governments announce strong opinions about Israel, and most of them are very negative. They look at the Jewish people through very different glasses. They see through the lenses of their own logic, through historical revisionism, humanism, secularism, and the opinion of the media. Personally, I believe that much of this is the doctrine of demons which is full of lies and half-truths. Those doctrines are designed to keep the world form participating in the ways of the Lord.

A person can be politically correct in the eyes of the world, but not have the right perspective. The only correct answers will come from God and what He has to say about Israel, which is recorded in the Bible. Isn't it time for us to listen to the One who made the heavens, the earth and all of humanity?

This is not a guessing game; discovering God's position and making that our own position is the only correct way to proceed. Every believer must fight against demonic deceptions, media manipulations and even the common wisdom of man, if it does not line up with God's Word. Regardless of human opinion, the King of Heaven has the final word concerning Israel. The earth and all within it belongs to Him. May all who read this book say this: "No matter how much I have to change, I declare that I am on the Lord's side. His words are my words and I will follow them with all that is in me. I aim to bring His truths into my life."

Who, of God's children, does not want to walk in step with Him?

CHAPTER FOUR

THE SPIRITUAL FIG TREE

I LOVE FRESH FIGS

MY mother, Miryam Magdaline Wyns is a Jewess. Before her marriage to my father, her name was Magdaline Katz. She was born in Tel Aviv in 1933, just fifteen years before the nation of Israel was reborn. When she was five days old, she was taken in and later adopted by Lydia and Derek Prince. She was raised in the Holy Land in the cities of Ramallah and Jerusalem.

Mom loved fresh figs. I remember when she and Dad went with my wife, Joy, and me on a Mediterranean Cruise and travelled north into the Aegean Sea. We stopped at the Port of Ephesus, and the four of us hired a taxi to search out the Biblical ruins of Ephesus. Along the twenty mile ride we discovered an abandoned fig tree on a forsaken stretch of the road. I asked the driver to stop and I ran back and plucked a big, juicy yellow fig from the tree. Mom and I shared it, and it was the best fig I have ever eaten. I loved sharing things with my mother. She was great, always opening her heart to others, and through her life I discovered many little details about my Jewish roots.

Several years ago she passed away. It was a very painful time in my life. While looking through her home, I discovered a huge half-gallon, unopened tin of fig jam in the back of a kitchen cupboard. That summer my breakfasts consisted of toast smothered with Philadelphia cream cheese and Mom's fig jam. I just about lived off it; it was so good. I love fresh figs and really thick fig jam. That year I planted a fig tree in my back yard as a memorial to my mother. For the past two years, Joy and I have collected fresh figs from the tree. Joy made fabulous preserves and produced the very best fig jam. The legacy continues.

GOD LOVES FIGS

We know God loves figs because He loves His chosen people Israel and has likened them to a fig tree. Talking of figs and Israel, Jesus told this parable.

> *A man had a fig tree planted in his vineyard and he went to look for fruit on it, but he did not find any. So he went to the man who took care of the vineyard, "For three years now I've been coming to look for fruit on this fig tree and haven't found any. Cut it down! Why should it use up the soil?" "Sir," the man replied, "leave it alone for one more year, and I'll dig around it and fertilize it. If it bears fruit next year, fine! If not, then cut it down." (Luke 13:6-9)*

The vineyard is the world and all of the nations, and the fig tree is Israel. The man who owns the vineyard is Jesus, sent by God the Father. He planted Israel among the nations; Israel is not an accident, but a deliberate planting of the Lord. For three years, Jesus came looking for fruit on the fig tree, but He found none. He said, "cut it down." The Holy Spirit, who is the gardener, said, "Give it one more year." Figs represent the spiritual fruit that God was looking for in Israel. After the season of Christ's ministry, it was cut down. Jesus cursed Israel (see Matthew 21:43). Thank God, that is not the end of the story for Israel.

JESUS CURSES THE FIG TREE

Jesus cursed the tree because He was giving His disciples an illustration. The fig tree is Israel, and it withered. As in the parable, He came looking for fruit on Israel's tree. It was not the season for figs, so Jesus knew He would not find any fruit. He cursed it. He was showing His disciples what was happening to Israel.

"As they were leaving Bethany, Jesus was hungry. Seeing in the distance a fig tree in leaf, he went to find out if it had any fruit. When he reached it, he found nothing but leaves, because it was not the season for figs. Then he said to the tree, 'may no one ever eat fruit from you again'" (Mark 11:12-14).

"In the morning, as they went along, they saw the fig tree withered from the roots" (Mark 11:20).

THE RESURRECTION OF THE FIG TREE

Later, Jesus' disciples asked Him when the end of the age would come. He gave them many signs, and, once again, He told them about the fig tree and Israel.

> *At that time ... They will see the Son of Man coming on the clouds of the sky, with power and great glory. ...* Now learn the lesson of the fig tree: As soon as its twigs get tender and its leaves come out, *you know that summer is near. Even so, when you see all these things, you know that it is near, right at the door. I tell you the truth, this generation will certainly not pass away until all these things have happened." (Matt. 24:30, 32-34; emphasis added)*

One of the signs that points to Jesus' return is the emergence of the fig leaves on the fig tree. If the fig tree is Israel, then what are the leaves? Some people believe that Israel's becoming a nation in 1948 and her people returning to the land are the leaves of the fig tree. The generation that sees the emerging leaves of Israel will certainly not pass before the Lord returns.

More than a generation has passed since 1948, and the Lord has not returned. Did we miss something?

I think this conclusion is missing a key component regarding the prophecy. The leaves are not pointing to the natural rebirth of Israel, but to her spiritual rebirth. First comes the natural, and then the spiritual follows. For more than sixty years we have witnessed the natural rebirth of Israel, but soon her spiritual revival will come. The eyes of the Jewish people will open, and millions of Jews will receive the revelation that Jesus is Messiah. They will receive Him and be saved. The generation that witnesses this Jewish revival will certainly not pass away before the Lord will return. The spiritual leaves must emerge on the fig tree and not just the natural ones.

RABBINICAL REVIVAL

Several years ago, Joy and I met with a group of international intercessory leaders in Mexico. One of the speakers was our good friend Lance Lambert. He is one of the most respected Holy Spirit-filled Messianic Jews in Israel. He is an international Bible teacher and was a very dear friend to my grandfather, Derek Prince.

He told a story and asked that we not share it so that those involved would be protected. So many years have passed since then that I know that no one will be wrongfully uncovered by the telling of this story anymore. Let me now share it with you.

Years ago, Lance's secretary received a phone call from the secretary of a prominent Jewish rabbi who taught at one of the Rabbinical Yeshivas (a school of the rabbis) in Israel. He said that the rabbi was coming to visit Mr. Lambert and would be at his house at eight o'clock that evening. Lance waited and at eight o'clock, on the dot, he heard a knock at his door. Upon opening it, he saw a Jewish rabbi standing before him. He was dressed in black and wore a white starched shirt. He had a huge grey beard, and ringlets hung from the corners of his head. The rabbi had a large fur hat and pantaloons. He was a genuine son of Abraham - the real deal.

After sitting down and having some refreshments the rabbi said the following: "I have had a dream about Jesus - that He is Messiah. I have believed and I have surrendered my life to Him. I have come to you to learn what you have to teach me about Jesus. I have many questions to ask about the New Testament as well."

For hours they sat and talked until it seemed they had covered all of the rabbi's questions. Then they sat in quiet reflection for some time. Finally

Lance asked, "Now that Jesus is your Savior and Lord, what will you do? Will you leave the Yeshiva?"

The rabbi responded, "Where would I go? I am not a Baptist, a Catholic or a Pentecostal, and, besides, there are nineteen other rabbis who have also received Jesus as Messiah. We meet regularly for study and fellowship."

REJOICING AND ANTICIPATING

We are rejoicing with all that God is doing behind closed doors. I cannot say that the fig tree is sending out her spiritual leaves quite yet, but her twigs are definitely greening up.

The word of the Lord is final. Israel's spiritual revival will come after her physical restoration. Her spiritual restoration is a follow-up to her aliyah (her physical homecoming), and when the spiritual happens, keep your eyes on the eastern skies. The generation that witnesses the Jewish revival shall see the return of the King.

CHAPTER FIVE

WHOEVER BLESSES ISRAEL
IS BLESSED

A BIBLICAL PROMISE

IT was not only because of Abraham that God joined himself to the Jewish people. The joining with Israel was God's plan long before Abraham was born; nevertheless, God chose Abraham and called him His friend.

To be called God's friend is the greatest title a person can posses. It is better than being a king, president, pastor, millionaire, famous movie star, or CEO. If you can be anything, be God's friend. It is also good to be related to someone who is God's friend. You can be blessed by association, for blessings and curses are generational.

The Lord tells the people of Israel that they have been chosen because they are Abraham's descendants, and Abraham is God's friend. We read: "But you O Israel, my servant, Jacob, *whom I have chosen*, you descendants of Abraham my friend, I took you from the ends of the earth, from its farthest corners I called you. I said, 'You are my servant; *I have chosen you and have not rejected you*'" (Isa. 41:8-9; italics added).

Even through the darkest times, when Israel was far from God, the Lord said that He would choose her again.

"This is what the Lord Almighty says: 'My towns will *again* overflow with

prosperity, and the Lord will *again* comfort Zion and *choose Jerusalem'"*
(Zech. 1:17; italics added).

"The Lord will inherit Judah as his portion in the holy land and will *again*
choose Jerusalem" Zech. 2:12; italics added).

The Lord promises that He will restore Israel as if she had never been
rejected. He says:

"I will strengthen the house of Judah and save the house of Joseph. I will
restore them because I have compassion on them. *They will be as though I
had not rejected them,* for I am the Lord their God and I will answer them"
(Zech. 10:6; italics added).

No matter how we look at it, God says that He will continue to choose and
bless Israel. Listen to what He says the following to Abraham about these
blessings:

"I will make you into a great nation and I will bless you; I will make your
name great and you will be a blessing. *I will bless those who bless you, and
whoever curses you I will curse"* (Gen. 12:2-3; italics added).

Isaac, Abraham's son, spoke the same words over his son. He said to Jacob,
Abraham's grandson, who is also called Israel, "May those who curse you be
cursed and those who bless you be blessed" (Gen. 27:29).

The prophecies that tell us about blessing or cursing Israel continue in the
Scriptures:

"Balaam saw that it pleased the Lord to bless Israel … the Spirit of the Lord
came upon him and he uttered this oracle: … May those who bless you be
blessed and those who curse you be cursed" (Num. 24:1,2,9).

Moses prophesied as well. The following verses are part of a prophetic word
from Moses concerning the children of Israel. He said that God would

gather the Israelites back to Himself and back to their land, and, at that time, whoever curses Israel will be punished and cursed. We read:

> *When all these blessings and curses, I have set before you, come upon you and you take them to heart wherever the Lord your God disperses you among the nations, and when you and your children return to the Lord your God and obey him with all your heart ... then the Lord your God will restore your fortunes ... and gather you again from all the nations ... He will bring you to the land that belonged to your fathers, and you will take possession of it. He will make you more prosperous and numerous than your fathers ...* The Lord your God will put all these curses on your enemies who hate and persecute you. *(Deut. 30:1-2, 3, 5, 7;* emphasis added)

NATIONS BEWARE

The nation of Israel is not the same as any other nation. How individuals and nations treat her will determine a level of God's blessings or curses on them. This is not the only reason that blessings or curses come to a nation, but it is a significant one. The consequences for blessing or cursing Israel are far reaching. This position has been established by the Lord God Almighty, and it must not be overlooked.

Throughout history, the consequences for nations who bless or curse Israel have proven to be true. Today the United States has a record of standing with Israel. They have not done it perfectly; nevertheless, they have stood with her. This is one of the main reasons why God has blessed the United States. If the U.S. government pressures Israel to divide her land and give portions of it to others, or if they treat her unjustly or persecute her, it will cause trouble for the nation; they will reap a whirlwind of judgment and curses. Every nation that has turned against Israel has fallen, and this dynamic will become more pronounced in the days ahead as God's timing to restore and bless Israel unfolds.

RUSSIA AND AMERICA

The recent histories of Russia and America demonstrate what happens when a nation blesses Israel and what happens when a nation curses Israel. They have two very different stories to tell. I cannot go into a full report regarding their histories, but I think, for most people in the western world, it is self-evident. John P. McTernan says this in his book, *As America Has Done To Israel*:

> *America and Russia provide a good test of accuracy of the Bible regarding the treatment of the Jews. Russia has a long and well-established history of hating Jews. America has a long and well-established history of accepting and blessing Jewish people.* [4]

The nations of America and Russia are similar in many respects. They are both huge countries with large populations and expansive areas of farmland. They have abundant natural resources such as coal, iron, lumber, oil, and other minerals; they have tremendous rivers. Both nations also have historical Christian roots. [5]

From 1917 until today, Russia has been a "living hell." Communist tyrants such as Lenin and Stalin rose to power, killing tens of millions of people. Millions starved to death and millions died in prison camps. [6]

> *Russia remained in a living hell until communism fell in 1989. Even after the fall, Russians are still suffering from poverty and disease. Russians have the lowest life expectancy in the Western World. The country paid a fearful price for violating God's word about blessing the Jews.* [7]

> *From 1948 onward, the United States became the new nation's best friend. America continues to vote with Israel in the United Nations. The United States supplies Israel with its latest military equipment. Russia continues to curse Israel. The Russians always vote against Israel in the United Nations, and Russia continues to supply Israel's enemies with weapons to attack the Jewish state.* [8]

The United States became the leader of the free world - the nation with both the greatest military power and the greatest economic power. The nation with the finest universities and medical centers. [9]

The contrast between America and Russia is clear. Russia was cursed in every area while America was blessed. [10]

JUDGING THE NATIONS

Throughout history God has been blessing and cursing people in response to how they have treated Israel, but the final and most definitive judgments will come at the end of the age. As the Great Tribulation ends, the Lord will gather the nations together to judge them on how they have treated Israel. The following words are from the prophet Joel:

In those days and at that time, when I restore the fortunes of Judah and Jerusalem, I will gather all nations and bring them down to the Valley of Jehoshaphat. There I will enter into judgment against them concerning my inheritance, my people Israel, for they scattered my people among the nations and divided up my land. They cast lots for my people and traded boys for prostitutes; they sold girls for wine that they might drink. (Joel 3:1-3)

It will happen just before the Second Coming of Christ, two hundred million troops (see Revelation 9:16), representing all the nations, will gather to fight the people of Jerusalem. They will think they are gathering to fight against Israel's domination over her Arab neighbors and her intolerance toward other religions. At that time, Israel will refuse to participate in the pluralism of the world. They will be portrayed as narrow-minded. They will state that their God is the only true and living God, the only one who should be worshipped. They will reject all other religions and make their claim that what the Bible has promised them does, in fact, belong to them. They will possess their land, and the nations will rise up against the Jews to take them by force, to humble them and to assimilate Israel into the global community.

The nations will not know that God is mustering them; He is gathering them for judgment. They will march across the Valley of Armageddon (see Revelation 16:16). Joel calls it the Valley of Jehoshaphat, which simply means the Valley of Judgment. The Valley of Armageddon is known today as the Valley of Jezreel. It is situated about sixty miles north of Jerusalem, between Mount Carmel and Nazareth.

God will judge the nations for scattering the Jews, dividing up their land and abusing His Jewish children. He will destroy those who have done evil when He appears at what we call the Second Coming (see Revelation 19:11-15). The birds of the air will feast on the dead bodies of the enemies of God while their spirits will be thrown into Hades. There they will wait in torment for one thousand years and then stand before the Great White Throne of God's judgment.

BLESSINGS ARE AVAILABLE

Judgments are coming, but so are blessings. The blessings of the Lord are much more powerful than His judgments (see Exodus 20:5-6). For a full and detailed description of how we can receive God's blessings, I encourage you to order a copy of my book *Blessings or Curses for the Next Generation.* (See details at the back of this book).

If you bless Israel, you will be blessed. To bless Israel is to protect and defend her and her people. It is to help support her financially and to help the Jews return to their land. It involves praying for her peace and helping her obtain, keep and restore her land. It may involve helping the poor and oppressed who live in her lands and also making her enemies your enemies.

In short, if you encourage the Jewish people, God will bless you. Look at all of the promises that the Bible says belongs to them. Help fulfill them, and God will bless you. The Lord has chosen Israel again, and He calls you to choose her as well. Whoever blesses the Jews and the nation of Israel blesses the descendants of Abraham. God is committed to blessing Israel. It is a good idea to be in step with Him.

CHAPTER SIX

ISRAEL'S AMAZING INHERITANCE

THE ROMAN ROAD

THE biblical book of Romans is the longest letter in antiquity. Paul writes this letter to the church in Rome because the Gentile Church in Rome is already leaning toward the error of Replacement Theology (the theory that the Gentile Church has replaced Israel in the purposes of God). The key to understanding the purpose of the book of Romans is found in chapters 9-11. In these verses we are taught to have a right attitude toward Israel.

I have discovered that many bible schools who teach Romans as part of their curriculum skip lightly over these three chapters as if they are not important. Nothing, however, could be further from the truth. These chapters are not of secondary importance; in fact, they provide one of the main focus points and three of the most pivotal chapters of the entire book. All other chapters point to and support the argument of these three chapters.

The book of Romans teaches people everywhere how they must come to God through Christ and how they can mature in God through the gospel and grace of Christ. Pains are taken by Paul to explain that Jews and Gentiles come to God in the same way and can only be saved through Christ's merits. The same carnal struggles that one group has, the other has. Both must depend on and follow the Holy Spirit to find their destiny and calling, and neither Gentiles nor Jews should lift themselves into a position of supremacy over the other.

The ancient Roman Church was waving the supremacy flag over the fallen Jews, as do many churches today. Paul lets them know that God's covenantal blessings and the special calling for Israel are still very much alive and that the Gentile Church should not boast because Israel is suffering and they are blessed. Chapters 9 to 11 are the heart and soul of the book of Romans. These three chapters are the main reason why Paul is writing such a lengthy letter. In short, the book of Romans is an apologetic in defense of Israel's destiny and call.

The next few chapters of this book will focus on Romans 9:1-5. You will feel Paul's heartbeat and catch the revelation that God has given him for Israel.

PAUL BARES HIS HEART

Upon reading and understanding Romans 9:1-5, you will have to settle these questions: Is Paul speaking his own ideas or God's and is the Bible the absolute word of God for humankind? A Christian knows that all that is written in the Bible is the inspired word of God, including these three chapters in Romans. Paul's writings in Romans are indeed a revelation from heaven.

Paul writes the following: "I speak the truth in Christ – I am not lying, my conscience confirms it in the Holy Spirit – I have great sorrow and unceasing anguish in my heart. For I could wish that I myself were cursed and cut off from Christ for the sake of my brothers, those of my own race, the people of Israel" (Rom. 9:1-4).

The chapter begins with Paul baring his heart as he is in pain for the Jewish people. He identifies them as his brothers, the people of his own race, the people of Israel. It is impossible to misunderstand him; he is not talking here about the Gentile Church, but he is talking about the Jewish people.

He is in pain because Israel is not claiming her appointed inheritance or her blessings. Paul even says that he wishes that he could be cursed and cut off from Christ if it would mean the restoration of his own people. He is speaking rhetorically, for Paul knows very well that there is only one name under heaven that can save someone and only one sacrifice that can pay for a person's sins - the name and sacrifice of Jesus. His words are highly emotional; they express his deep love and earnest desire for Israel. With this impassioned introduction, he begins to tell us what belongs to Israel. In the next two verses, he describes Israel's amazing inheritance. See if you can identify eight monumental blessings that Paul says belong to Israel today.

EIGHT MONUMENTAL BLESSINGS FOR ISRAEL

Theirs is the adoption as sons, theirs the divine glory, the covenants, the receiving of the law, the temple worship and the promises. Theirs are the patriarchs, and from them is traced the human ancestry of Christ, who is God over all, forever praised! Amen. (Rom. 9:4-5)

In my study, I work with seven different translations of the Bible. Each translation describes these eight blessings and infers that they belong to Israel today. These verses do not say that Israel has somehow lost these blessings. This is a New Testament, not an Old Testament, passage of scripture, and Paul is making a positive statement about Israel in the strongest way he can.

Here is Israel's eight-fold inheritance:

1.   The Adoption as Sons
2.   The Divine Glory
3.   The Covenants
4.   The Receiving of the Law
5.   The Temple Worship
6.   The Promises
7.   The Patriarchs
8.   The Human Ancestry of Christ

In the next chapters, we will study these eight blessings. We will look at each of them individually, and you will be amazed at what actually belongs to Israel today.

THE NUMBER OF RESURRECTION

In the Bible, God gives us loads of revelation to emphasize truth from many different angles. One of His dynamic tools for giving us revelation is found in His use of numbers. Every number has a special meaning with God; for example, five is the number for grace, six is the number for man, seven is the number for completion and eight is the number for resurrection.

It is no accident that Israel's inheritance is summed up in eight powerful phrases because eight is the number for resurrection, and they are the resurrection people. Every blessing that was ever promised by God to Israel can be found in these eight themes.

Eight is the number for resurrection, and Israel fit the bill. Until 1948, Israel was a dead nation, and Hebrew was a dead language. By God's sovereign will, Israel was brought back to life; she was raised from the dead. That is why her number is eight.

In 70 AD the Romans demolished Jerusalem, and most of the surviving Jews were eventually scattered across the face of the earth. They had no homeland, no central government and no unifying network for their culture or traditions. No other nation could have remained in existence after almost two thousand years of being banished from their homeland. They faced demonic persecution and extreme isolation, yet God sustained them. Israel has been brought back from the brink.

Like cutting eight beautiful, long-stemmed roses from the garden and putting them in a vase, we will take the teachings of Israel's blessings and put them on display for you to see. Then you will discover God's covenantal heart toward Israel. You will see that Israel is the apple of His eye. Right now Israel is not living in the good of what God has promised her, but one day she will. Then the whole world will come to the brightness of her rising, and the Church will partner with her and see the glory of God cover the earth as the waters cover the sea.

CHAPTER SEVEN

THE ADOPTION AS SONS

ISRAEL - A NEW TEACHING FOR SOME

I T may be a shock to the system when seasoned Christians first discover what actually belongs to Israel. Gentile believers know that the Bible reveals God's definitive word on a subject, but when they discover Israel's inheritance according to the New Testament, it is sometimes difficult to absorb. Many pulpits of modern-day Christendom have, by-and-large, failed to focus on Israel's blessings because of the historical rhetoric of Replacement Theology that has blinded the Church and hidden the truth.

Years ago, I was asked to speak about Israel's modern-day biblical blessings to a group of twenty-five pastors and elders at a large church in the south of England. They had more than a thousand people in the congregation, and I had preached to the entire congregation at the Sunday morning service, but not about Israel. The leaders and I were good friends, but we were miles apart on the subject of God's chosen people. Knowing my position, they asked me to reserve the subject for their senior leaders only. They met for prayer and fellowship behind closed doors on Monday morning, and I was asked to share about Israel in the end times.

I was delighted; I found that some were open to my teaching, but since they had not heard anything quite like it, they were cautious about embracing it. Others were adamantly opposed to any thought of Israel's being special, and the questions that followed came fast and furiously. One advantage I had was that these pastors had almost never spoken directly about Israel to their congregation. They did not have an anti-Israel message or a Replace-ment Theology book that one of them had written that they would have to defend. When ministers have overtly taught Replacement Theology, only a supernatural act of God can correct the error. Those leaders have raised their colors on the mast, and changing them publically can be difficult and somewhat embarrassing.

The leaders whom I was addressing on this particular Monday morning had simply ignored the subject of Israel, but they still had a problem to overcome because their worldview was full of Replacement Theology. They had taken every promise of blessing in the Bible that was given to Israel and spiritual-ized it to fit the Church.

If these leaders took my presentation to heart, it would mean a huge shift in their approach to the Scriptures. Many details of their teachings would no longer ring true, and their church congregation would need to be instructed to rethink the scriptures and receive them in a new light. I felt like the pro-verbial fox who had been chased and was now surrounded by twenty-five British hunting hounds.

I remember one bright young pastor in the group asking me to make further comment on Romans 11:13-16. He wanted me to once again explain about the first fruits, the dough and the root. Look at these verses for yourself. Paul says the following:

> I am talking to you Gentiles. Inasmuch as I am the apostle to the Gen-tiles, I make much of my ministry in the hope that I may somehow rouse my own people to envy and save some of them. For if their rejection is the reconciliation of the world, what will their acceptance be but life from the dead? If the part of the dough offered as firstfruits is holy, then the whole batch is holy; if the root is holy, so are the branches. (Rom. 11:13-16)

I explained that Paul was making the point that Israel's beginnings were holy, and God promises that her future will be holy as well. In this incidence, the firstfruits and the root refer to the Jewish patriarchs. Paul is referring to such national leaders as Abraham, Isaac, Jacob and Moses. In the context of this Scripture passage, the patriarchs are both the firstfruits and the root. Because of their holiness, an anointing for holiness comes to future generations. This is further confirmed in Romans 11:28-29. Here the Scriptures teach that God's gifts and call for Israel are irrevocable because of the patriarchs: "… as far as election is concerned, they are loved on account of the patriarchs, for God's gifts and his call are irrevocable" (Rom. 11:28-29).

Word got back to me that the young pastor was beginning to see something new, but later he asked his senior pastor if the root represented the Jewish patriarchs in this verse. The pastor dismissed the notion, stating that Christ is the root in the scriptures.

I was saddened but not surprised to hear of this. Of course, Christ is referred to as the root of Jesse and David in other Scriptures, but He is not the root in this verse. It is obvious that Paul is referring to the Jewish patriarchs. Without adequate exegesis of these verses, the pastor simply put the subject in his predetermined theological box. His bias hindered the flow of fresh understanding and revelation, and he remained unchanged.

This was only one small point among many, but the same defense mechanism was used over and over again. Replacement Theologists dismiss New Testament references to Israel's future blessings or just put the Gentile Church in place of the Jews whenever references to Israel's blessings are made. I know that the Holy Spirit is helping the Church to adjust on this subject, and we will see more of a shift toward blessing Israel in the days ahead. One day the penny will drop, eyes will be opened and the Church will see and partner with God's end-time purposes for Israel.

On one of our great pilgrimages to Israel, we took our Christian tour group to the shop of a Jewish rabbi in the Jewish Quarter of the old city of Jerusalem. The rabbi was sharing when, suddenly, one Gentile man in the group spoke out. He said, "You Jews must accept Christ. You are blind and need the veil to be removed from your eyes."

The rabbi responded politely, "I know what the New Testament says about the Jews being blind to Messiah, and maybe what you say is true, but I think we are all blind in some way or another, for no one sees everything. You are just as blind as I am. The New Testament says that we all see through a glass darkly."

Even though our Gentile friend spoke the truth, so did the rabbi, and I think the other Christians in the room were more appreciative of the heart and attitude of the rabbi than they were of the argumentative Gentile.

A NEW TESTAMENT DOCTRINE

If we will have the posture of an inquisitive student, we will be on our way to discovering what the Bible says about Israel's amazing inheritance. The first in the list of eight blessings is the adoption of sons.

Paul says of the people of Israel, "Theirs is the adoption as sons" (Rom. 9:4).

The adoption as sons refers to God's adopting people to be a part of His family. When anyone believes in Christ and confesses Him as Savior, that person is adopted as God's son. Paul says that this right belongs to the Jewish people. He does not say that this blessing used to belong to the Jews, but that it still belongs to them today.

The adoption of sons is not an Old Testament doctrine, so when Paul says that this belongs to the Jews, he is referring to the present and not their past. The word adoption is only mentioned five times in the whole Bible and each time it is in the New Testament. It is a New Testament doctrine.

The word adoption, in the Bible, refers to one who is brought into sonship with respect to God. The word adoption is found in Romans 8:15, Romans 8:23, Romans 9:4, Galatians 4:5 and Ephesians 1:5. In each of these verses the word adoption is used in the same way. It refers to a person's being made part of God's family through Jesus Christ.

Romans 8:23 adds an additional aspect to the adoption process to complete it. It tells us that the adoption process continues as the Holy Spirit begins to live within us and that it is finalized when we are raised from the dead and given a new body. To the Jewish people belongs the adoption as sons. The Scriptures tell us that salvation belongs first to the Jews and then to the Gentiles.

SALVATION FIRST FOR JEWS

Paul is not saying that the adoption of sons only belongs to the Jews. He is the apostle to the Gentiles and knows that salvation is available to all people, but he says it *first* belongs to the Jews. We cannot take it away from them. If anyone is in the company of the elect of God, it is the Jew. Today, they remain God's chosen people.

When Jesus came to earth, He even instructed His disciples not to preach to the Gentiles, but only to the Jews. This changed after Acts 10, when the Gospel opened up to the Gentiles, but it was specifically extended to the Jews first. We read, "These twelve Jesus sent out with the following instructions: "Do not go among the Gentiles ... Go rather to the lost sheep of Israel" (Matt. 10:5-6).

When talking to the Samaritan woman at the well, Jesus said, "Salvation is from the Jews" (John 4:22).

God's salvation has come to the Jews and has moved through them to the people of the world.

Paul said, "I am not ashamed of the gospel because it is the power of God for the salvation of everyone who believes; *first for the Jew*, then for the Gentile" (Rom. 1:16; italics added).

The adoption of a Jew into the family of God involves the same process as for Gentiles. Jesus is the door and the only way to God the Father. There is no other name under heaven whereby a person can be saved. Romans 9:6-8 and verse 32 tell us that, in God's eyes, not *all* of Israel is considered Israel. Jews, like everyone else, must have the appropriate faith to receive God's salvation. Their adoption as sons is not automatic, but certainly it is intended for them and graciously extended to them. To them belongs the adoption as sons.

ISRAEL MUST CLAIM HER BLESSINGS

Even though these eight blessings belong to Israel, they are of no benefit unless Israel claims and embraces them. It is like the person who has won an enormous amount of money from the national lottery. Although I do not participate in lotteries, permit me to use them as an example for the sake of illustration.

When someone wins the lottery, he must claim his prize. The people responsible want to contact the winner. Millions of dollars belong to the right ticket holder, but it is of no good unless the winner comes for the money. So it is with the Jews; these amazing blessings belong to them, but they must claim their prize.

The winning ticket says, "Enter only through the name of Jesus," and many Jews have not yet accepted that reality. That is why Paul was so frustrated when he wrote theses verses. It is only a matter of time, however, before all of Israel will be saved. Then all of her promised blessings will come to her. They already have the promise, for the gifts and calling for Israel are irrevocable (see Romans 11:28-29). To them belongs the adoption as sons.

CHAPTER EIGHT

THE DIVINE GLORY

AN EXTRAORDINARY STATEMENT

ISRAEL'S amazing inheritance is outlined for us in Romans 9:4-5. It is an extraordinary list, and if we stop and look at these verses long enough, we will be surprised to discover the vast scope of Israel's blessings. The most dynamic item in this inventory of eight blessings is the one discussed in this chapter. It is the second blessing on the list, and it tells us that Israel is a recipient of God's glory. Paul says, "The people of Israel ... theirs [is] the divine glory" (Rom. 9:4).

THE GLORY OF GOD

Over the past forty years, I have preached many sermons on the glory of God. I have never done this subject justice, and I do not think that any preacher ever has.

It is the challenge of every good teacher to adequately communicate profound truths in a simple way, but to be successful, the teacher must not reduce the depth or meaning of that truth. I think that is impossible to accomplish when describing God's glory. As soon as we begin to describe it with any human language, we reduce its potency.

God's glory is bigger than what we can explain, but I will try. The glory of God is described in so many different ways in Scripture. It is God's presence coming like a cloud that filled the temple. Glory is that all-inclusive word that humans use to describe God's radiant beauty, His power, greatness, love, character, wisdom, and, in fact, all that He is. If we could put all of God's amazing attributes together and find a word to describe what we have discovered, we would use the word *glory*.

God's glory is more than His shining greatness because the words shining and greatness are inadequate. He does more than shine, and He is more than great. It is because we are human, and confined in time and space, that we cannot grasp this. God is not natural; He is supernatural. He is uncontained, unlimited and far beyond the scope and reason of science or imagination. When we talk of God's glory, we talk of that other-worldy aspect of who God is and what He can do.

Here on earth we have qualities of greatness. We have fame, excellence, magnificent beauty, extra-ordinary skill and even genius, but none of these comes close to describing glory. They are the best of our human qualities, but they are flawed. God's glory, on the other hand, is perfect. It is awesome. He is not only worthy of adoration, but He is worthy of the highest form of worship.

GLORY FOR HUMANS

If we get as close as we can to understanding God's glory, we find it is greater than the greatest of all things combined. It is the most powerful and the most brilliant quality that could be possessed or known. If it is not that, it is not God's glory.

Moses went up on Mount Moriah to meet with God, and God gave him the Ten Commandments. While there, Moses asked God if he could see His glory. God told him than no one could see Him and live; nevertheless, He let Moses see His back. When Moses came down from the mountain, his hair was white, and his face shone so brightly that no one could look at him. The people were afraid, and Moses had to wear a veil over his face so that the Israelites could come near. A bit of God's glory had spilled over onto Moses.

When God's glory filled the temple, the priests could not enter. When they came close to the cloud, their legs gave way, and they were unable to stand.

At times, God's glory was described as fire. It was like flashing lights coming from brilliant gem stones. Everyone who has seen God's glory has only seen a small portion of it. It has been released only in part so that a human can have a taste without paying for it with his life. All of this changes one day. In eternity we will be like Jesus and will be able to see God face to face.

Revelation states the following: *"No longer will there be any curse.* The throne of God and of the Lamb will be in the city, and his servants will serve him. *They will see his face*, and his name will be on their foreheads" (Rev. 22:3-4; italics added).

Right now we cannot see God face to face. We live in a fallen, sin-cursed world. From the time of Adam, sin has resulted in curses, and curses have separated us from God. When, finally, every curse is removed, we will be able to see God face to face. Then we will live with Him on this earth. We will experience amazing fellowship with Him and serve Him in extraordinary ways. For now, our lives are moments of opportunity and training. The closer we walk in fellowship and friendship with Jesus, the more we become like Him. The process is called sanctification or being made holy. The Scripture says, "Those he called, he also justified; those he justified, he also glorified" (Rom. 8:30).

To be called, justified and glorified is a process that leads to purpose. When God calls you and you respond, He removes your sin and begins a work of glorification in you. His goal is to fill you with His glory, one measure at a time.

GOD'S GLORY FOR THE JEWS

God will never give all of His glory to any human, but any amount of His glory is fabulous. God promises that His glory (in part) will be given to the Jewish people. Romans 9:5 tells us that to them (the Jews) belongs the divine glory. In front of the word *glory*, He places the word divine so that we will not reduce it to some human quality, such as fame, skill or genius. Paul says that it is the God-glory that belongs to Israel.

Some people teach that God will not share His glory with any human. They come to this conclusion because of a verse that I feel is greatly misunderstood: "I am the Lord; that is my name! I will not give my glory to another or my praise to idols" (Isa. 42:8).

This Scripture teaches us that God will not share His glory with other so-called gods; He will not give His praise to idols. He is not saying that He will not share His glory with humans; in fact, sharing His glory with humans is a key aspect of His great eternal plan. That is why He made us in His image and why we will, one day, be like Jesus.

The amazing thing is that God's glory, in part, will come upon Israel. Just look at what the prophet Isaiah says: "Arise, shine, for your light has come, and the glory of the Lord rises upon you. See, darkness covers the earth and thick darkness is over the peoples, but the Lord rises upon you and his glory appears over you. Nations will come to your light, and kings to the brightness of your dawn" (Isa. 60:1-3).

This verse is a prophecy given for the Jewish people. Two verses earlier we discover that the prophecy is aimed at Israel. We read: "'The Redeemer will come to Zion, *to those in Jacob* who repent of their sins,' declares the Lord. 'As for me, this is *my covenant with them*,' says the Lord. ... 'the *glory of the Lord* rises upon you ... *His glory appears over you* '" (Isa. 59:20-21, 60:1; italics added).

This does not mean that God's glory is just for the Jews. It is available to the Gentile Church as well. Gentiles have been grafted into God's family, and they will receive most of the blessings that God has promised Israel (see Romans 11:19). The blessings that the Gentile believers will receive include His glory.

It is important to line things up according to God's time clock, as discovered in the Scriptures. It will help us to be in step with Him if we understand His plan. That knowledge helps us, equips us and enables us to partner with God for the coming of His glorious kingdom.

In Isaiah 60:1-2, we discover that God's glory comes at a time when darkness covers the earth and gross darkness covers the people. All of this tells us that His glory will come upon the Jews while darkness is still on the earth. The glory comes before the Second Coming and before the millennial reign of Christ. God's glory, as prophesied in Isaiah, may even come upon the Jews in our lifetime, and if it does, it will simultaneously come to the Gentile Church.

WHAT GOD'S GLORY WILL LOOK LIKE

As we understand God's plan, we begin to agree with Him in prayer and participate with Him in His victory. Extraordinary dynamics will transpire in Israel as the glory of the Lord comes upon the Jewish people. We will share more details about this later in the book. I also recommend, for further study on the subject, you read the book of Zechariah. (While the book of Revelation describes the end times and what will happen to the devil, the Church, the world and Israel, Zechariah specifically describes the end times for Israel.) As I read Zechariah, I especially love chapter 12. It is about God's glory coming upon Israel to provide supernatural military supremacy. (I also encourage you to order our audio teaching on Zechariah 12. You may find our contact information in this book and ask for the CD called "Israel's National Defense.")

Israel's supernatural defense is just the beginning of God's glory coming upon Israel. Before the Lord returns, God's glory will be seen on many fronts. Israel will experience supernatural protection, an amazing increase of land and population, extraordinary financial wealth, a world-changing spiritual revival, amazing fame and honor among the nations, many miraculous signs and wonders, and a powerful anointing of God's presence moving upon her ministers. In short the glory of the Lord will overshadow the Jewish community.

Then a spiritual revival will sweep the nations of the world. The Church will experience many of the same signs and wonders that will be displayed in Israel. Believers from every nation will experience increased anointing for miracles, and multitudes of new believers will come to salvation. The world will witness a new visitation of the presence and power of the Holy Spirit. A season full of worship and rejoicing will come to those who love God Almighty and the Lamb.

The end-time revivals will come, but they will not be sustained. The work of the cross and all of the biblical prophecies must be fulfilled before the return of the Lord. God's people will rule the nations of the earth for a season. This will not last, however, for after a season of God's displaying of His glory on His people, He will lift His hand and allow Satan's armies to rise and be exposed. The devil will employ the arts of the Antichrist, and his most vile coworkers will do their worst. Then, the Lord will destroy them. He will begin the process of ending evil and rebellion as He rides to earth on resurrection day. These prophetic truths can be discovered in Revelation 7, 11, 13 and 19. (For a detailed study, see my book, *Unexpected Fire*.)

This present season of time favors you and your children. Get ready; prepare yourself for the increased anointing of the Holy Spirit in Israel, in the world and in your family. The glory of the Lord is coming.

CHAPTER NINE

THE COVENANTS

AGREEMENTS FROM HEAVEN

THE next amazing blessing in our list involves the covenants. The Bible says that the covenants belong to Israel. We will discover this as we continue to study Romans 9:4. A covenant is an agreement, a promise, a binding contract. Two parties make an oath to bless each other, and then a contract or covenant is established, and it must not be broken.

God is a covenant-keeping God, and He is always faithful to keep His part of any covenantal agreement. Every person on the planet is blessed because of Him, but in order to receive sustained blessings from God, a person must agree to make a covenant with Him. They must promise their lives to the Lord and walk in His ways. It is like a marriage agreement. A covenant made with God operates like this: you give your life and all that you have to God, and He will give all that He has to you. This is so extensive that one day those who make a binding covenant with God will become joint heirs with Christ; they will inherit all things. Humans are the real beneficiaries of this two-way agreement. God gets our devotion, friendship and fellowship, but what we get in return is an unlimited amount of resources plus the awesome opportunity of friendship and fellowship with Him.

The Bible is divided into two parts, the Old Covenant and the New Covenant. Each represents a powerful contract that God has made with humankind. These two major covenants, however, are not the only covenants that God has made with people. The Bible tells us of seven main covenants that God has made with the inhabitants of earth. They are as follows:

1. The Noahic Covenant (Gen. 9:1-17)
2. The Abrahamic Covenant (Gen. 15:9-21; 17:1-8)
3. The Old Covenant (Heb. 8:8-9)
4. The Mosaic Covenant (Exod. 19:5; 24:1-4; Deut. 29:1-15; Josh. 8:30-35)
5. The Levitical Covenant (Num. 25:10-13; Jer. 33:21; Mal. 2:4-5)
6. The Davidic Covenant (2 Sam. 7:5-16, 23; Ps. 89:3-4, 28-29)
7. The New Covenant (Heb. 8:8-12; 10:6-17; Jer. 31:31-37)

There are many covenantal blessings that have been promised to Israel. The earth will never again be completely destroyed by a flood; Israel will receive her land; Israel will be treasured among the nations; Israel will become prosperous; the Living God will be her God; they will have a lasting priesthood and countless ministers from their descendants; they will have eternal salvation and eternal life; they will be established forever; and God will protect them, watch over them and live among them.

THE COVENANTS BELONG TO ISRAEL

Paul was an outstanding student of the Scriptures, and more importantly, he was filled with the Holy Spirit. He understood that the covenants belonged to Israel, so he declared this fact as part of his defense in his letter to the church at Rome. He said of the people of Israel, "Theirs [are] … the covenants" (Rom. 9:4).

This is the third blessing in this eight-part list of what belongs to Israel. The specific covenant that is most misunderstood by believers is the New Covenant. It seems that some Christians do not realize that the New Covenant was, in fact, given to Israel. When I visit church congregations and we are having fellowship with some of their leaders, the questions and discussions often focus on Israel. I like to ask this question: "To whom was the Old Covenant given?" The answer is always, "Israel". Then I ask, "To whom was the New Covenant given?" The answer from leaders is often, "To the Gentile

Church". This of course is not who the New Covenant was first given to, so I take them to the Scriptures.

> *"The time is coming," declares the Lord, "when I will make a new covenant with the house of Israel and with the house of Judah. It will not be like the covenant I made with their forefathers when I took them by the hand to lead them out of Egypt, because they broke my covenant, though I was a husband to them," declares the Lord. "This is the covenant I will make with the house of Israel after that time," declares the Lord. "I will put my law in their minds and write it on their hearts. I will be their God and they will be my people. No longer will a man teach his neighbor, or a man his brother, saying 'Know the Lord,' because they will all know me, from the least of them to the greatest," declares the Lord. "For I will forgive their wickedness and will remember their sins no more." (Jer. 31:31-34; emphasis added).*

From this Scripture in Jeremiah, we see that God initiated the New Covenant with the people of Israel. This, however, is an Old Testament Scripture, so let us look further in the New Testament. The following verses are from the book of Hebrews. (Later in our book, we will look at this again.)

> *"The time is coming," declares the Lord, "when* I will make a new covenant with the house of Israel and with the house of Judah. *It will not be like the covenant I made with their forefathers when I took them by the hand to lead them out of Egypt, because they did not remain faithful to my covenant, and I turned away from them," declares the Lord. "This is the covenant* I will make with the house of Israel *after that time,"* declares the Lord. I will put my laws in their minds and write them on their hearts. I will be their God and they will be my people. No longer will a man teach his neighbor, or a man his brother, saying, 'know the Lord.' Because they will all know me, from the least of them to the greatest. For I will forgive their wickedness and will remember their sins no more." Heb. 8:8-12; emphasis added)*

This verse is also repeated in Hebrews 10:16-18. The New Testament Scriptures are almost identical to the Old Testament passage. It is conclusive; the

New Covenant was given to Israel, to the house of Judah. This teaching was presented in the Old Testament and confirmed in the New Testament. The New Covenant was given to those whose forefathers were led by God out of Egypt.

The New Covenant was not given to the Gentiles, but to Israel. This does not mean that the Gentile Church is left out in the cold. Like many blessings that God gave to Israel, the New Covenant is extended to those from every nation who will open their hearts to Jesus and believe in the work that He did for them on the cross. The New Covenant blessings are now available to all believers.

THE NEW COVENANT TEACHER

Through the New Covenant, God promises that His Word, which was written on tablets of stone and other external surfaces, will now be written on people's hearts; it will be internalized. The Holy Spirit will come and live inside of God's people. All who receive the New Covenant may have a personal relationship with the Living God. They may fellowship with the Lord and know Him intimately.

Under the Old Covenant, God sent His Word to His people through special leaders, such as priests and prophets. Under the New Covenant, a major paradigm shift occurs; the Holy Spirit comes to all believers, and He becomes their personal teacher. It is not that we cannot be taught by other teachers, priests or prophets, but we now have the ability to judge what we are taught because the Holy Spirit speaks to us from within. He lets us know if what they are saying is right or wrong, and, more important than that, He gives us direct revelation so that many truths will come to us directly from God and not through another person.

When I preach a sermon, I know that I am teaching God's Word, but more importantly, I know that the Holy Spirit is teaching. Sometimes, the Holy Spirit will teach things to individuals that I am not teaching in my sermon. The people are not only judging what I am delivering, but hearing more than what I am saying because the Holy Spirit is speaking to them. The Holy Spirit becomes the primary teacher for every New Covenant believer.

Jesus makes a powerful statement, telling us that His sheep hear His voice, that He leads the sheep and a stranger they will not follow (see John 10:1-10). The Holy Spirit of the New Covenant is the Spirit of Jesus, and He gives us the opportunity to hear His words directly. This gift of the Holy Spirit is available to all of God's people, Jew and Gentile alike, because of the New Covenant.

THE CHANGER AND THE COMFORTER

The Holy Spirit brings more than words of instruction. He brings comfort, supernatural gifts of miraculous power, character changes called the fruit of the Spirit and amazing guidance and personal direction. In short, under the New Covenant, the Holy Spirit becomes our personal trainer. It is the indwelling voice of the New Covenant that enables a person to walk in fellowship with Christ. This is the main purpose of the New Covenant.

Paul says that the covenants belong to Israel, but, in case you did not catch it earlier, here is a reminder. In the tenth chapter of the book of Acts, we discover that the New Covenant has been extended to the Gentiles. Every person from any nation has a personal right to enjoy the benefits of the New Covenant. Those blessings can be claimed when any person accepts Jesus Christ as his or her Lord and Savior. (They start with every kind of earthly blessing and go on to eternal and everlasting ones). Give thanks to God for the Jews, for Paul says that to them belong the covenants, and if you are a believing Gentile, then you have been grafted in.

CHAPTER TEN

THE RECEIVING OF THE LAW

A s we look at the list of eight blessings that belong to Israel, we find that one of them is easy to acknowledge. It is the fourth blessing. It says that to the Jewish people belongs the receiving of the Law.

This reference is not pointing to just any law, but to the Jewish Law, or, as it is more commonly called, the Law of Moses. This is the law that was given to Israel while they were wandering in the wilderness. It has been added to, or extended by, the rabbinical or spoken Law. Rabbinical Law emerged after the first temple was destroyed, when many Jews were exiled from the land of Israel. They needed an adaptation to help them maintain a consistent form of religious behavior, and they needed guidelines to help them maintain a new pattern for God-centered worship. They were cut off from their priests, and they did not have access to temple life, so their worship had to find different expressions. It was adjusted so that it could be better exercised in their daily lives, in their homes and in their synagogues.

The Bible gives us the original, unaltered form of the Jewish Law as God gave it to Moses. That expression of the Jewish Law was ordained by God. We cannot be sure that any additions or adjustments to the Law were given by God. They may have been, but only God knows.

Regardless of our perspective on the matter, the truth remains that Paul affirms that the Mosaic Law was given to the people of Israel. He says, "the people of Israel. Theirs is … the receiving of the law" (Rom. 9:4).

The Law was given, by God, to the Jews for a number of reasons:

1. It sustained them through centuries of persecution.
2. It gave the Jews a moral code that most of the world has adopted.
3. It illustrates the ways of the Lord as He walks with humanity.
4. It is a teacher to bring the Jews to grace.
5. It exposes man's failures by uncovering the roots of sin.

Let us look further into these five blessings of the Law and see why the law is a special gift from God to the Jewish people.

A SPECIAL GIFT

Most Gentile believers who understand what is involved in the keeping of the Mosaic Law are glad that the Law was given to the Jews and not to them. With more than six hundred dos and don'ts, the keeping of the Law is a very heavy burden. Whoever keeps it will not become more holy because of it, but they will definitely be busy and focused. In order to properly observe Jewish Law, one must be consumed with lots of protocol. The Law involves every detail of a Jew's life; from the food he eats, to the clothes he wears, and to the many details about his personal behavior and social boundaries. The life of an observant Jew is the life of a programmed person who does not belong to himself. It was God's plan to give the Law to the Jews.

It is this burdensome Law that has been such a special gift for Israel. It may seem obvious and rudimentary to say it, but God knew exactly what He was doing when He gave them the Law. This is what kept them through almost two thousand years of exile and persecution. The Law enabled them to maintain their culture and be identified as a separate people when they were in distant lands far away from Jerusalem.

Imagine if the traumas of Israel had fallen on the people of Cuba. Both Israel and Cuba are nations that are relatively small. Think about it; if the people of Cuba were scattered around the world for almost two thousand years, what would have happened to them? After just five hundred years of intermarrying and being absorbed by other countries, would you be able to find a single Cuban anymore? Probably not! If the Cubans no longer had a homeland to give them identity, would they still exist after, let's say, one thousand years? Hold that thought and add to the mix the pressures of an international ethnic cleansing agenda. The Jews were a perpetual target for hatred and murder; for centuries, they faced the worst kind of persecution and genocide attempts. Hundreds of thousands and even millions were killed through the centuries. Because of this, many changed their names and denied their Jewish identity so they could hide themselves from public view. They wanted to stay alive and be left alone. What if all of those pressures came upon the Cubans? I think it would be impossible for them to survive. I doubt that a single person on the planet would still be identified as Cuban after nineteen hundred years of exile and persecution among the nations.

Yet this is exactly what happened to Israel, only they endured and survived. After such a long period of time, they were miraculously reborn as a nation in 1948. That is an amazing phenomenon, and it happened because the people of Israel had the Law. The requirements and restrictions of the Law gave the Jews their identity and their culture, no matter where they lived.

God gave them the Law and threatened them with curses, death and annihilation if they forsook it. The Law kept them God-focused and separate from other people while they were living in foreign lands. Then, when God so decided, the sound went out, and the Jews were called back to their homeland. They became a nation again, but it could not have happened without the receiving of the Law. Without it they would have been lost. They would have been absorbed in the tossed salad and the cross-cultural mix of the world. The Law was faithful to distinguish them and identify them from other people. In hindsight, it was a very special gift from God.

A SPIRITUAL CODE FOR THE WORLD

By and large, the world adopted the moral and ethical guidelines of the Mosaic Law. Although there is a growing departure from it, and no nation has ever followed it perfectly, the godly guidelines of civilization have historically come from the Law of the Jews.

When the Jews first began to live under the guidelines of the Ten Command-ments, for example, the rest of the world was worshipping idols, murdering other people, stealing, sleeping with their neighbors' wives and exercising every form of cruelty, corruption and indecency. Little by little, the nations adopted the moral guidelines of the Jewish Law. The receiving of the Law has not only blessed Israel; it has blessed the nations of the world.

A PATTERN AND A SHADOW

The Law is not only the glue that held the Jews together for thousands of years, and it is not only a moral code for the world, but, because of the keeping of the Law, the Jews have become a picture book of God's blessings for all the world to see. The Law is full of shadows and types that illustrate the devotion and lifestyle that God desires from His people. Everything, from the circumcision of the flesh, to tassels at the hem of a Jew's garment, speaks of some spiritual dimension that God intends for humanity. These symbols are not the realities, but an illustration of them, and while the Jews are to show forth the illustrations, both Jews and Gentiles are called upon to live in the realities of what each illustration points to. The book of Hebrews says, "The law is only a shadow of the good things that are coming – not the realities themselves" (Heb. 10:1).

It seems that God has chosen a people to be a picture book to show forth the shadows and symbols of His requirements and blessings. It is amazing to think that a people are called to illustrate, through symbolism, the call of God on our lives.

THE APOSTLES' DOCTRINE

After Jesus died and the Holy Spirit was sent to the Jewish people on the day of Pentecost, the New Testament Church emerged. The believers, at that time, were all Jews, and they went from house to house sharing life with one another and exploring the blessings of the New Covenant.

"They *devoted themselves to the apostles' teaching* and to the fellowship, to the breaking of bread and to prayer" (Acts 2:42; italics added).

These early saints were Jews. They knew the Old Testament Scriptures and the doctrines of the Jewish faith. They were now learning something new. They called this fresh teaching "the apostles' doctrine." It was different from what they had known before; it involved the teachings that took them from the shadows of the Law to the realities of Christ. From these new teachings and revelations, the book of Hebrews was written. *The book of Hebrews is a basic summary of the apostles' doctrine.*

The book of Hebrews talks about better things. It reveals ten aspects of Jewish Law that have been adjusted, upgraded and fulfilled under the New Covenant. Here is a list of these ten shadows of the Law and what they have become in Christ.

1. *Animal sacrifices* are replaced by the sacrifice of Christ on the cross (Heb. 7:27; 9:7-23; 13:10).
2. *The way into the Holy of Holies* (the presence of God) is not through a curtain or veil, but through the body of Christ, who died on the cross (Heb. 10:20, 29-30).
3. The *High Priest* is no longer a man here on earth, but Jesus, who is before the throne of God, in heaven (Heb. 2:17-18; 3:1-2; 4:14-15; 5:5,10; 7:26-28; 8:1-3; 9:11).
4. *The priesthood* is not relegated to the Levites alone, but to all believers (Heb. 7:11, 12, 21-22).
5. *The sanctuary* is not only a room in the temple, but also God's throne room in heaven (Heb. 8:5, 9:24).
6. *The Law* is not written on stone, but on our hearts (Heb. 8:10).
7. *The Sabbath* is not just a day, but also a position of rest through faith in Christ (Heb. 4:8-11).
8. *The New Covenant* completely replaces the Old Covenant (Heb. 8:6-13; 10:16-18).
9. *The natural city of Jerusalem* has a spiritual counterpart called the New or Heavenly Jerusalem (Heb. 11:8-16; 12:22).
10. *The Temple* is not only a physical building, but also a spiritual building. We are the new temple; the Holy Spirit lives in us, and

He is writing the Word of God on our hearts and minds (Heb. 8:15-16).

A SCHOOLMASTER THAT LEADS TO GRACE

The Law is a schoolmaster that leads us to God's grace. It tells us what not to do, and it exposes our sin when we fail. The Law helps us see that we are frail. It is unbendable; it is perfect, but we are not. Jesus came not to destroy the Law, but to fulfill it. The Bible tells us that we cannot be righteous by attempting to keep the Law. All of us will fail, and all of us will commit sin.

The Law exposes the root of our sin, and then it points us to Christ for help. Only His grace can save us. The Law is a schoolmaster that leads us to His grace.

The Law was given to Israel, and it has been a great blessing to them. They can never become holy or be saved from hell through the keeping of the Law. That does not mean, however, that they should forsake it. The Jews have a special role to play in God's great plan. Their lives continue to be a symbolic illustration for all the nations to see. It is their calling to be a separate people, to obey the Law and to do the things contained in it. They must discover the book of Hebrews and adjust to the fullness of the Law that is taught there; nevertheless, they will carry the shadows and types contained in the Law to demonstrate the patterns and ways of the Lord throughout eternity. To the Jews belongs the receiving of the Law.

GENTILES AND THE LAW

The Law is good and holy, but the Gentile Church is not required to keep all of the details that are written in the Law. If anyone tries to be righteous by keeping the Law, whether Jew or Gentile, they are cursed because only through faith in Christ can a person become righteous.

The Jews, nevertheless, are to keep the Law (with the appropriate adjustments written in the book of Hebrews) for the purpose of illustration and service to God. The Gentiles are not called to bear the burden of the Jewish

Law with all of its regulations for any reason. Those who choose to keep that Law will add a burden to their lives that God does not require of them. The Gentiles and the Jews, nevertheless, are required to follow the moral code and the teachings of Christ and the apostles as recorded in the New Testament. Those teachings are more than shadows; they are substance and realities that all of God's people should follow.

CHAPTER ELEVEN

THE TEMPLE WORSHIP

INCLUDED in the joblist that God has given to the Israelites is temple worship. It is one of the eight blessings that Paul tells us belongs to them: "To the people of Israel … belongs the temple worship" (Rom. 9:5).

Most Gentiles have no idea what this means, so this chapter will focus on bringing understanding to this teaching.

UNDERSTANDING REAL WORSHIP

Upon hearing of this Jewish responsibility of temple worship, many Christians will have more questions than answers. As they think of temple worship, many can only relate to the songs they sing during their Sunday morning church services. They might picture a group of volunteer players and singers who gather to lead the congregation in spiritual songs every Sunday. Many of them are young people who come with guitars, a keyboard and a set of drums, and they play their best for the Lord. I love to see people worshipping the Lord with all of their hearts.

Things have changed, for just fifty years ago there would have been no drums or guitars in most churches. The only instruments allowed in many churches back then were pianos and organs. Other instruments were considered worldly, undignified and even sinful. Our Gentile temple worship has experienced a radical facelift. When our parents were still children, the church hymnal was the primary source of songs for Sunday morning. Today, many young believers sing only choruses, and the only hymn they have heard is "Amazing Grace." We should note that without the modern young singers and instrumentalists, many of our forefathers knew how to worship the Lord with all of their hearts.

Whether we reflect on our present forms of worship or that of our grandparents, we are still far removed from the biblical reference to temple worship. If we want to understand what the Bible is referring to when it says that *temple worship belongs to Israel*, we must go back in history. We must leave our Christian evangelical perspective for a moment and explore a much broader understanding of worship. It will help if we first understand what worship really is.

Worship is the daily dedication of our lives unto God. To the woman at the well in Samaria, Jesus said, "The Father is seeking such to worship Him … and those who worship Him must worship in spirit and in truth" (John. 4:23,24).

Jesus was not talking about singing before a congregation on Sunday morning when He called this woman to be a worshipper. He was not recruiting her as a new lead singer for the Sabbath worship service. Jesus was calling her to a life of adoration and service unto the Lord. That is what worship is. Paul explains worship as the total surrender of our lives to God. He says, "I urge you, brothers, in view of God's mercy, to offer your bodies as living sacrifices … to God -*this is your spiritual act of worship*" (Rom. 12:1; italics added).

Singing heartfelt songs unto the Lord is a wonderful aspect of celebration, and it is an expression of our worship. If our daily lives, however, are not dedicated in obedience unto the Living God, then our Sunday singing, no matter how stirring or emotional it is, is not real worship.

TEMPLE WORSHIP

Understanding what it means to live a life of worship and combining that with the details of temple life that God gave to the Jews will help us appreciate the term *temple worship*. Some Christians believe temple worship for the Jews is an old religious tradition of spiritual insignificance. Paul, however, does not think so; he presents temple worship as a magnificent honor and a solemn, God-ordained responsibility that was given to the Jews. He lists temple worship as one of eight amazing dynamics that points to the unique blessings that God has given to Israel.

A major part of temple worship is connected to the appointed feasts of the Lord. Leviticus 23 reveals what God ordained as appointed holy days or feast days for His people. Before we discard the Jewish feasts as Old Testament relics, we should see what God says about their significance in the future. For example, the Feast of Tabernacles is one of the Jewish feasts that is celebrated in the Millennium. Every Christian community, nation and Jew will be required to observe and celebrate this feast after the return of Christ. The prophet Zechariah explains in the following passage:

> "Then the survivors from all the nations ... will go up year after year to worship the King, the Lord Almighty, and to celebrate the Feast of Tabernacles. If any of the peoples of the earth do not go up to Jerusalem to worship ... they will have no rain. ... This will be the punishment ... of all the nations that do not go up to celebrate the Feast of Tabernacles" (Zech. 14:16-19).

These verses refer to the thousand-year reign of Christ. All of the people of the earth will celebrate at least some of the Jewish feasts at that time. That is the real temple worship.

GOD'S APPOINTED FEASTS

The Jewish feasts are God appointed holidays (holy days) for His people. They were designed by God, and they are not like the arbitrary dates of bank holidays that a nation might assign to her people to remember or celebrate an event or person in order to have a day off work. These are the feasts of the Lord. Leviticus 23 tells of their importance: "The Lord said to Moses, 'Speak to the Israelites and say to them: "These are my appointed feasts, the feasts of the Lord, which you are to proclaim as sacred assemblies"'" (Lev. 23:1-2).

The 23rd chapter of Leviticus reveals seven amazing feasts of the Lord. They are divinely appointed, and they include the following:

1. Passover
2. Unleavened Bread
3. Firstfruits
4. Weeks
5. Trumpets
6. Day of Atonement (Yom Kippur)
7. Tabernacles

Besides the seven feasts that are mentioned in Leviticus, we could also include the observances of the Sabbath, Hanukkah and Purim as holy days of the Lord.

Each of the God-appointed feasts involves detailed activities of solemn remembrance that require the usual daily activities to grind to a halt. These spiritual activities include acts of dedication to the Lord by individuals, families, priests, politicians and the nation as a whole. Some of the feasts last for an entire week and require months of preparation before the actual feast days arrive.

The preparation and observance of the appointed feasts involve a large portion of the Jewish calendar. They require a year-round focus of obedience and personal sacrifice. While every devout individual in Israel cannot give all of his time to these functions, rabbis and priests can. This is the main focus of temple worship, but not all of it. Add to the observances of the feasts the daily religious activities of the priests and Levites, and you will start to understand the meaning of temple worship.

I will not take the time to elaborate on the details involved in the observances of the feasts, but let me say that they are very involved. There are other books that focus specifically on this theme. If you are interested, I recommend *The Feasts of the Lord*, by Kevin Howard and Marvin Rosenthal. It is published by Nelson Books.

LITURGICAL TEMPLE LIFE

Today, the Jews cannot experience the full expressions of temple life, for there is no temple in Jerusalem. They only celebrate, at home and synagogue, an adaptation of temple life, but it is far from complete. There are many synagogues around the world, but these are not temples. There can only be one Jewish temple, and it must be built in Jerusalem on the temple mount. Scripture tells us that the temple will be built again, and the Jewish people will play an important role in the future of the planet because they will lead the nations in the God-ordained focus of temple worship.

Many details regarding temple life have been adjusted by the Lord. We have become aware of this by studying the book of Hebrews. For example, animal sacrifices for the removal of sins are finished. Jesus is the Lamb of God who died for the sins of the world, and no other sacrifice is required or acceptable to God.

Messianic Jews, those who recognize and receive Jesus as their Messiah, realize that the Law is completed in Christ. They are still Jews, but they are completed Jews. Jesus is their Lord, and they study God's Word to discover their adjusted function under the New Covenant.

Although God forbids any other blood sacrifice except His Son, the Bible tells us that devout Jews, who have not yet received Jesus as Messiah, will reinstate animal sacrifices at the end of the age. For sure, this is not God's way, but it will happen because many Jews still believe that the keeping of the Old Testament Law, in its original form, is God's plan for them. When Jesus comes, He will reveal everything to them, and even these misguided Orthodox Jews will be changed. Those who are already Messianic will come to full understanding, and the others who are devout but have not accepted Christ will see Him for who He is and believe that He is their Messiah.

Temple life will be redefined by the Lord, so it will not be exactly as it was under the Old Covenant. The Levitical priests were promised by God that they would have priests among their descendants for all eternity, and so they shall. To the Levites He said, "Their anointing will be to a priesthood that will continue for all generations to come" (Exod. 40:15).

They have been commissioned by God to continue the temple worship. It is their honor and their responsibility. The Lord will restore the temple and its temple worship, and the Jews will serve the Lord by administrating the temple worship for the nations of the world.

Gatherings for future temple worship may resemble, in some ways, the liturgical and sacramental life of modern Catholics or Christian Orthodox churches without the focus on Mary, idols or saints. The format of the Catholic order of service, although different from the Jews, has its roots in Jewish temple worship.

Other liturgically structured church groups, less well-known than the Catholics, may be even closer to the temple worship that is coming. I have a deep appreciation for the Charismatic Episcopal Church. Their priests wear robes, and they have structured liturgy and sacramental presentations but they also have lively singing, prayer for the sick, evangelistic outreaches and powerful charismatic preaching. They exercise the gifts of the Spirit, study God's Word and have genuine fellowship in the Spirit. Their doctrine is similar to the doctrine of charismatic evangelicals, but they add many of the formal expressions that one might see in a Catholic church. I think that Pentecostals, Baptists and other evangelicals might be surprised to see what is instituted by the Lord concerning temple worship in the Millennium.

The phrase in the New Testament that refers to the temple and all that happens within the temple is "David's Tent". The Lord has promosed to rebuild David's tent. The Lord says, "After this I will return and rebuild David's fallen tent. Its ruins I will rebuild and I will restore it" (Acts 15:15).

IN CONCLUSION

To the Jews belongs the temple worship. All of Jewish religious life is designed to be an illustration for the world to see and enjoy. Right now, their religious life may seem stiff and lifeless to some, but in time it will become an anointed demonstration of worship. The Jews have the task of being a walking picture book and a living parable. The original traditions of their religious activities and their lives were designed by God. They have reflected man's interaction, fellowship and worship to Him and God's requirements and obligations for humankind. These religious traditions have now been adjusted by the New Covenant, and they will be further adjusted in the Millennium.

At the top of Israel's religious responsibility lies the temple worship. The ordinances, liturgy, sacraments, offerings, music, readings, kosher requirements, order of activities, procedures and ceremonies that will take place in the new temple will be officiated and orchestrated by the Jews. As a people, the temple worship is, and will be, one of their eternal responsibilities. It is their honor, privilege and blessing to fulfill this calling.

The people of God from among the nations will join with Israel as they lead the temple worship. All of our lives, at some point, will focus on and celebrate the Feasts of the Lord. They will be our new national holidays. Together we will adore the Lord and enjoy the Jewish festivals that illuminate the glories of the Father and of Jesus the Lamb. To the Jews belongs the temple worship.

Chapter Twelve

THE PROMISES

PROMISES FOR THE JEWS

INCLUDED in God's list of blessings for Israel are the promises. Paul says, "To Israel belongs the promises" (Rom. 9:3).

A promise is a step up from good intentions; it is a solid commitment made by one person to another. Throughout the Bible, God made powerful promises to the people of Israel. There are more than one hundred different promises that He gave to them.

When God makes a promise, He keeps it. The following are some examples of God's promises:

For He remembered His holy *promise* given to His servant Abraham. (Ps. 105:42; italics added).

"The days are coming," declares the Lord, "when I will fulfill the gracious *promise* I made to the house of Israel and to the house of Judah." (Jer. 33:14; italics added).

Do not leave Jerusalem, but wait for the gift my Father *promised*. ... The *promise* is for you and your children and for all who are far off – for all whom the Lord our God will call. (Acts 1:4; 2:39; italics added).

Christ has become a servant of the Jews on behalf of God's truth, to confirm the *promises* made to the patriarchs. (Rom. 15:8; italics added).

This Melchizedek ... collected a tenth from Abraham and blessed him who had the *promises*. (Heb. 7:1,6; italics added).

Throughout my life I have had many promises extended to me by different people, and some of those promises were not kept. Sometimes, people had good intentions, but they were simply unable to keep their promises. I know that the best promises come from God, for He is able and determined to keep them. God made many promises to the Jews, and He keeps His promises.

PROMISES OR COVENANTS

In Paul's dynamic list of eight blessings for the Jews, we find both covenants and promises. These two words seem to be similar, and they are even used interchangeably in some Scriptures. Galatians 3:17 says, "The law, introduced 430 years later, does not set aside the *covenant* previously established by God and thus do away with the *promise*" (Gal. 3:17; italics added).

The Lord is talking about something that could be set aside (the covenants) and, in the same sentence, something that could be done away with (the promise). Here, the terms are used interchangeably.

Technically speaking, a covenant is a binding testament, like a will or a deed. In society, it usually refers to a contract involving land or material goods that are owed because of a binding agreement. It involves two or more people. Each group must keep its part of the covenant contract.

A promise is an assurance that a person is determined and commited to fulfil what he announces. A promise is giving one's word to perform in a certain way. It may be as simple as giving one's word to be on time for an event. A promise is different from a covenant because it does not require a commitment from both parties; it may be a commitment from just one party who has given his word to bless the other party. You can make a promise with no conditions. A covenant always involves conditions, and it requires two or more parties to fulfill those conditions, which are obligations of the covenant.

So a covenant is a two-way agreement, while a promise may be a one-way agreement. God has established covenants with Israel that require her covenantal response. God has also extended promises to the Jews, and He will keep those promises, no matter what the people of Israel do. He has given both covenants and promises to the Jews. Sometimes promises and covenants overlap. Then God decides to fulfill His part of the covenant even though the other party fails. Much of what God has decided to do for Israel falls into that category.

PROMISES ONLY FOR JEWS

In the New Testament, God extends covenants to all people, no matter what nation they come from. At first, these blessings were given to the Jews, but, according to God's eternal plan, the covenants have now reached the Gentiles. The most famous of those covenants is the New Covenant. Peter said, "I now realize how true it is that God does not show favoritism but accepts men from every nation who fear him and do what is right" (Acts 10:34).

And Paul wrote to the Gentiles and said, "And you [Gentiles] … have been grafted in among the others [the Jews] and now share in the nourishing sap [God's blessings] from the olive root [the Jewish patriarchs]" (Rom. 11:17).

A special blessing has been extended to the Jews, and they are the recipients of a few promises that God will keep no matter what the Jews or anyone else does. Those promises will not be broken, and they are only for Israel. Listed below are seven promises that have a specific application for the Jewish people. They are prophetic promises that the Jews will receive in the last days:

1. People around the world will pray for Israel's restoration.
2. The Promised Land will be given to Israel.
3. The Lord will bring the Jewish people to their land.

4. Israel's financial fortunes will be restored.
5. A national revival will come to Israel.
6. Israel will be honored among the nations.
7. The Lord promises to judge the nations for how they have treated Israel.

Let us look at these promises, one at a time.

PROMISE NUMBER ONE

People around the world will pray for Israel's restoration.

Isaiah says, "I have posted watchmen on your walls, O Jerusalem; they will never be silent day or night. *You who call upon the Lord*, give yourselves no rest, and give him no rest till he establishes Jerusalem and makes her *the praise of the earth*" (Isa. 62:6-7; italics added).

This promise is being fulfilled in our lifetime; people from around the world who call upon the Lord are praying for Israel. This prayer movement is an international phenomenon and it has emerged in just the last fifty years. Before then, small groups of Christians were praying for the Jews, but now a massive ground swell of saints, from every nation, are praying that Jerusalem will become the praise of the earth.

PROMISE NUMBER TWO

The Promised Land will be given to Israel.

There are forty-six different passages of Scripture where God promises to give Israel her land. Here are a couple of them:

"Then you will know that I am the Lord, when I bring you into the land of Israel, the land I had sworn with uplifted hand to give to your fathers" (Ezek. 20:42).

"He remembers his covenant forever, the word he commanded for a thousand generations, the covenant he made with Abraham, the oath he swore to Isaac. He confirmed it to Jacob as a decree, to Israel as an everlasting covenant: To you I will give the land of Canaan as the portion you will inherit" (Ps. 105:8-11).

The language of covenants and promises could not be stronger or more enduring than the language God used to commit to Israel in this verse. If this verse did not impact you in a profound way, I suggest that you may not have grasped its significance. Read it again. The land is promised to Israel with a covenant *forever*. It is commanded for a thousand generations.

Stop and think of this for a minute; if a generation is twenty years, there are five generations in a one-hundred-year period and fifty generations in one thousand years. If Adam lived six thousand years ago, there are only three hundred generations of humanity since the time of Adam and Eve. If God's covenants for Israel were commanded for a thousand generations, it means they extend beyond the time of mortal man; they reach into eternity.

He made this covenant with Abraham, which He swore by an oath to Isaac and confirmed by a decree to Jacob. God will give the Jews their land. This is so powerful that Scripture calls it an everlasting covenant. No demon, angel or human will be able to stop the covenant that God has made with Israel.

God even reveals the size and boundaries of the land that He promised to them. Genesis tells us, "On that day the Lord made a covenant with Abraham and said, "To your descendants I give this land, from the river of Egypt to the great river, the Euphrates – the land of the Kenites, Kenizzites, Kadmonites, Hittites, Perizzites, Raphaites, Amorites, Canaanites, Girgashites and Jebusites" (Gen. 15:18-21).

The parcel of land that God promised to Israel is significantly larger than what they possess today and what the Jewish people have ever possessed. It will reach from the Nile River (although some say that it is a different river in Egypt) to the Euphrates, not far from Bagdad in Iraq. It covers all the land of the Hittites and all of the other nations that are mentioned. The Promised Land, which will become the land of Israel, includes Turkey, Lebanon,

Jordan, parts of Iraq and Syria. We will look at this subject in more detail as we study Israel's national defense, later in the book.

God's promises are absolute. I am not worried about Israel's future, but the future of the Arab nations around her. As they attack Israel, they will inadvertently injure themselves, and Israel will gain more and more parcels of land as she defends herself. God's promise of the land is not negotiable.

PROMISE NUMBER THREE

The Lord will bring the Jewish people to their land.

The prophet Isaiah said, "He will raise a banner for the nations and gather the exiles of Israel; he will assemble the scattered people of Judah from the four quarters of the earth" (Isa. 11:12).

Zephaniah the prophet spoke the Word of the Lord when He said, "Sing, O daughter of Zion; shout aloud O Israel: Be glad and rejoice with all your heart O Daughter of Jerusalem! ... At that time I will gather you: at that time I will bring you home" (Zeph. 3:14,20).

We call the gathering of the Jews to their homeland, the *aliyah*. Isaiah gives us more details about it; he says, "Your sons hasten back to you and those who laid you waste depart from you. ... This is what the Sovereign Lord says: "See, I will beckon to the Gentiles, I will lift up my banner to the peoples; they will bring your sons in their arms and carry your daughters on their shoulders" (Isa. 49:17,22).

This is happening right now; Gentiles, who are Christians, are working hard to bring the Jewish people back to their land. Many believers who cannot participate in the physical act of transporting Jews to Israel are sending money to organizations that administrate the *aliyah*. In some cases, however, the Gentiles themselves are travelling to places like Russia and are actually carrying infirmed and tired Jews in their arms as they help them get on buses and planes for their journey to the Promised Land. It is exactly as the prophecy said it would be: "They will bring your sons in their arms and carry your daughters on their shoulders."

PROMISE NUMBER FOUR

Israel's financial fortunes will be restored.

Zephaniah prophesies the word of the Lord to Israel; he says, "'At that time I will gather you; at that time I will bring you home. I will give you honor and praise among the peoples of the earth *when I restore your fortunes* before your very eyes,' says the Lord" (Zeph. 3:20; italics added).

Besides Zephaniah, the prophet Joel tells us about the financial blessings that are promised to Israel. Joel says, "In those days and at that time, *when I restore the fortunes* of Judah and Jerusalem, I will gather all nations" (Joel 3:1; italics added).

Moses also prophesied regarding the fortunes of Israel:

"Then the Lord your *God will restore your fortunes* and have compassion on you and gather you from all the nations where he scattered you" (Deut. 30:3; italics added).

Since 1948, the year that Israel became a nation, she has risen from obscurity to be one of the wealthiest nations in the world. Her creative genius in agriculture and computer technology combined with her diamond sales, tourism and amazing marketing skills have brought Israel out from the poverty status that some of her neighbors cannot seem to shake. We should understand that Israel will continue to grow financially, for the Lord has promised to restore her fortunes before her very eyes.

The following is an excerpt from an article written by Barbara Yaffe for the Vancouver Sun:

> *I wrote a column recently on a newly published book, titled* Start Up Nation, *that documents the Israeli economic miracle.*

The tiny country, with so very few natural resources and surrounded by enemies, has a per capita GDP of about $28,000 and boasts the highest ratio of university degrees to population in the world.

Fully 70 percent of Israel's waste water is recycled — more than any other country in the world. And Israel is the birthplace and world leader in drop irrigation, a technology that has transformed desert into farmland.

Israel's success will give hope to other developing nations who start their journey with very little but hope, and Monday's news [that Israel has been accepted as a member of the Europe-based Organization for Economic Cooperation and Development] *will also serve as a measure of vindication for a country that too often is vilified for trying to preserve itself as a homeland for the Jewish people.*[11]

PROMISE NUMBER FIVE

A national revival will come to Israel.

Israel's coming revival is the theme of this book, so I will not say much about it at this time. Here, however, are some Scriptures that point to this promise.

And I will pour out on the house of David and the inhabitants of Jerusalem, a spirit of grace and supplication. They will look on me, the one they have pierced, and they will mourn for him as one mourns for an only child, and grieve bitterly for him as one grieves for a firstborn son. … On that day a fountain will be opened to the house of David and the inhabitants of Jerusalem, to cleanse them from their sin and impurity. (Zech.12:10; 13:1)

When the full number of the Gentiles has come in then all of Israel will be saved. (Rom. 11:26)

The Jewish revival is the real emergence of the fig leaves that will usher in the return of the Lord. Within one generation of Israel's spiritual revival, Jesus will return (see Matthew 24:34).

PROMISE NUMBER SIX

Israel will be honored among the nations.

Of the seven promises for Israel, this one is the least talked about by preachers and perhaps the most difficult to believe. We hear of Israel's restoration and of the world at war with the Jews, but I do not hear Bible teachers talking about Israel's honor among the nations. God has promised this to Israel. Here are some prophetic verses that point to this forgotten truth.

"Arise, shine … Nations will come to your light and kings to the brightness of your dawn" (Isa 60:1,3).

"'At that time I will gather you; at that time I will bring you home. I will give you honor and praise among all the peoples of the earth when I restore your fortunes before your very eyes,' says the Lord" (Zeph. 3:20).

"This is what the Lord Almighty says: 'In those days, ten men from all languages and nations will take firm hold of one Jew by the hem of his robe and say, "Let us go with you, because we have heard that God is with you."'" (Zech. 8:23).

PROMISE NUMBER SEVEN

The Lord promises to judge the nations for how they have treated Israel.

Like the other six promises in our list, this one is specifically for Israel. It does not apply to the Gentile Church. At the end of the age, God promises to judge the nations, not only because of their wicked behavior or how they responded to Christ's call for salvation, but also because of how they have treated His chosen people, the Jews.

The prophet Joel gives us this prophetic word:

In those days and at that time, when I restore the fortunes of Judah and Jerusalem, I will gather all nations and bring them down to the valley of Jehoshaphat. There I will enter into judgment against them concerning my inheritance, my people Israel, for they scattered my people among the nations and divided up my land. *They cast lots for my people and traded boys for prostitutes; they sold girls for wine that they might drink."(Joel 3:1-3; emphasis added).*

God calls the Jewish people His inheritance, and He is jealous to have them for Himself. Those who hurt the Jews are in big trouble with the Lord. Many nations have already earned a heavy sentence of judgment, for they have been so hostile toward God's chosen people. Notice the three things that will cause a nation to be judged:

1. Driving the Jews from their homeland.
2. Dividing up the land that belongs to the Jews.
3. Treating the Jewish people as chattels so they can be traded and sold as material goods.

For many centuries, the European nations were guilty of these three crimes against the Jews. Today, it is not common practice to buy and sell Jewish people. Trying to divide their land, however, and trying to force the Jews to evacuate parts of their land are very real battles that they are facing right now.

Even the United States has shifted her policies and is putting much pressure on Israel in this regard. This is very dangerous for America, and many Christians in the land are deeply aware of the trouble their nation is in. If the White House continues on its present course of defiance toward Israel, catastrophic judgments will increase in America, and the United States will be included in the ultimate judgments that will fall on the valley of Jehoshaphat. Today, we call that valley, the valley of Armageddon.

PROMISES IN REVIEW

By way of review, here are the seven promises that the Lord has extended to Israel:

1. People around the world will pray for Israel's restoration.
2. The Promised Land will be given to Israel.
3. The Lord will bring the Jewish people to their land.
4. Israel's financial fortunes will be restored.
5. A national revival will come to Israel.
6. Israel will be honored among the nations.
7. The Lord promises to judge the nations for how they have treated Israel.

CHAPTER THIRTEEN

THE PATRIARCHS

OWNING THE PATRIARCHS

IN the dynamic list of Israel's inheritance, Paul tells us about the patriarchs. They include the ancient heroes of the Bible, like Noah, Abraham and Moses. Abel worshipped, Enoch walked, Noah worked and Abraham went. In fact, all of the patriarchs obeyed God. They accomplished His will and were blessed because of it. For better or for worse, Paul says that they are the ancestors of the Jews, and today the Israelites recognize the patriarchs as the heroes of their nation. They have given them their history. Paul says, "The people of Israel … Theirs are the patriarchs" (Rom. 9:5).

BLESSES OR CURSES SHOULD NOT BE OVERLOOKED

Although many blessings were promised to us when we received Christ as Savior, not all of them came to us immediately. We have our sins removed, and the penalty of hell is removed, but that does not mean that everything in our lives has instantly become perfect. Most Christians have discovered that many changes still take time, and all of them require steps of obedience. Every blessing is promised to us when we surrender our lives to Jesus, but most of those blessings come to us through a process called sanctification. Our salvation has many components to it, and we have stuff to work through. That is why the Bible says, "Continue to work out your salvation with fear and trembling, for it is God who works in you to will and to act according to his good purpose" (Php. 2:12-13).

Some people have more work to be done than others because they have a lot of spiritual baggage. The Bible speaks of blessings and curses (judgments). Blessings bring favor, but curses bring difficulties. Blessings and curses are two opposite laws of human behavior. The Bible calls this dynamic, "sowing and reaping." If we do right, we are blessed but if we commit acts of evil, we will be cursed. Many people accept the idea of blessings but refuse to accept the fact that curses are also real. Many curses linger even after a person becomes a Christian. Through salvation, a person receives grace to enter the pearly gates when they die, but that does not mean that all of their baggage in this life has been instantly removed in. Every pastor knows that people have ongoing problems even after they become saved. Some of those problems stem from their ancestors' sins and some judgments remain because of their own sin. If, for example, people were involved in witchcraft, they will have a battle to be free of its consequences, even after salvation. They need curses broken off of their lives.

The opposite is also true; if people have ancestors who walked with God, they will receive blessings that they did not earn. The Jewish patriarchs were blessed by God, and those blessings have been passed on to their descendants. Israel's patriarchs are so important because they have released blessings to the whole nation. Let's study this a bit further.

Blessings and curses come into our lives from three major sources.

1. Blessings or curses will come to us because of our behavior. Blessings stem from extraordinary kindness that we show to others, but curses come if we commit evil acts of wickedness. Judgments or privilege comes because of our behavior. Whatever we sow, we reap, and what goes around, comes back around to us. That is the reality of blessings and curses. We are forgiven through Christ, and curses can be broken off of our lives through Christ. Sometimes a person is forgiven, but the issue of curses is not dealt with. Those people struggle with unnecessary hardship.

2. Blessings or curses also come upon nations and communities because of the policies andthe behavior of political leaders. Entire

nations are blessed or judged by God. We can also be under blessings or curses because of the actions of authority figures who are
over our lives. This could include teachers, pastors, politicians and
even, in some cases, the bosses we work under. Their behavior
affects the well-being of countries, cities, schools, churches and
places of employment. That is why some countries struggle in great
poverty while others are blossoming with prosperity.

3. The third way that blessings or curses can come to us is by the sins
   or the valiant acts of our ancestors. In the details of the Ten Commandments, we read that curses go to four generations, but God's
   blessings can go for a thousand generations (see Exodus 20:4-5).
   Our fathers, mothers, grandparents, great-grandparents and even
   our great-great-grandparents have left us a legacy of blessings or
   curses. Their behavior, like our own, has far-reaching consequences.
   For further study on this subject, I recommend my book, *Blessings
   or Curses for the Next Generation.*

THE PATRIARCHS

The patriarchs of the Bible lived valiant lives before God. The Lord blessed
them and promised that their blessings would be passed on to their descendents. The Jews have a bright future because God made fantastic promises
to the patriarchs.

A young man may deserve to be fired from his job because of his poor behavior, but the boss may spare him because he really appreciates the young man's
father. God honors authority, especially fathers and mothers who perform
extraordinary acts of kindness. Regarding Israel, Paul says, "As far as the
Gospel is concerned they [the Jews] are enemies ... but as far as election is
concerned, *they are loved on account of the patriarchs*, for God's gifts and His
call are irrevocable" (Rom. 11:28-29; italics added).

The Jews have had a mixture of blessings and curses passed on to them. They
have suffered throughout history because of their sin. Their sin brought great
calamity upon them, but they also have many testimonies of exceptional

deliverance, and the greatest blessings are still ahead of them. Their story is not yet over; they have many blessings waiting for them in the bottom of the bag because of the patriarchs. God will bless Israel and fulfill all of the promises that were given to her because He honors the forefathers.

OTHER PATRIARCHAL BLESSINGS

There are many blessings that the Jews have received. It is because of the patriarchs that God calls the Jewish people the natural olive branches, while Gentile believers are called the wild olive branches. The patriarchs provided a spiritual greenhouse to nurture the people of Israel at a time when the rest of the world was growing wild in the wilderness, far from the blessings of God. All Gentiles who come to God have the Jews to thank for their spiritual heritage. Gentile believers are supported by the patriarchal roots of the Jewish tree.

> *If some of the branches have been broken off, and* you, [Gentiles from the Church in the city of Rome] *though* a wild olive shoot, *have been grafted in among the others and now share in the nourishing sap from the olive root* [the Jewish patriarchs], *do not boast over those branches.* [the Jews] *If you do, consider this: You do not support the root, but* the root supports you.... *After all, if you were cut out of an olive tree that is wild by nature, and contrary to nature were grafted into a cultivated olive tree,* how much more readily will these, the natural olive branches, be grafted into their own tree! *(Rom.11:17-18,24; emphasis added).*

The Jewish patriarchs gave the nation of Israel the stories and examples of greatness that we find in the Bible. The stories of Abraham's obedience, Moses' leadership and Joshua's courage are ever before us. All of the heroes of the Bible, with few exceptions, are ancestors of the Jews. They are their patriarchs. Phinehas was a Jew, and David was a Jew. Daniel, Shadrach, Meshach and Abednego, (Hananiah, Mishael, Azariah) were Jews. Elijah, Elisha, Hannah, Deborah and Nehemiah were Jews. The list goes on and on; the Jews have, by far, the richest heritage of godly leadership in the world. Most other nations have adopted these patriarchs as their own spiritual fathers and mothers. They have become the examples of faith and obedience for the whole world. We owe the Jewish patriarchs a great debt.

TEACHINGS OF THE BIBLE

Besides their heroic acts of obedience and faith, the patriarchs brought us God's Word. They are the world's most famous teachers. They gave us the Ten Commandments, which have formed the moral foundation for Western civilization. They taught us about faith, love and intimacy with God. Even Jesus and the apostles quoted the teachings of the Old Testament patriarchs. Their instructions have brought life to the Jewish people and brought life from them to the entire human race. There are no people in all of history who compare in greatness with the Jewish patriarchs.

The patriarchs taught us to care for widows, orphans, immigrants and the poor. They taught us to be honest in business and to show fidelity within marriage. They taught us not to shed innocent blood, to steal or to lie. All of these teachings and many more were first given to the Jews because they are the natural olive branches; they have grown up under the influence of their patriarchal roots. They were born into an environment designed to groom them to be men and women of God. Like plants growing in a greenhouse, they were nurtured, manicured, fertilized and watered. They received the nourishing sap that came up from the roots; because the patriarchal roots were blessed, the entire nation has been blessed (see Romans 11:16).

It is no wonder that so many Jews have become great international leaders in so many different fields of science. Some have not used their impartation for the glory of God; nevertheless, the Jews have become a nation of amazing inventors, creators, leaders and entrepreneurs. They received this great inheritance because God has blessed the patriarchs.

The Jews make up a very small percentage of the world's population. There are twelve million Jews on earth, and that means that only 0.2 percent of human beings are Jews. Even though their relative numbers are so small, they have earned 22 percent of all Nobel Prizes."[12] This is an amazing statistic.

Many more blessings will come to the Jews, for the gifts and call of God for Israel are irrevocable (see Romans 11:28). Even through their worst times, they continued to exhibit amazing qualities. In the future they will shine brighter than they ever have in the past, because to them belong the patriarchs, and God loves the patriarchs.

CHAPTER FOURTEEN

THE HUMAN ANCESTRY
OF CHRIST

AN UNSPEAKABLE PRIVILEGE

"To the people of Israel … belongs the human ancestry of Christ" (Rom. 9:5).

This is an unspeakable privilege, and the importance of it has not yet been realized. Imagine if you were related to the Queen of England or the President of the United States or to some famous movie star or athlete. You would have celebrity status by association. You would be invited to fancy dinners, and you would meet prominent people. You would gain financial blessings and be in the public eye. People would recognize you and want to be with you just because you were related to that famous person. It would be a privilege and an honor for you to be part of the family of a real celebrity.

The Jews can claim the human lineage of Christ. At this time, many Jews do not accept Jesus, and those who do bear His rejection as well as His blessings, but the rejection will be short-lived. In the future, the name of the Lord will be the only name of adoration on the planet. He will be known and received by all as the King of kings and the Lord of lords (see Zechariah 14:9).

The Jews already have celebrity status because of Jesus, but most of them have not grasped the immense blessing of this association. One day they will, and that will bring dignity and honor to every Jew. If it were not significant,

Paul would not have included it in his list of extraordinary blessings that belong to Israel.

EVEN IN HEAVEN

Many Christians take no thought of the Jewish identity of Jesus, but God Almighty and all of heaven still see Him as a Jew. In God's throne room, Jesus is known as the Lion of the tribe of Judah and the root of David. His Jewish identity remains intact to this very day and for all of eternity. We could say, "There is a Jewish God-man in the heavens." John recognized this in his vision of the end times and recorded it in the Book of Revelation. We are given a picture of the throne room in heaven, and there, standing before God's throne, is a very Jewish Jesus. We read, "Then I saw in the right hand of him who sat on the throne a scroll ... Then one of the elders said to me, "Do not weep! See, *the Lion of the tribe of Judah, the Root of David*, has triumphed. He is able to open the scroll and its seven seals" (Rev. 5:1,5; italics added) (see also Revelation 22:16).

We understand that Jesus came to earth and became human. In order to do so, He had to be associated with one nation and people group, for every person is part of some clan. Without a link to other humans, we cannot be human. Even on the cross, Pilate had these words written: *King of the Jews.*

The fact that Jesus came to the Jews is understood, but to think of Him as still being a Jew will definitely stretch the perspective of some people. When Jesus returns to the planet, He will stand on the Mount of Olives in Jerusalem. He will defend the Jewish people and set up His earthly kingdom. His throne will be in Jerusalem on the temple grounds, and the Jewish people will administrate the temple worship around Him. He is still the King of the Jews. No wonder the Jews are the apple of God's eye and the sheep of His pasture. It is no wonder that He will watch over Israel and keep Jerusalem as a Jewish city. No wonder He will judge the nations on how they treat Israel. He says, in not so many words, "Don't mess with my people."

We have a saying that blood is thicker than water; in other words, at the end of the day, your relatives mean more to you than your friends. You will stand by them, support them and defend them, if possible. It seems that Jesus has chosen Israel to be His blood relatives. The people of the earth should be careful how they treat them.

A JEW BY CHOICE

Jesus does all things well, and nothing that He does is a mistake. He did not stand before a map of the world, close His eyes, and put His finger on a nation like a school boy playing pin the tail on the donkey. He did not choose Israel randomly or haphazardly. He chose Jerusalem, decisively, even before the foundations of the earth were formed. Jesus planned to be a Jewish baby, to be raised in a Jewish family, to live according to the Law of Moses and to, one day, become a Jewish King who will rule the entire universe from the land of Israel. He is the very glory of His people Israel. Simeon saw this when he dedicated Jesus in the temple, eight days after His birth. We read, "He [Simeon] took Him up in his arms and blessed God and said: 'A light to bring revelation to the Gentiles, And *the glory of your people Israel*" (Luke. 2:28,32 NKJ; italics added).

Jesus is the glory of His people, Israel. It is no small thing that to the Jews belongs the human lineage of Christ. It is, by far, their biggest claim to fame. It is an unspeakable honor and a most awesome privilege. It is no wonder that God promises to walk with them in the coming days. It is no wonder that the nations of the earth will rally around the Jews and people of every nation will take hold of a Jew and want to go with him to Jerusalem.

To the Jews belongs the human ancestry of Christ. Don't mess with the Jews; they have a powerful big brother, and He loves His family.

THE JEWISH INHERITANCE

Paul gave us eight dynamic blessings that belong to the Jews today. The list gives us a picture of Israel's complete inheritance, and it is absolutely amazing. Everything that God has promised to Israel is included in this list. To help us get a grasp of their extraordinary privilege, I have recorded the list again for us to see and remember.

To Israel belongs the following:

> The Adoption of Sons
> The Divine Glory
> The Covenants
> The Receiving of the Law
> The Temple Worship
> The Promises
> The Patriarchs
> The Human Lineage of Christ

Pray that the Jews will come into their inheritance. When the Jews receive their inheritance, it means that God's blessings will come to every nation and human being who has claimed the name of Christ for themselves. Whoever blesses Israel will be blessed, and through them all the nations of the earth will be blessed (see Genesis 12:1-2).

CHAPTER FIFTEEN

CAN PAUL TEACH YOU?

CONCLUSIONS

IT is fitting to pull this section of the book together and conclude it by doing a study of Romans 11. It is one thing to take a verse from here and there throughout the Bible to make a case, but it is a special study when you can take a chapter and go through it, verse by verse, keeping everything in context.

THINGS DONE IN IGNORANCE

For centuries many in the Church have held wrong attitudes toward Israel, and God has overlooked such ignorance as He overlooked the ignorance of the heathens. The time will come, however, when God will no longer overlook ignorance. He commands all people everywhere to repent. Read below how God has overlooked things in the past because of ignorance.

"Therefore since we are God's offspring, we should not think that the divine being is like gold or silver or stone - an image made by man's design and skill. *In the past God overlooked such ignorance,* but now he commands all people everywhere to repent" (Acts 17:29-30; italics added).

Paul also realized that he was, at one time, working against God, but the Lord was merciful to him because what he did, he did in ignorance. Paul said, "I thank Christ Jesus my Lord who has given me strength, that he considered me faithful, appointing me to his service. Even though I was once a blasphemer and a persecutor and a violent man, *I was shown mercy because I acted in ignorance* and unbelief" (1 Tim. 1:13; italics added).

The Bible tells us that God overlooks some things because of a person's ignorance. That is how it is with many believers who have previously sided against Israel. They did it in ignorance, and God has overlooked it, but the day is fast approaching when He will expect better of His children. Those believers who continue to be anti-Semitic in the future will pay a heavy price. Paul warns us about having wrong attitudes toward the Jews.

Hopefully our study of Romans 11 will help align attitudes with the precepts of God's Word concerning Israel.

ROMANS' AMAZING CHAPTER

Paul writes to the church in Rome like a father who is gently correcting a child who is making a huge mistake. The Church there was becoming anti-Semitic; they were turning against the Jews, lifting themselves up in pride, and moving away from the purposes of God. The Roman letter is an apologetic to help adjust their wrong attitudes. Paul is an amazing teacher and he lays out a persuasive argument, point by point, in this chapter. Let's look at the points he makes.

Here are the sixteen major points concerning Israel that Paul gives to the Gentile Church in Romans 11:

1. God has not rejected Israel, for Paul is an Israelite, and God did not reject him.
2. Even though the Jews are unworthy, God has a remnant among them.
3. Israel, who fell away, will one day be completely restored to God.
4. The falling away of the Jews became the doorway of salvation for the world.
5. Paul is qualified to teach the Gentile Church about the Jews because he is the apostle to the Gentiles.

6. When Israel comes back to the Lord, resurrection and revival will come to the nations of the Gentiles.

7. The nation of Israel is holy because their ancestors, the patriarchs, were holy.

8. All Gentiles (wild olive branches) can be grafted into the Jewish olive tree to receive the blessings of God that flow from the patriarchs (the roots of the tree).

9. The Gentile Church should not be prideful against the Jews.

10. If the Jews believe, they will be grafted in again.

11. Gentiles should not be ignorant of God's promises for the Jews, or they will become conceited and prideful.

12. A certain number of Gentiles will be saved, and then revival will come to Israel.

13. God loves the Jews because of the patriarchs.

14. Many Jews are enemies of the gospel.

15. God's gifts and calling for the nation of Israel are irrevocable.

16. God's mercy, for Jews and Gentiles, is absolutely amazing.

We will now look at Paul's points, one at a time.

Paul's Point - Number One

God has not rejected Israel, for he is an Israelite, and God has not rejected him.

Romans 9 - 11 (the heart of the letter) focus specifically on God's undying covenantal promises for Israel. The eleventh chapter starts with the following all-important question, and immediately, without hesitation, Paul throws down a strong answer to his own question.

"I ask then: Did God reject his people? By no means! I am an Israelite myself, a descendant of Abraham, from the tribe of Benjamin. God did not reject his people, whom he foreknew" (Rom. 11:1-2).

Paul's Point - Number Two

Even though the Jews are unworthy, God will always have a remnant from among them, who will remain faithful.

Paul uses God's encounter with Elijah, which is specifically focused on the Jewish people, to make this point. He says the following: "Don't you know what the scripture says in the passage about Elijah – how he appealed to God against Israel: "Lord, they have killed your prophets and torn down your altars; I am the only one left, and they are trying to kill me?" (Rom. 11:3).

Paul takes us back in time to where Elijah is so upset with Israel that he makes a case against the Jews before God. The response that God gives Elijah, however, is worth noting. He says, "And what was God's answer to him? I have reserved for myself seven thousand who have not bowed the knee to Baal" (Rom. 11:4).

God had some faithful Israelites that Elijah did not know about. Paul immediately leaps forward to his present time, making the point that if God still had some Jews who walked with Him during Elijah's time, then surely He has many Jews who walk with Him now. He goes on, saying, "So, too, at this present time there is a remnant chosen by grace. And if by grace, then it is no longer by works; if it were it would no longer be grace" (Rom. 11:5-6).

Paul starts to adjust our attitudes by telling us that God was still with Israel in Elijah's day, and He is still with His people today. It has to do with His grace, not works. This, however, does not mean that every Jew is saved, but only those who have received His grace.

I am always amazed when I see pastors teach from these verses about Elijah. They speak of God's remnant, but the pastors usually refer to themselves and their church as the remnant. Few, if any, talk about Israel being the remnant, even though the Israelites are the focus of Paul's teaching in these verses.

The book of Romans was written twenty-two years after Christ's death and resurrection, and conservative calculations estimate that there were more

CAN PAUL TEACH YOU?

than fifty thousand Jews who were, at that time, born-again believers in Jesus. God has certainly not rejected the Jews. Later in the chapter, he gives us this telling phrase: "If some of the branches have been broken off" (Rom. 11:17).

Notice that only some of the branches were broken off, not all of them.

ISRAEL'S RECOVERY

Paul's Point - Number Three

The nation of Israel who fell away, will one day be fully restored to God.

Paul says the following: "Again I ask: Did they stumble so as to fall beyond recovery? Not at all! Rather, because of their transgressions salvation has come to the Gentiles to make Israel envious. But if their transgression means riches for the world, and their loss means riches for the Gentiles, how much greater riches will their fullness bring!" (Rom. 11:11-12).

Paul's Point – Number Four

The falling away of many Jews has become the doorway of salvation for the world.

Paul states that when the Jews come back to the Lord, the blessings and spiritual riches for the nations will be even greater. Paul is absolutely unrelenting as he teaches about Israel's restoration. He goes on to restate this point even more emphatically. He says this: "I am talking to you Gentiles, inasmuch as I am the apostle to the Gentiles ... For if their [the Jewish people's] rejection is the reconciliation of the world, what will their acceptance be but life from the dead?" (Rom. 11:15).

Paul's Point – Number Five

Paul establishes his qualifications to speak to the Gentile nations about Israel's blessings.

He wants us to know that the Lord and the apostles commissioned him as the apostle to the Gentiles. He has the necessary revelation and the authority to teach the nations about the kingdom of God. With that powerful affirmation, he teaches the importance of standing with the Jews as they receive their covenantal blessings.

If the Church had received Paul's teaching on this subject (remember, he was their assigned apostle) from Romans 11, then the Jews would not have suffered the Crusades, the backlash of the Reformation, the Spanish Inquisition and perhaps not even the Holocaust. It is very late in time, but let's receive his teachings now.

Paul's Point – Number Six

> When Israel comes back to the Lord, there will be a resurrection from the dead for the Gentile Church.

In this verse, Paul not only infers that Israel will be returning to the Lord, but he gives us his sixth point. Israel's coming reival will be the catalyst for the greatest international revival in all of history.

TWO OLIVE TREES

At this point, Paul shifts his presentation in Romans 11 to introduce us to the two kinds of olive trees in the world. In this section of his teaching, we discover that every person on the planet is growing on one of these two trees. There is a cultivated olive tree, namely Israel, and a wild olive tree, a picture of all Gentile nations. He says the patriarchs are the firstfruits and the root of the Jewish olive tree. Notice that verse 24 refers to the cultivated olive tree as the Jewish tree. Paul says, "If the part of the dough offered as firstfruits is holy, then the whole batch is holy; if the root is holy, so are the branches" (Rom. 11:16).

Paul's Point - Number Seven

The nation of Israel is holy because their ancestors, the patriarchs, were holy.

First he uses the example of a lump of dough that rises to be a big batch. The ingredients of the final batch are the same as the ingredients in the original lump of dough that it came from. Note that he is talking about holiness. Then he comes to the illustration of the olive tree. He tells us that because the root is holy, so the branches will also be holy. There is a generational blessing of holiness that is on the Jewish people because their forefathers, the patriarchs, were holy.

This does not mean that all Jews are saved just because they are descendants of Abraham and the patriarchs. Some Jews (some branches) have been broken off because of unbelief. From God's perspective, they are no longer Israel. God defines an Israelite as one who is a natural Jew, but to qualify he must also have the faith of Abraham (see Romans 9:6-9).

Paul's Point – Number Eight

The Gentiles (those who have come from a wild olive tree) can be grafted into the Jewish olive tree and receive the blessings of God that flow from the patriarchs.

Paul says: "If some of the branches have been broken off, and you, though a wild olive shoot [Gentiles], have been grafted in among the others and now share in the nourishing sap from the olive root" (Rom. 11:17).

Some Jews have been broken off from their own tree and some Gentiles have been added or grafted in, and they are now sharing in the nourishment that was promised to Abraham, Isaac, Jacob, Moses, Daniel and David. Godly nourishment comes up from those patriarchal roots, and it has become available to every person on the planet. It comes when an individual receives salvation through Jesus Christ. The nourishing sap includes the gift of the Holy Spirit and all that the Holy Spirit brings, plus the benefits of eternal life that are given to those at the end of the age.

This does not mean that Christians become Jews; they should not be called "spiritual Israel." Gentiles do not become Israelites when they become saved. They become part of the commonwealth of Israel. To understand this, think of Canada and England. Canada is part of the British Commonwealth, but that does not make a Canadian person English. Read Ephesians 2:12 in the King James or the New King James Version to understand the word commonwealth.

STRONG WARNINGS FOR GENTILE PRIDE

Paul lets us know that the blessings of God have come to the Gentiles, but he also gives the Gentiles some strong warnings. Here is an all-important warning from the teacher.

Paul's Point – Number Nine

Paul instructs the Gentile Church not to be prideful against the Jews.

Paul says the following:

"*Do not boast* over those branches [the Jews]. If you do, consider this: You do not support the root, but the root supports you. You will say then, "Branches were broken off so that I could be grafted in." Granted. But they were broken off because of unbelief, and you stand by faith. *Do not be arrogant*, but be afraid. For if God did not spare the natural branches, he will not spare you either" (Rom. 11:18-21; italics added).

Paul warns the Gentile Church not to be proud. This teaching has been ignored by many preachers over many centuries, and this oversight has caused much harm. Paul says not to be boastful because some Jews were broken off and some Gentiles have been grafted into the Jewish tree. He also says that the Church should not be arrogant because if God removed some of the natural Jewish branches, he can also remove Gentile ones; after all, Gentiles are wild branches, but the Jews are the natural branches.

Paul's Point – Number Ten

If the Jews believe - they will be grafted in again.

Paul says, "If they [the Jews] do not persist in unbelief, they will be grafted in, for God is able to graft them in again. After all, if you were cut out of an olive tree that is wild by nature, and contrary to nature were grafted into a cultivated olive tree, how much more readily will these, the natural branches, be grafted into their own olive tree?" (Rom. 11:23-24).

The key to Israel's revival is faith; they must not persist in unbelief. When they believe again, they will be brought back into the family of God. They will be grafted back into their own tree. This is one of the reasons why Paul tells the Gentile Church not to brag over the failure of the Jews and the success of the Church. One day the Jews will come back and take their rightful place. They are God's chosen people.

Notice that the Gentile Church has been grafted in, *contrary to nature*. This is because they are wild branches, and wild branches will always produce wild, inferior fruit. Farmers only graft cultivated branches that bear great fruit onto a wild stock, but never the other way around. *Contrary to the laws of nature*, God has taken wild branches that produce lousy olives and grafted them into a good tree. They should still produce lousy olives, but a miracle has happened; the wild branches (Gentiles) will bear great fruit.

Paul's Point – Number Eleven

Paul tells the Gentiles not to be ignorant of God's promises for the Jews. He says that if the Church is ignorant they will become conceited and prideful.

We read, "I do not want you to *ignorant of the mystery*, brothers, so that you may *not be conceited*: Israel has experienced *hardening in part* until the full number of the Gentiles has come in. And so all Israel will be saved" (Rom. 11:25-26; italics added).

To be ignorant is to lack knowledge and understanding. Paul says that if we lack understanding about the Jews, we will likely become conceited and prideful. He tells us that there is a mystery that we must understand. Then he tells us what the mystery is. He says that one day all of Israel will be saved. (Once again, refer to Romans 9:6-9 to discover who true Israel is. It is those who are Israelites by blood and birth, who also have the faith of Abraham.)

Paul has given four words of warning to the Gentile Church about Israel; he says the following:

1. Do not boast.
2. Do not be arrogant.
3. Do not be ignorant.
4. Do not be conceited.

It is time to listen to the teachings of Paul and come into step with the purposes of the Lord for Israel.

ISRAEL'S REVIVAL

Many preachers know that Israel has been hard-hearted and cut off, but some fail to grasp the mystery that one day all of Israel will be saved. Even here, in this verse, we are reminded that Israel has experienced a hardening in part, but not in whole. Not everyone in Israel has become hardhearted; it has happened only in part.

Paul's Point – Number Twelve

> *A certain number of Gentiles must come to Christ, and then revival will come to Israel.*

God knows how many Gentiles will come to Christ because of His foreknowledge. He tells us that when a certain number of people come to Jesus from among the nations, suddenly a great revival will fall on Israel. All of Israel will be saved. Again, refer to Romans 9:6-8 to discover who true Israel is. When Paul says "All of Israel," he is likely referring to the vast majority of Jews, but he is not likely referring to every single individual Jew in the nation.

IRREVOCABLE PROMISES

Paul's Point – Number Thirteen

God loves the Jews because of the patriarchs.

Paul says, "As far as the gospel is concerned, they are *enemies* on your account; but as far as election is concerned, *they are loved on account of the patriarchs,* for *God's gifts and his call are irrevocable*" (Rom. 11:28-29; italics added).

God loves the patriarchs. They followed Him with great faith even without the benefit of all the Scriptures that we have today. Their obedience was so great that all of their descendents have been blessed. The jews are honored to have such heroism in their ancestry.

Paul's Point – Number Fourteen

Many Jews are enemies of the gospel.

God loves the Jews, even though they are enemies of the gospel. Since the days of Christ and His disciples until this Roman letter was written, the Jews persecuted the Christians. The Jewish leaders were jealous of the Christians because so many Jews were turning to Christ through the preaching of the gospel. The Jewish hierarchy did all they could to trouble the growing Church. They came after the members of the Church with heavy persecution, but their campaign only lasted for forty years. The Jewish persecution of the Church lasted from the ministry of Jesus in 30 AD and continued until 70 AD, when the Roman Emperor ordered the destruction of Jerusalem. After that, the Jews had no power to be a force of persecution against anyone. In fact, from that time on, they became the persecuted ones, and that persecution has lasted for almost two thousand years.

Today, once again, many Orthodox Jews have become enemies of the gospel.

Some of them do all within their power to discredit the message of Christ and His followers. They specifically target Messianic Jews (those Jews who believe that Jesus is their Messiah). Christians, and more to the point, Christ-believing Jews, are persecuted in Israel by many ultra Orthodox Jews today. They are enemies of the gospel.

Paul's Point – Number Fifteen

> *God's gifts and call for the nation of Israel cannot be taken away from them.*

When we consider all of the points that he presents in this chapter, we discover that Paul makes a profound statement. He tells us that God's gifts and call for Israel are irrevocable. That means that no matter what they have done, God's covenant blessings for the Jewish people, as a nation, cannot be taken away from them; they cannot be removed. Their gifts and calling cannot be revoked.

I do not think that this verse applies to every Christian. I have seen many Gentile pastors lose their gifts and calling. I do not want to name names, but I am sure that you know of pastors and other church members who have lost the godly blessings that they once had.

The verse is written about the Jews. Their calling and gifts, as a nation, cannot be lost.

Paul's Point – Number Sixteen

> *God's mercy, for Jews and Gentiles, is absolutely great.*

Read verses 30 to verse 36 to end the chapter. Paul says that God will show fresh mercy to the Jews through the mercy He gave to the Gentiles. In other words, it is time for God to use the Church to love and witness to the Jews so that they may come to their promised blessings and to salvation.

PAUL'S CONCLUSIONS

Like Paul, we conclude, without a doubt, that God still loves the Jews. He has not taken His covenant from them. He has many promises to give them, and one day He will bring the entire nation of Israel back to Himself through faith in Jesus their Messiah.

For the purposes of review, here is the list of points gleaned from the teachings of Paul in Romans 11. There are many other details that could have been included, but here are the sixteen major points concerning Israel that Paul gives to the Gentile Church.

1. God has not rejected Israel, for Paul is an Israelite and God did not reject him.
2. Even though the Jews are unworthy, God has a remnant among them.
3. Israel, who fell away, will one day be completely restored to God.
4. The falling away of the Jews became the doorway of salvation for the world.
5. Paul is qualified to teach the Gentile Church about the Jews because he is the apostle to the Gentiles.
6. When Israel comes back to the Lord, resurrection and revival will come to the nations of the Gentiles.
7. The nation of Israel is holy because their ancestors, the patriarchs, were holy.
8. All Gentiles (wild olive branches) can be grafted into the Jewish olive tree to receive the blessings of God that flow from the patriarchs (the roots of the tree).
9. The Gentile Church should not to be prideful against the Jews.
10. If the Jews believe, they will be grafted in again.
11. Gentiles should not to be ignorant of God's promises for the Jews, or they will become conceited and prideful.
12. A certain number of Gentiles will be saved, and then revival will come to Israel.
13. God loves the Jews because of the patriarchs.
14. Many Jews are enemies of the gospel.

15. God's gifts and calling for the nation of Israel are irrevocable.

16. God's mercy, for Jews and Gentiles, is absolutely amazing.

In the first section of the book, we have examined Israel's restoration. We will now move into the second section of the book and study the theme of Israel's national defense, according to the Scriptures.

PART TWO

ISRAEL'S NATIONAL DEFENSE

CHAPTER SIXTEEN

THE ONE-NEW-MAN ANOINTING

A PROVISION OF THE CROSS

MANY glorious provisions were bought for us on the cross, but some have been overlooked and, therefore, have rarely been taught from church pulpits. When Jesus died on the cross, He took upon Himself everything that was bad about us, and He gave us everything that was good about Him. Here are some of the wonderful provisions that were provided for us on the cross:

> He took our sin and gave us His righteousness.
> He took our sickness and gave us His health and the gift of healing.
> He took our rejection and gave us His acceptance.
> He took our sorrows and gave us His joy.
> He took our curses and gave us His blessings.
> He took our shame and gave us His glory.
> He took our judgments and gave us His justification.
> He took our prison sentence and gave us His freedom.

Wise saints know that all of God's provisions were made available to us through the cross. Although all of these things are immediately ours at salvation, it still takes a lifetime of yielding to Christ to fully apprehend and enjoy these provisions. Some of them we will not experience until we are with Him in eternity.

There is one specific provision that was paid for on the cross that I did not give in the list above. It is often overlooked, yet it is so important. On the cross, Jesus broke down the wall that divides Jews and Gentiles. He destroyed the enmity between the two, making one new man. The following is a powerful Scripture passage that highlights the one-new-man provision that was paid for on the cross.

> *Remember that you ... Gentiles ... were without Christ, being aliens from the commonwealth of Israel and strangers from the covenants of promise ... But now in Christ Jesus, you who once were far off have been brought near by the blood of Christ. For He Himself is our peace, who has made both one, and has broken down the middle wall of separation, having abolished in His flesh the enmity, that is, the law of command- ments contained in ordinances,* so as to create in Himself one new man from the two, *thus making peace, and* that He might reconcile them both to God in one body through the cross, *thereby putting to death the enmity. And He came and preached peace to you who were afar off and to those who were near." (Eph. 2:11-17 KJV; emphasis added).*

Here then is a powerful provision of the cross that has been largely ignored. Through His cross, Jesus destroyed the animosity and the wall of hostility and separation between Jews and Gentiles and made them one new man. Even though the provision was paid for, the world has never seen the one-new-man blessing.

WE HAVE NOT SEEN IT

Here are seven facts that will help us understand the difficult history of the one-new-man proposal.

1. Long before Christ came and died on the cross, there was enmity between Jews and Gentiles. Symbolically, biblically and histori- cally, Jews and Gentiles represented the saved and the unsaved. The Jews were the people of God, and the rest of the world was lost. The devil understood this. He recognized the God-ordained, two- camp distinction (the Jewish saved and unsaved Gentiles) and he

did all within his power to hurt and even destroy the Jewish people because God had chosen them. On many occasions genocide attempts were aimed at the Jews from the Gentile nations.

2. When Christ came, He singled out the Jews for special family status, special VIP treatment which included salvation. Jesus said that He came to minister only to the Jews. On one occasion He called the Gentiles dogs, and on other occasions, He told His disciples not to go to minister to the Gentiles. He emphasized the wall of partition between the two peoples. He said to His disciples, "Do not go among the Gentiles or enter any town of the Samaritans. Go rather to the lost sheep of Israel" (Matt. 10:5-6).

3. A few determined Gentiles broke through the wall of separation to receive God's blessings, but they were the exception. Enmity existed between Jew and Gentile, and orthodox Jews looked down their noses toward people of other nations.

4. After Pentecost, the Lord began to extend salvation to all peoples. In Acts 10, Peter goes to the house of Cornelius, the Roman centurion, and salvation is officially released to the Gentiles. Rivalry among the apostles emerges during this transition time. The Jews began to accept the Gentile Church, but they were legalistic and controlling, and they put themselves in a position of superiority over the Gentile believers.

5. Then the Messianic Jewish apostles and elders opened their hearts toward the Gentiles and determined that the Gentiles, who were coming to Christ, did not have to keep all of the Jewish laws to be disciples. In Acts 15 they made provision for Gentile involvement in the faith. Animosity toward Gentiles was largely dealt with, but the Gentiles begin to reverse the roles. They begin to look down on the Jews, and enmity between the two groups resurfaced and grew rapidly.

6. Christians began to persecute the Jews. An attitude of superiority was embraced by the Gentile Church, and they begin to treat the Jews as inferior, as Christ-killers. The book of Romans is Paul's apologetic to tell the Gentiles that God has not rejected His chosen people, the Jews. We have just studied the heart of the matter in Romans 11. The Church, by and large, ignored Paul's warning. The Church became arrogant and conceited, and a doctrine of Replacement Theology (which states that the Gentile Church has replaced Israel as God's chosen people) became a popular Church teaching. This has lasted for almost two thousand years. Great enmity and excessive persecution from the Gentile Church has been poured upon the Jews from the time of the early Church until now.

7. During the last one hundred years God has been turning the tide of enmity in preparation for the one-new-man blessing. The hearts of His people in the Gentile Church have been shifting in love and favor toward Jews. In our lifetime a prophetic phenomenon is unfolding, the Gentile Church is beginning to honor Israel. The Church is beginning to recognize Israel's promised inheritance and to pray for them and stand with them.

8. The Jews, however, have high walls of resistance because they do not trust the Gentile Church. On their part, the enmity toward Christians is very high. Christians have persecuted and killed them in the name of Christ for hundreds of years. They are not impressed by the message of love that the Church extends to them.

9. Jesus died on the cross to destroy the enmity between Jewish and Gentile believers, but the world has never seen the dynamic fulfillment of that provision. We need a massive *revival*, supernatural *restoration* and Holy Spirit *revelation* coming to both camps in order for the one-new-man miracle to emerge.

THE ONE NEW MAN IS INDISPENSABLE

The Almighty has a powerful, end-time plan that will prepare the way and usher in the return of the King. It is the birth of the one new man. Jesus told us not to be afraid of the end-time traumas for these were just the beginnings of labor pains (birth pains). Jesus says, "Nation will rise against nation and kingdom against kingdom. There will be famines and earthquakes in various places. All these are *the beginning of birth pains*" (Matt. 24:8; italics added).

These labor pains are for the birthing of the one new man. In Revelation 12:2-5 we find another picture of the end times. Here the bride of Christ is about to give birth. The one new man will come forth as the new baby. The devil, called the dragon, wants to destroy this one new man, but he will fail. The provision of the one new man was paid for on the cross. The middle wall of hostility was broken; the prophecy of the one new man must come to reality.

This is God's way of using weak humanity to expose and overpower the devil. In Christ, the one new man shall emerge to overcome the devil, to release world-wide revival and even to rule the nations of the world for a short season, before the return of Christ. Later, in the same chapter of Revelation that speaks of the man-child's (the one new man) being born, we discover that he (the people of God) overpowers the devil. We read, "They overcame him [the devil] by the blood of the Lamb and by the word of their testimony; they did not love their lives so much as to shrink from death" (Rev. 12:11).

Both of God's covenant peoples, believing Jews and believing Gentiles, will finally join together in the miraculous grace of Holy Spirit unity. They will be the most powerful human force the world has ever seen. Authority, miracles, wisdom, resolve, and godly character will come together in this one new man. God's glory will come upon His people, and the devil will be pushed back. All mankind will finally see what the Church and Israel are supposed to look like. This is the glory of the one-new-man phenomenon. It is God's amazing plan, and it was paid for on the cross two thousand years ago.

THE ONE-NEW-MAN RULES

Before closing this chapter, we will briefly look at the governmental rule and also the specific identities that make up the one new man. First of all, let me talk about the rule of the one new man. The reality of the one new man will soon emerge. The two expressions of God's people, Jews and Gentiles, joined together in unity, will become all that the Bible promised. The glory of God will come upon them, and they will be powerful. They will release miracles, bring morality and rule the world. The two groups (redeemed Jews and Gentiles) that make up the one new man are the two olive trees and the two lampstands that stand before the Lord of the earth.

> *These are the two olive trees and the two lampstands that stand before the Lord of the earth. If anyone tries to harm them, fire comes from their mouths and devours their enemies. This is how anyone who wants to harm them must die. These men have power to shut up the sky so that it will not rain during the time they are prophesying; and they have power to turn the waters into blood and to strike the earth with every kind of plague as often as they want. Now when they have finished their testimony, the beast that comes up from the Abyss will attack them, and overpower and kill them. (Rev. 11:4-7)*

After a short reign of power and godliness over the planet, the Lord will allow the devil to retaliate. Like Christ on the cross, the one new man will become vulnerable to Satan's attacks. The antichrist spirit will emerge, and the world will have a final opportunity to choose between two kingdoms before judgment falls and the millennial reign of Christ begins.

The people who are still on the earth at this time will see enormous levels of power demonstrated by both kingdoms. They will witness the best of God's people and the worst of Satan's evil. When Jesus returns, He will bind the devil and his armies, and we will see the one new man rise again. Like Christ emerging from the grave, the one new man will serve the Lord throughout the thousand-year reign and then on into eternity.

TWO SPECIFIC IDENTITIES OF THE ONE NEW MAN

Secondly, let us take a brief look at the specific identities of both groups who make up the one new man. The one-new-man phenomenon does not remove the individual identities of each group. While Gentile believers are part of the commonwealth of Israel, they are not Israel; they are not even "spiritual Israel." Believing Gentiles are Abraham's seed by faith and therefore heirs of the promise along with Israel, but they still are not Israel. In heaven, in the Millennium and in eternity, the Gentile Church will be the Gentile Church and redeemed Israel will be Israel. They are both God's people and come together as one new man, but they do not lose their individual identities. Look at this verse:

"There is neither Jew nor Greek, slave nor free, male nor female, for you are all one in Christ Jesus" (Gal. 3:28).

The verse speaks of races, sexual gender and position in society. We do not think that men and women lose their identites even though they are one in Christ. The women are still women and the men are still men. They are one redemptively, but their identities and their different functions remain. So it is with the Jews and the Gentiles. Each has a different role to play in the purposes of God. They are one in Christ, but they retain their separate identities.

THE ONE NEW MAN IS MORE

The coming forth of the one new man involves the Gentile Church and Israel. Together, they will be involved in the most miraculous encounters every seen. They will experience more anointing for ministry than at any other time in history. They will rise to world-wide leadership in the political realm. They will shift human morality toward godliness in every society on the planet. They will change the spiritual atmosphere around the world. They will welcome the partnership of angels and the see the manifest power of the Holy Spirit in the greatest of all revivals. They will be worshippers and people of prayer, and for a God-appointed length of time, they will be unstoppable. This will be a time when God demonstrates to people, angels, demons, powers and principalities in every realm that the work of the cross was completely effective. Before Jesus returns, His glory shall be released upon the world through the one new man.

During this short space of time, two things must happen. First of all, darkness will be bound, and secondly, the last opportunity for salvation will be extended to millions of people at the end of the age. While the one new man is so powerful, the devil cannot rise, and his evil cannot be fully exposed. That is why God's grace will suddenly be lifted off of the one new man. Satan will release his most powerful forces, and many people who are still in his camp will turn to the Lord when they see his wickedness. Many hardened sinners are still within the reach of salvation, and God, in His mercy, will go after them.

The world in the Tribulation will literally fall apart, and the extreme disasters and chaos combined with the malice of the antichrist will effectively push some last-minute-comers into the grace of Christ. Then Christ will come to bind the devil and begin His millennial reign on earth. We will study these end-time realities more fully in the last chapters of the book.

CHAPTER SEVENTEEN

JEWS WITH NO MILITARY DEFENSE

SPECIAL THANKS

A s we begin the subject of Israel's national defense, I want to show you a brief picture of Jewish persecution over the past nineteen hundred years. This will serve to emphasize and contrast the miracle of their military status today. It will show us what God has rescued her from.

In one sense, I wish I did not have to write this chapter, but I know it is necessary, for many who are reading this book have no knowledge of Jewish history. Please be prepared; this chapter is heartbreaking. For the Jews, things are better now, but it was not always that way. For centuries the Jews were attacked by other peoples, almost to the point of annihilation.

I wish to give thanks, special honor and acknowledgement to the person who gathered most of the information that I am presenting to you in this chapter. Thank you Sister Pista, of the Evangelical Sisterhood of Mary in Darmstadt, Germany, for your hard work and for your booklet entitled "The Guilt of Christianity Towards the Jewish People." (To contact the Sisterhood or get a copy of this booklet, write to: Evangelical Sisterhood of Mary, P.O. Box 13 01 29, D-64241 Darmstadt, Germany.)

AN ANTI-ISRAEL WORLD

Since the time of Maccabeus until 1948, the Jews did not rule Jerusalem, and even in that period of time (the time of the Maccabeus revolt) the Jewish rule over the land was short-lived. The fact is; that it was not since before the days of Nebuchadnezzar when he conquered the city more than twenty-five years ago that the Jews ruled their capital city. The devastation of the city began almost six hundred years before Christ.

"In 586 BC, he [Nebuchadnezzar] destroyed Jerusalem and led the captive Jews to Babylon. He ended the rule of the Kings of Israel. From 586 BC onward, Israel ... was at the mercy of one empire after another. The Babylonian, Persian, Greek, and Roman empires all ruled over Jerusalem."[13]

This was just the beginning; Gentile oppression against the Jews did not even stop with the coming of Christ. Sadly, it has been the Church, who, throughout history, has partnered with ungodly governments to launch the greatest attacks of persecution against the Jews.

THE CHURCH ATTACKED THE JEWS

One hundred years after the birth of Christ, during the days of the early Church fathers, the Church played a devastating role in persecuting Jews. The so-called letter of Barnabas began an attack against the Jews. Concerning the Jews, it read, "Do not add to your sins and say that the covenant is both theirs and ours. Yes! It is ours; but they thus lost it forever." [14]

Prominent Church leaders like Ignatius of Antioch (70-107 AD), Tertullian (160-220 AD), Justin (100-165), Hippolytus (170-236), Origen (185-254), Eusebius (263-339), and Chrysostom (344-407) were extremely anti-Semitic, adding to the pain and persecution of the Jews. Even Augustine wrote this concerning the Jews: "Let them live among us, but let them suffer and be continually humiliated."[15]

Then, around the year 325 AD, we discover the following: "During the fourth century, Constantine, the first Christian emperor, officially declared that the land of Israel no longer belonged to the Jewish people. From that time forward, he said, it belonged to the Christian Church."[16]

One historian said,
"The popular Christian doctrine has always been that anyone, whether pagan or Christian, who has at any time persecuted, tortured or massacred Jews has acted as an instrument of Divine wrath."[17]

"For centuries, severe repressive measures continued to grow against the Jews. Emperor Justinian I (483-565) removed the laws that protected Jewish religious and civil rights and instituted harsh restrictions against them."[18]

"In the seventh century, Byzantine Emperor Heraclius imposed forced baptisms upon the Jews in order to secure unity within his realm."[19]

Over the centuries, this edict was repeated with devastating results for the Jews.

In 1096, the Christian Crusades began, and they brought great pain, suffering and death to the Jewish people.

"Approximately a quarter to one-third of the entire Jewish populations in Germany and northern France were murdered during the first Crusade."[20]

The following is one account of hostilities that were perpetrated against the Jews during the Crusades.

> In Jerusalem the Jews fled from the Crusaders, locking themselves in the main synagogue, where all 969 were burnt to death. Outside, the Crusaders, who believed they were avenging the death of Christ, sang, Christ, We Adore Thee, holding their Crusader crosses aloft. Earlier that day, as the Crusaders ran over the mutilated bodies of those slaughtered, one leader, Raymond of Anguilers, quoted Psalm 118:24: 'This is the day that the Lord has made; let us rejoice and be glad in it.' The Crusaders intended to make Jerusalem a Christian city.[21]

In the time of the Christian Crusades, hundreds of thousands of Jews were killed. And those who survived were forced into servitude, especially in Germany.

"During the first two Crusades, German Jews appealed to the crown for help. In return for royal protection they were made 'serfs of the Imperial Chamber.' Required to pay large sums of money for this privilege, the Jews eventually became a very real source of royal revenue. As the king's property, they could be – and were – bought, loaned and sold to pay off creditors."[22]

"Sadly, the protection for which the Jews paid such a high price did not always materialize ... At the time of the third Crusade one of the most tragic anti-Jewish riots in England occurred in York."[23]

Here is an account of the violent anti-Semitism that occurred in York:

> *Crusaders, before setting out to follow their King, plundered the posses-sions of the Jews, who fled into the royal castle where they were besieged by the warriors – many of whom were deeply in debt to their quarry. The climax was reached when a stone, thrown from the castle, killed a monk. ... When the Jews saw the fury of the besiegers and felt their fate to be sealed, they took their own lives, cutting one another's throats. When the mobs gained access to the tower, the few Jews left, who begged for baptism and deliverance, were slaughtered. The total casualties have been estimated variously from 500 to 1500. From this scene of carnage, the attackers converged on the cathedral and burned all the records of financial obligations to the Jews kept in its archives.[24]*

In 1135, Pierre Abelard wrote a telling report about the Jews. He said:

> *No nation has ever suffered so much for God. Dispersed among the nations, without king or secular ruler, the Jews are oppressed with heavy taxes as if they had to repurchase their very lives every day. To mistreat the Jews is considered a deed pleasing to God. Such imprisonment as is endured by the Jews can be conceived by the Christians only as a sign of God's utter wrath. The life of the Jews is in the hands of their worst*

enemies. Even in their sleep they are plagued by nightmares. Heaven is their only place of refuge. If they want to travel to the nearest town, they have to buy protection with the high sums of money from the Christian rulers who actually wish for their death so that they can confiscate their possessions. The Jews cannot own land or vineyards because there is nobody to vouch for their safe keeping. Thus, all that is left them as a means of livelihood is the business of money-lending, and this in turn brings the hatred of Christians upon them.[25]

Catholic Popes also took a lead role in anti-Jewish propaganda and persecution: "In 1021 Pope Benedict VIII had Jews executed. He blamed them for a hurricane and an earthquake." [26]

The Jews were even blamed for natural disasters and plagues.

When the Black Death (1347-1350) broke out in Europe, the Jews were held responsible: they had poisoned the wells. In southern France, northern Spain, Switzerland, Bavaria, Rhineland, eastern Germany, Belgium, Poland and Austria the charge was believed – and over 200 Jewish communities throughout Europe were destroyed. The extent of the tragedy can best be gauged by the reported 10,000 casualties in Poland – where the Jews escaped comparatively lightly. Considerably more than 10,000 were killed in three German towns (Erfurt, Mainz and Breslau) alone.[27]

During this time in history the Jews were accused of desecrating the sacred elements of the Holy Communion (the bread and wine of the Lord's Supper). In Germany and the surrounding countries, this led to an increase in Jewish persecution. We find that, "In 1298 the host-desecration accusation caused Rottingen's entire Jewish community to be burned at the stake. Their attackers went on to massacre Jews elsewhere in Germany and also in Austria. According to estimates, 100,000 were murdered, and some 140 Jewish communities decimated."[28]

This doctrine of blame was prevalent in most European countries, including Czechoslovakia. "In Prague, in 1389, a priest carrying a wafer host was accidently sprayed with sand by Jewish children at play. As a result 3000 Jews were massacred."[29]

Europe was on fire with hatred toward the Jews. Some of the worst attacks against them took place in Span. "In medieval Spain ... In 1391 ... 50,000 Jews died in riots instigated by the preaching of Ferrand Martinez."[30]

This was led by the King and Queen. We might say that they were very religious, but not very godly. "In 1480 King Ferdinand and Queen Isabella of Spain established a tribunal to purge the Church of those who clandestinely clung to their Jewish faith. Wholesale arrests followed. In 1481 the first victims were burned at the stake."[31]

This slaughter of Jews and other so-called "enemies of the church" was called the *Spanish Inquisition*.

"Over the years an estimated 30,000 marranos [Jews converted to Christianity, whom they called pigs] were consigned to the flames. The Spanish Inquisition had a long history from the fifteenth century until the threshold of the nineteenth."[32]

"Ferdinand and Isabella expelled all Jews from Spain in 1492 in order to consolidate their Christian realm. Many of the 300,000 refugees fled to Portugal. There they were permitted to stay for a few months, but at a great price. Afterwards they were temporarily enslaved by King John II (1481-1495), then – freed by his successor – brutally and forcibly baptized."[33]
To better understand the gruesome reality of the anti-Jewish Spanish Inquisition, see the recently released movie *Goya's Ghosts*, directed by Milos Forman.

Even our beloved Martin Luther (1483-1546), who at first spoke well of the Jews, turned radically and even violently against them. He wrote: "All the blood kindred of Christ burn in Hell, and they are rightly served, even according to their own words they spoke to Pilate ... Verily a hopeless, wicked, venomous and devilish thing is the existence of these Jews, who for fourteen hundred years have been, and still are, our pest, torment and misfortune. They are just devils and nothing more."[34]

Luther published another writing in 1542. It was called "Concerning the Jews and Their Lies." In it he wrote the following:

> *Firstly, their synagogues should be set on fire ... Secondly, their homes should be likewise broken down and destroyed ... Thirdly, they should be deprived of their prayer-books and Talmuds ... Fourthly, their rabbis must be forbidden under threat of death to teach any more ... Fifthly, passport and travelling privileges should be absolutely forbidden to the Jews ... Sixthly, they ought to be stopped from usury ... Seventhly, let the young and strong Jews be given the flail, the axe, the hoe, the spade, the distaff, and spindle, and let them earn their bread by the sweat of their noses ... We ought to drive the rascally lazy bones out of our system ... therefore away with them ... To sum up, dear princes and nobles who have Jews in your domains, if this advice of mine does not suit you, then find a better one so that you and we may all be free of this insufferable devilish burden – the Jews.[35]*

Luther's writings were later used by Hitler to fuel his attacks against the Jews. They were used to help bring about the Holocaust.

I have only given a brief and insufficient representation of Jewish persecution that happened in our distant past. Much more evil was hurled against the Jews during that time period than what I have been able to share. The teachings and practice of anti-Semitism and Replacement Theology were so strongly instilled over the centuries that they were the common way of thinking for the Church, even during our more recent history. Because these teachings had been promoted, pushed and repeated for almost two thousand years, they became part of the very theological fabric of the Church.

Even throughout the nineteenth and twentieth centuries, it was popular and normal for many Christians to treat the Jews with utter contempt. Many pastors, still today, hand out fragments of Replacement Theology in their teachings, and worse than that, some church leaders are absolutely deceived and captivated by the ancient stronghold of that wicked anti-Jewish doctrine.

MORE RECENT HISTORY

For a more recent picture, here are some details of Jewish persecution that have taken place over the past four hundred years.

Multitudes of Jews had left Germany and the surrounding nations during the Crusades and the time of the Black Death. They fled to Poland. This temporary haven eventually became a living hell for the Jews.

"In 1648 Eastern Orthodox Cossacks from the Ukraine devastated Poland, the Jews were singled out for special cruelties."[36]

A report was written about the Jews during that time.

"Some were flayed alive and their skins were tossed to the dogs as meat. Others were severely wounded and then thrown onto the streets ... Others were burned alive. Babes in their mother's arms were stabbed to death ... Large numbers of Jewish children were thrown into the water in order to make the fords more level."[37]

"In Poland, from 1648-1658, until then perhaps the bloodiest decade in Jewish history since biblical times, some 100,000 to 500,000 Jews were murdered, and 700 Jewish communities destroyed. Refugees fled in droves to other European countries."[38]

Then we learn about Russia; the Church and the government of Russia persecuted the Jews excessively over the past two hundred years.

"Under Nicholas I (1825-1855) the situation for the Jews worsened. Military conscription began at age 12 for Jewish youths and could be extended up to 25 years. They were sent to remote areas. Every method was employed, including torture and verbal abuse, to make them renounce their faith and accept Christianity."[39]

"During the reign of Czar Alexander III, Russia's first major pogrom began at Easter 1881 and spread to a hundred Jewish communities. The czar's anti-Semitic advisor intended to solve the Jewish problem by causing a third to emigrate, a third to die, and a third to disappear (i.e. to be converted)."[40]

"Pogroms and accompanying mass emigrations continued under Czar Nicholas II (1894-1917), who regarded the Jews as Christ-killers ... Even after World War II, pogroms occurred in Poland, despite the horrors of the Holocaust and the greatly decimated Jewish population."[41]

The Nazis of World War II (1939-1945) targeted and killed half of the Jewish population in the world. Six million were murdered, and more than one million of those were children under the age of twelve. The people of Germany, at that time, were divided almost equally between Lutheran Protestants and Catholics. Although some individuals resisted the anti-Semitism, many in both churches collaborated with the Nazis or just stood by as Hitler attacked and destroyed the Jews. Because anti-Semitism was so ingrained through the Church, it seemed that most of the world did not care about the plight that was unfolding for the Jews. At the beginning of World War II, as great numbers of Jews were already being threatened and killed by Hitler, many tried to flee from Europe. Very few nations around the world would help them.

"At the Evian-les-Bains conference in France, specifically convened by President Roosevelt in July 1938 to discuss the lot of European Jewry, only three of over thirty nations (Denmark, the Dominican Republic, the Netherlands) volunteered to take in a few thousand Jews. Nazi informers reported back to Hitler: 'You can do what you like with the Jews, nobody wants them'."[42]

In the time just prior to and during the war, boatloads of desperate Jews sailed to Cuba, South America, the United States and Canada, but they were turned away and had to return to Europe, where many met their death.

In 1985, Edward Flannery, a Catholic priest, wrote the following:

> *The sin of anti-Semitism contains many sins ... was not this Christianity's supreme defection: that the Christian people to whom persecution was promised by its master (John 16:2-4) were not the most persecuted*

*people in Christendom, but rather was it the people from whom He
came? And the ultimate scandal: that in carrying the burden of God in
history the Jewish people did not find in the Christian Churches an ally
and defender but one of their most zealous detractors and oppressors? It
is a story that calls for repentance.*[43]

GOD-ORDAINED CHANGE HAS COME

For thousands of years the Jews have been defenseless. They were attacked,
persecuted and killed, but the time for change has come. The world is still
anti-Semitic, but the time has come for God to shield His people. With all
that has happened, it is a miracle that the Jewish people have endured for
these two thousand, five hundred years. Now the time of their promised
blessing has begun. The plan of the Lord is at work to protect them as a
nation, to cleanse them of their sins, to remove the curse from them, and to
bless them with unspeakable abundance.

Israel's military defense will grow much stronger than what it is today. The
Bible tells us that it will even become a spiritual force (see Zechariah 12).
Never again will the people of Israel be defeated. I am very glad to begin this
section of my book. It is focused on the biblical prophecies regarding Israel's
national defense. We will start this section by discovering that Jerusalem has
become an immovable rock. I know this will help prepare you and inspire
you for your partnership with the Lord and with the Jews for this present
time and for the future.

CHAPTER EIGHTEEN

JERUSALEM - AN IMMOVEABLE ROCK

AN AMAZING CHAPTER

ZECHARIAH 12 brings us amazing insights about Israel's national defense. It starts with God's telling us that He has something to say about Israel. The chapter then takes us through the stages of Israel's growing military strength and finally ends with Israel's spiritual revival.

There are four separate stages of military growth mentioned in this chapter. Each is greater in strength than the one before, and all of them involve the supernatural power of God that is sent to help Israel. The stages begin with what seems to be just a well-orchestrated natural defense, but the stages of military progress end with miraculous, supernatural power from heaven.

These stages of national defense are prophetic mandates; they are God's promises to the Jewish people. Her enemies should take careful note of these prophesies. In this chapter, we discover a very clear description of Israel's national defense for the end of the age. The NIV is the version that I am using; however, a deep study of any other translations will reveal the same basic message. The NIV, nevertheless, gives the message to us in plain, easy-to-understand English. We will move, verse by verse, through Zechariah 12, and, as we proceed through this section of the book, I invite you to see if you can discover the four progressive stages of Israel's national defense for the end times. Israel does not deserve the amazing blessings that will come to her. They come because God has chosen her and therefore she will be blessed. That is the way of grace; all of humanity is blessed because of God's grace. I encourage you to open your Bible, get an NIV if you can, and follow along as we put the pieces together for Israel's national defense at the end of the age.

THE ALMIGHTY SPEAKS

This is how the chapter begins:

> *This is the word of the Lord concerning Israel. The Lord, who stretches out the heavens, who lays the foundations of the earth, and who forms the spirit of man within him, declares: "I am going to make Jerusalem a cup that sends all the surrounding peoples reeling. Judah will be besieged as well as Jerusalem. On that day, when all the nations of the earth are gathered against her, I will make Jerusalem an immovable rock for all the nations. All who try to move it will injure themselves." (Zech. 12:1-3)*

Before God tells us what He has to say about Israel, He introduces Himself. He says that He is the God who made the universe with all of its galaxies and planetary systems. He goes on to say that He is the One who made the earth with every animal, blade of grass and drop of water that exists on it. Then, to top it off, He says that He put the breath of life in every human being. We get the idea; He is the Mighty One, the Omnipotent Creator of everything. We owe Him our allegiance. After giving us this awe-inspiring introduction of Himself, He tells us to listen to what He has to say about Israel.

Israel is a hot topic on the global scene. God has chosen her and made her a flashpoint issue that will reveal people's attitudes toward Him. A good father might say, "How you treat my daughter is how you treat me. If you abuse her, you abuse me. If you are kind to her, you are kind to me. Do not tell me that you respect me if you mistreat my daughter."

The Lord says, "I tell you the truth, whatever you did for one of the least of these brothers of mine, you did for me" (Matt. 25:40).

In essence, the Almighty says, I made everything in the universe and on the earth; I even made you, so put every other voice on the shelf and listen to what I have to say about Israel. He is using Israel as a test to determine where people stand with Him. If they follow His directives concerning Israel, they will be blessed, but if they choose their own agendas over His, they are saying, by their actions, that He is not their God. The people who take that stand are in deep trouble.

There are many voices that have lots to say about Israel. We hear preachers, politicians, news commentators, national governments, terrorists, humanists, Jews and Gentiles, but the time has come for us to hear what God Almighty says about Israel. He does not have just another opinion; His Word is the final word on the matter, and He is extremely persistent. So now that the Lord has our attention, let us hear what He has to say.

A CUP OF REELING

The Lord will make Jerusalem a cup that sends all of the surrounding peoples reeling. The word *reeling*, used in this case, infers angry intoxication. It gives us a picture of Israel's irate neighbors who are fuming drunk with hatred toward the Jews. Although it is an awful dilemma for Israel, this Scripture is being fulfilled right now.

Jerusalem, the seat of Israel's government continues to claim her God-given inheritance, and the nations around her are furious. The Palestinians within Israel want the Jews out of Samaria, East Jerusalem and Gaza, but the Jews continue to build homes for their people, especially in East Jerusalem. The Arab nations are outraged with Israel's present position, and Iran repeatedly lashes out with threats of destroying the Jewish homeland completely and wiping Israel off the map once and for all.

God loves people; He made every person in His image, and He hates racism. He has a place for every people group on the planet; the Arab peoples included. He is the One who designs and makes the nations. He has decided that the Holy Land belongs to Israel, and those who challenge that decision will find they are fighting against the God of the universe. He has declared that Jerusalem will be an immoveable rock among the nations.

STAGE ONE - AN IMMOVABLE ROCK

Throughout this chapter we read the words, "on that day." This means, "at this time," or "during this era or season of history." This helps us place this chapter into a specific time period. When He says that "on that day" something will happen, He is saying that there is a season coming when He will do something different. So the Lord says,

"On that day, when all of the nations are gathered against her, *I will make Jerusalem an immovable rock* for all the nations. *All who try to move it will injure themselves*" (Zech. 12:3; italics added).

To find out when this Scripture will be fulfilled, we must ask ourselves this question: On what day or season has Israel or Jerusalem ever been an immovable rock? The answer is very telling. The people of Israel have always been moved and shoved. They have been driven off and scattered about for two thousand, five hundred years. Throughout the centuries they have been a very movable rock. They have been distributed among the nations, and Jerusalem has been trodden under the foot of foreign Gentiles right up until 1967.

The change began in 1948 when half of Jerusalem came under Jewish rule. For the first time since the book of Zechariah was written, Jerusalem has now become an immovable rock. This is that day that the Bible predicted; Jerusalem cannot be moved. This is the day that the Scriptures refer to when they say, "On that day ... I will make Jerusalem an immovable rock."

This fact causes Zechariah 12 to line up with the day and time in which we live. This chapter of the Bible does not fit any other time in history before now. All that takes place in this chapter will happen very soon. Fasten your seat belts and watch Israel's national defense grow. It will be the most dynamic and relevant fulfillment of prophecy before the coming of the Lord.

It will usher in the tribulation period, release a Jewish revival, and open the door for Messiah to return to the earth.

I love the next part of this verse; we have already witnessed its truth: "All who try to move it [Jerusalem and Israel] will injure themselves" (Zech. 12:3).

This is a phenomenon, and the world has witnessed it happening since 1948. As soon as Israel became a nation on May 14, 1948, five Arab nations attacked her. The Israeli War of Independence lasted until January of 1949, and the Scriptures began to unfold. All of the nations that attacked her injured themselves. This held true even though their combined force was much greater than that of Israel's. That war was just the beginning, for each time Israel has been attacked since then, her attackers have been the ones who have suffered the most. It has happened over and over again since 1948; all who have tried to move the Jewish people from their seat of government in Jerusalem have ended up injuring themselves.

The most obvious example of this happened during the famous Six Day War on June 9, 1967. Egypt, Jordan, Syria and Iraq were preparing to attack Israel. In response, Israel bombed 452 Egyptian planes within three hours. Then the Jewish people warned Jordan not to attack, but Jordan's King Hussein attacked by opening fire and occupying the United Nations building in Jerusalem. Syria and Iraq joined in, and all of them suffered great losses. The war was over in just six days, and it was the greatest military victory for Israel in all of her history.

While defending herself, Israel gained and occupied the Sinai Peninsula in Egypt, all of Gaza, Samaria and Judea on the West Bank of the Jordan, and they took the entire Golan Heights from Syria. For the first time since the days of Nebuchadnezzar, they occupied and finally ruled the entire city of Jerusalem. Of course, all of these lands are Israel's property by right, according to the God of the Bible. Since that war they have given back the Sinai in Egypt, but more than forty years later, Israel has extended her borders and kept the Golan, Samaria, Judea and the all-important city of Jerusalem. Israel has become an immovable rock, and all who attack her will injure themselves.

Since then, other wars have been fought on Israeli soil, and they have not all been as successful as the Six Day War, but the final result lines up with the Word of God. All who have attacked her have injured themselves and have sustained far more damage than what they have brought upon Israel.

We know that more wars will come, but Israel will continue to be victorious. The damage to those nations that attack her will increase even more than in the previous wars. God is stepping things up with regard to Israel's national defense, so the nations that surround her should be warned.

Even as I write, the White House, under the combined leadership of President Obama, Vice-President Biden and Secretary of State Hilary Clinton, has put immense pressure on Israel to give up her lands and to stop building Jewish homes in the eastern half of Jerusalem. They think this will bring peace to the Middle East, but it won't. The U.S. government does not understand what they are doing; to oppose Israel's occupation of the Holy Land is to oppose the Living God. We pray that America, who in the past has been a strong supporter of Israel, will once again turn her policies around so that she will stand with Israel and be blessed.

Concerning Iran, we have two words to say: "Watch out." Iran's nuclear threat against Israel will backfire and the nation will suffer. Israel may attack, the United Sates may attack, a natural disaster may land on their doorstep, but in one way or another, Iran will not go unharmed if it pursues its present course to hurt Israel. To touch Israel is to touch the apple of God's eye. In another age Iran would possibly have gotten away with it, but not now. This is the day foretold by Zechariah; God is watching over Jerusalem.

The Lord God Almighty says, "On that day ... I will make Jerusalem and immovable rock ... all who try to move it will injure themselves" (Zech 12:3).

We are already at stage on of Israel's national defense for the end times. Let us now move on and study stage two of Israel's national defense.

CHAPTER NINETEEN

THE LEADERS OF JERUSALEM

ISRAEL'S NATIONAL DEFENSE – STAGE TWO

ZECHARIAH 12 continues to reveal God's end-time program for Israel's national defense. This chapter in my book is dedicated to stage two - the empowerment of Israel's leaders. It begins with the words of Zechariah 12:4-6.

On that day ... I will keep a watchful eye over the house of Judah, but I will blind all the horses of the nations. Then the leaders of Judah will say *in their hearts, 'The people of Jerusalem are strong, because the Lord Almighty is their God.' On that day* I will make the leaders of Judah *like a* firepot in a woodpile, like a flaming torch among the sheaves. *They will consume right and left all the surrounding peoples, but Jerusalem will remain intact in her place. (emphasis added)*

The words "on that day" are mentioned again, twice in these verses. What day are we referring to? The answer has already been given; the day when God makes Jerusalem an immovable rock among the nations. That is our present season, for no previous season in history fits the description of Jerusalem's being immovable.

A WATCHFUL EYE

God's eye is on Israel today like never before. He will keep a watchful eye over the Jewish people from this day forward. His gaze is focused and purposeful because He must complete the preparations for the coming of His Son to the Holy Land. That means He will guard and protect Israel because Jerusalem must be a Jewish city when Jesus returns and His feet touch the Mount of Olives. It cannot be a French city, a British city, a Jordanian city or a Palestinian city. The Scripture says that God will keep a watchful eye over Judah. The name Judah used in this reference refers to all of the Jewish people. Notice how the terms *Israel, House of Judah, House of David* and the *People of Jerusalem* are used interchangeably throughout the Scriptures. All of these terms refer to the Jewish people, the Jewish people of Israel.

The Scripture says that the Lord will blind all the horses of the nations that are attacking Israel. Horses were high-tech military might in the days of Zechariah. They point to the power of horse cavalries and highly advanced chariot armies. The armies with the most horses had the leading edge of military might in ancient times.

This prophecy points to our modern military capabilities. It might include everything from high-tech intelligence gathering, to the release of so-called computer-guided smart weapons. The Lord says that He will make the enemies' most advanced weapons dysfunctional. Their horses will be blind. I believe that their high-tech intelligence and sophisticated weapons programs will be so damaged, perhaps by a nuclear pulse, that the enemies of Israel will have to revert to conventional warfare. They will be like an ancient chariot army whose horses have become blind and are forced to attack using only their foot soldiers. It is instructive to see that during the battle of Armageddon, two hundred million soldiers gather in the Valley of Jehoshaphat (see Joel 3:1-3, and Revelation 9:16). This is not a picture of modern warfare but one of outdated infantry maneuvers. In the battle of Armageddon, when the world marches on Jerusalem, some have mounts, but they seem not to have the high-tech weapons that we have come to expect in our present time.

THE LEADERS OF ISRAEL SPEAK

A dynamic shift is about to happen with the leaders of Israel. Since 1948, the leaders of Israel have been strong, and the present leader, Prime Minister Benjamin Netanyahu, is an outstanding commander in chief. He demonstrates strong military leadership for his people. I have heard many leaders of Israel say, "We are strong and we will defend ourselves and not back down," but I have not heard them add the words, *"because the Lord Almighty is our God."* That is what the Scripture in Zechariah says they will do.

We live in an era when, it appears, many Jews have lost their faith. Over the centuries, as the chosen people were scattered, persecuted, abused and murdered, it was so demoralizing and devastating that many lost their faith in God. Then when World War II came and the Nazis killed half of the Jewish population in the world, so many Jewish survivors were drained of their faith. They said in effect, "After all of this, how can we believe in God? Where was God during the Holocaust?"

That sentiment is beginning to shift because Israel is approaching her end-time revival. Change is in the atmosphere, and faith is returning to many people in Israel. When they see God protecting them with such unexplainable military might, they will realize that only the power of God is keeping them, and many will start to believe again.

Now, let me prophesy! Soon it will happen - you will see it on CNN, Fox News and BBC. A Jewish Prime Minister will be interviewed after a victorious battle and he will say, "The people of Jerusalem are strong, because the Lord Almighty is their God."

He will add, "Because our God is with us!"

When you see Israeli leaders on television and hear them speak these words, you will know that you are witnessing Biblical prophecy being fulfilled with your own eyes and ears.

A FIREPOT AND A TORCH

Look at the verse again: "On that day I will make the leaders of Judah like *a firepot in a woodpile, like a flaming torch among the sheaves.* They will consume right and left all the surrounding peoples, but Jerusalem will remain intact in her place" (Zech. 12:4-6; italics added).

The leaders of Israel will become violently reactive to the attacks that come at them from the surrounding nations. They will be like a firepot and a flaming torch. A firepot is a vessel that carries hot coals in it. It is used to start fires because it is not efficient or economical to keep a fire going all day and all night in the land of Israel. Wood and other fuels are too rare and too precious.

Of course, if you put a firepot in a wood pile, the stack of wood will heat up and suddenly burst into flames. That is what the leaders of Israel will be like; in fact, they are already like that now. As soon as a missile is launched against Israel, the newscasters are there to film Israel's reaction. We see helicopters zeroing in on the spot of the missile launch, and within minutes, the enemy faces the spontaneous wrath of Israel's explosive leadership. A fiery combustion follows, and we see a firepot in a wood pile; suddenly there are flames and devastation.

In case we pass over the point too quickly, it is emphasized with a second illustration. The leaders of Israel will be like a flaming torch among the sheaves. They consume, right and left all the surrounding peoples. A sheaf of wheat is an armful of wheat, still on the stalk, bundled and left to dry out in the hot Mediterranean sun. If a flaming torch comes among the sheaves, the field will burst into a roaring flame of fire within seconds. That is a present-day picture of the leaders of Israel, and they will fit the description even more so in days to come. They are a dangerous fire to their enemies.

At this time, it would be wise to check our own attitudes regarding Israel and decide whose side we will be on. God is on the side of His chosen people, and He will defend them. We must be careful that we are not swayed by the bias of the world, for if we stand against Israel, we will find ourselves standing against God. When we see Israel defending herself with harsh resolve, we must remember that it is God who has programmed her to respond like that at this time. The Scripture says, *"I will make the leaders of Israel a firepot …* and a flaming torch"* (italics added).

SYMBOLS OF THE COVENANT

If we study deeper into the Scriptures, we find even more importance to this fiery picture of leadership. We discover that God used the symbols of the firepot and the torch when He established His covenant with Abraham. That is when He promised the Holy Land to Abraham and his Jewish descendants. Read what God did and said when He made His covenant with Father Abraham; it is amazing.

> *When the sun had set and darkness had fallen, a* smoking firepot and a blazing torch *appeared and passed between the pieces* [of the sacrifice]. *On that day the Lord made a covenant with Abram and said, "To your descendants I give this land, from the river of Egypt to the great river, the Euphrates – the land of the Kenites, Kenizzites, Kadomites, Hittites, Perizzites, Rephaites, Amorites, Canaanites, Girgashites and Jebusites. (Gen. 15:17-19 (emphasis added)*

It is so significant that God uses the same two symbols (the firepot and the torch) to depict Israel's leadership when establishing His covenant regarding the possession and ownership of their Land.

It is now four thousand years since God established His covenant with Abraham, and His promise still stands today. In the covenant, God said that all of the lands of the nations around them would, one day, belong to Israel. These lands have been promised to Israel, the descendants of Abraham through Isaac.

Now, at this time in history, the promise is coming to pass and unfolding very quickly. Bible scholars know that the prophecies speak of many nations attacking Israel, but at this time, all of them will injure themselves. Israel's leaders will rise up and defend her. They will consume, right and left, all of the surrounding peoples. The leaders of Israel will be granted military supremacy over their enemies. God will give them a military advantage. The ability to consume Israel's enemies, on left and right, has not happened for the nation of Israel for two thousand, five hundred years. In the future we will see Damascus, the capital of Syria, fall (see Isaiah 17:1 and Zechariah 9).

Tyre and Sidon, the sea ports of Lebanon, will fall, and the strength of Gaza will utterly fail (see Zechariah 9). Those who attack Israel will face strong retaliation. They will be set upon with devastating resolve, for the leaders of Israel will rise up and send their armies after them. They will suffer harsh consequences. A further study to discover all of the lands of the nations that God promised to Abraham and Israel, shows that many of the nations that surround Israel will become part of the nation of Israel before the Lord returns.

In Genesis 15 we have the list of the nations and lands that will be given to Israel. It is logical to assume that the modern-day equivalent of these nations will attack Israel. Iran, Iraq, Lebanon, Jordan, Syria, Egypt and even Turkey will be among those who attack Israel, and all of them will fail and lose some of their land to the Jewish people.

Israel does not want war. For many years Joy and I have travelled through the land of Israel, and we have talked to many Jewish people about their situation. They just want to be left alone to live in peace. They are not interested in expanding their nation, but God is. When they are attacked, they will defend themselves and take possession of the lands around them as a buffer zone to protect their people. They will occupy those lands, and when Jesus returns those lands will be eternally secured as the land of Israel.

Notice the last few words in these verses. They repeat a powerful promise that was given earlier in the chapter. "But Jerusalem will remain intact in her place."

Settle it in your thinking - no nuclear bomb can land on Jerusalem. It cannot be destroyed anymore, and no one can move her government or her people. The Lord has a watchful eye on Jerusalem, and He will release supernatural power to protect her. It will become even more vibrant than what we have already discussed. The Scriptures give us much more on this subject. In the next few chapters, we will discover the vastness of God's awesome power that He will extend to develop Israel's national defense.

Chapter Twenty

SUPERNATURAL SOLDIERS

ISRAEL'S NATIONAL DEFENSE – STAGE THREE

ZECHARIAH 12 lays out four stages for Israel's national defense for the end of the age. Each level is more powerful than the one before, and level three is so supernatural that no one would believe it if it was not written in the Bible. I encourage you to open your Bible and see this for yourself. God's Word cannot be changed. It is not negotiable, and it tells us that Israel is moving quickly toward unbelievable military strength. Look with me at Zechariah 12:8

"On that day the Lord will shield those who live in Jerusalem, so *that the feeblest among them will be like David, and the house of David will be like God,* like the Angel of the Lord going before them" (Zech. 12:8; italics added).

GOD'S SHIELD

Once again, the Scripture reveals the time period when this word will apply. It happens, "On that day." What day? The answer is clear; it is this day that we are in right now because this is the day when Jerusalem is an immovable rock. At no prior season in history has Jerusalem been stable and unmovable.

Suddenly, sometime soon, Israel's military might will move to a whole new level. Not since the days when the walls of Jericho fell has Israel seen such obvious supernatural power applied to their military endeavors. In this season, the entire nation of the Jews will receive a power surge of biblical proportions; there is no other way to describe it. The nations of the world will witness their strength as their enemies are crushed and defeated with relative ease.

First, we see that God will shield Jerusalem. No weapon formed against Israel shall prosper, for the Lord is setting up a supernatural force field around her. That is the kind of shield that every individual, family and nation needs. We need God's protection against every natural and spiritual attack. No enemy can penetrate God's defense shield. Israel's upcoming defense shield is, first of all, a military one.

THE FEEBLEST ARE LIKE DAVID

God's heavenly shield is more than a defensive guard for Israel; it is also an empowerment for her people. The Scripture says that the feeblest among them will be like David, the warrior king. Who are the feeblest people in a nation? The weakest people in any society are the children, the handicapped and perhaps the seniors. The Lord promises that this group of citizens will become like David. Can you imagine attacking a nation where the grandmothers can beat you up? Who wants to battle children who are as strong as David or come against a land where even the handicapped are outstanding warriors?

I do not want to use natural reasons to explain the supernatural, but I have learned that sometimes that which seemed supernatural back in history can be explained by understanding modern technology today. These days we see the handicapped doing great things in the Special Olympics, so can't it happen in the military as well? Someone in a wheelchair can easily push the buttons on a computer and launch a missile. Even so, this prophecy may be about supernatural power alone. At any rate, the feeblest in Israel will be trained as excellent warriors. Maybe an attacking army will have to fight against the Jewish Mossad or another department of Israel's special forces, but first they must get past the children, the seniors and the handicapped.

Today, many more opportunities are available to people than in biblical times. To summarize, it is well within the realm of possibility in our day and age for seniors and the handicapped to be part of the military team. These wonderful seniors can be trained to use computer-fired weapons, and someone in a wheelchair can be highly skilled in military maneuvers if they have high-tech equipment. If we add to this scenario the miraculous power of God, then the extraordinary is not only possible, but it is certain.

The next statement in these verses, however, takes our feet off the ground; it is definitely supernatural. It involves those who are the most gifted warriors of Israel.

SOLDIERS, LIKE GOD

I do not want to be accused of mishandling God's Word or teaching some strange, false doctrine, so please read this Scripture verse for yourself. "And the house of David will be like God, like the Angel of the Lord going before them" (Zech. 12:8).

When the feeblest in the nation are like David, the house of David is given supernatural power to be like God. What an unbelievable statement, but this should not seem so strange to us. We have been reading about it and preaching it from our pulpits for years. Many have applied the following verses about God's rising glory to the Gentile Church, but this prophecy was given to Israel first. It is found in the words of Isaiah 60.

"Arise, shine, for your light has come, and the glory of the Lord rises upon you. See, darkness covers the earth and thick darkness is over the peoples, but the Lord rises upon you and his glory appears over you. Nations will come to your light, and kings to the brightness of your dawn" (Isa. 60:1-3).

Isaiah prophesied over Israel (see Isaiah 59:20,21), saying that the glory of the Lord would come upon her during a time when gross darkness was covering the earth. This event occurs not during the Millennium, for the world will not be covered in thick darkness at that time. And certainly, there has not been a season since the days of Isaiah when Israel has witnessed the glory of the Lord coming upon her so that nations and kings would come to the brightness of her dawn.

Scripture says that this level of military empowerment will cause the house of David to be like God, like the Angel of the Lord going before them. If the house of David will fight like God we should ask ourselves what happens when God fights. When God fights a nation, their walls crumble as if an earthquake hit, fire falls from heaven and devours people instantly, and a death angel moves through the enemy's camp in the night killing all the first-born. Thousands die in a blink of an eye when God attacks, and no earthly weapon or defense can stop His wrath. If the special forces of Israel have the supernatural power of God moving through them, then all opposing armies should keep their distance.

It is no wonder that all of the nations of the world will, one day, assemble their armies in a unified effort against Israel. It is a long shot, but militarily speaking, the only logical hope for the world to overpower Israel's military defense is to have a global united front against her. All of these steps lead to the battle of Armageddon, which is a battle of two entities: the world verses Israel. Many in the nations will not understand that it is God who they are fighting. Their global attacks against Israel are futile, for in the end, Jesus will descend from heaven and come to her defense (see Revelation 19).

GOD'S PEOPLE WILL SEE IT

The Church is presently experiencing a new love for Israel. Fresh revelation is flowing from our pulpits to tune and line us up with God's plan for Israel. Even longstanding Replacement Theology teachers are beginning to shift. Recently an old ministry friend phoned me to talk about Israel. He spoke with me on a long-distance phone call for a couple of hours. God was opening his eyes to Israel's part in the end times. He was excited but said that he lacked understanding and needed teaching on the subject. His searching questions came fast and furious as he threw them at me, one after the other. Before I could fully finish one thought, he was on to the next question. By the end of the phone call, he expressed such thanks. He said, "Peter, thank you. You have been preaching these truths for many decades, but some of us are just catching up now."

Part of the Church's upgrade on the subject of the Jews will come as they watch the rise of Israel's national defense. The governments of the world and the news media outlets will not admit that supernatural powers are protecting Israel, but the Church will see it. Prophets, pastors, apostles, teachers, evangelists and intercessors will shout for joy when they see stage three of Israel's national defense. They will recognize that the feeblest in Israel will be like David, and the house of David will fight with the power of God.

When this happens, new faith will surge in the Church around the world. Prayer meetings will be full, and evangelism will rise to new levels. Preaching will be more anointed, and the Church will move into partnership with Israel. Those who believe in Replacement Theology will shift their thinking, and many will become strong supporters of Israel. The one new man (Jews and Gentiles functioning as one in Christ) will soon emerge. Israel's amazing national defense is a forerunner to her spiritual awakening. Her revival will come like a resurrection from the dead.

CHAPTER TWENTY-ONE

GOD TAKES IT PERSONALLY

ISRAEL'S NATIONAL DEFENSE – STAGE FOUR

WE have been studying Zechariah 12. It is about Israel's national defense in the last days. We are discovering four stages or levels of God-directed military power that Israel will receive before the coming of the Lord.

THINGS ARE HEATING UP

Israel's first level of defense has already come, and the others are on the horizon. Faith is mounting in our hearts, and our eyes are on the Lord. He is telling us to look at Israel. As God's blessings fall on her, we are being educated with the details. Many people are beginning to ask when the tribulation period will begin.

Israel's spiritual revival will happen around the same time that the Tribulation begins. We are getting closer. No other Biblical sign is more telling than that of Israel's being restored and blessed. This fulfillment of prophecy will continue to unfold and be unstoppable until the end of the age. The final completion and fulfillment of Israel's prophecies will coincide with the return of the Lord at the end of the tribulation period.

We have already looked at the first three stages of Israel's national defense for the end times. They are as follows:

1. God shields the Jewish people, and Jerusalem becomes an immovable rock.
2. The leaders of Israel react powerfully to any attack against their people. Like a firepot and a flaming torch, they send their army out to consume the enemies who come against them.
3. The people of Israel receive supernatural power to defend themselves. The feeblest among them become strong warriors, and their mighty warriors become like God. Their army will be like the angel of the Lord.

Now we move to the fourth level of Israel's national defense as outlined in Zechariah 12. It is hard to believe that Israel's military strength can be stronger than what we have already discovered, but it will.

GOD IS ON THE MOVE

Please understand that these revelations about Israel's national defense are not my ideas. We are simply reading the Scriptures and believing what they say. Zechariah 12:9 says,

"On that day *I will set out* to destroy all the nations that attack Jerusalem" (Zech. 12:9; italics added).

After God shields Jerusalem, empowers her leaders, and gives supernatural capabilities to Israel's armies, He decides to get personally involved. The Lord says, "I will set out to destroy all the nations that attack Jerusalem."

It is as if God says, "I have had enough. The nations are not listening. I will now do more than just empower Israel to defend herself; I, the Lord God Almighty, will personally go out and attack her enemies."

This is stage four of Israel's national defense. God takes matters into His own hands. Now the surrounding nations are really in trouble. If they thought things were bad before, they did not have a clear understanding of the odds that were stacking up against them. Israel's enemies have just moved to a new level of suffering where it is impossible for them to have victory; God Almighty is coming after them, and He promises to destroy them.

NATIONS NOT IN THE MILLENNIUM

Many nations will be brought into the Millennium after the return of the Lord. Those who are accepted will find that their politics will be redesigned to reflect a kingdom-of-God lifestyle. The Bible calls these nations, "the nations of the saved", or "sheep nations" (see Matt 25:32-33). The scriptures differentiate between the sheep and the goat nations. Some nations are goat nations, and they will not make it into the Millennium. I think that some, although not all, of the nations who presently surround Israel may come to their final end and not be among those who enjoy eternity with the other nations of the world. Only God knows, but if that is true, then they are goat nations and will face such attacks from the Lord that they will be annihilated.

WHEN GOD GOES TO WAR

The book of Revelation gives us a picture of what it will look like when God goes to war against His enemies. There are earthquakes, fire and hailstones falling from heaven, volcanoes, hurricanes, tornados, disease, droughts, famines and all kinds of horrors and devastations.

In the book of Exodus, we read of the Death Angel moving through the streets of ancient Egypt. In the morning, all of the firstborn who were not protected by the blood of the lamb were dead. If God is going to war, we will see the beginning of the Great Tribulation. At that time, the wrath of heaven will be released against God's enemies. I think Israel's enemies will be among the first to experience God's wrath.

THE MUSLIM THREAT

The book of Revelation reveals three global wars, one at the beginning of the Great Tribulation, and two at the end of the book of Revelation. It is likely that the Muslims are contenders only in the first of these three wars. We will focus on the first war in a moment, but first let us briefly look at the last two great wars that are mentioned at the end of the book of Revelation.

The last two wars happen as God finalizes His judgments with the devil and humanity. Both of these wars involve armies' coming from every nation to fight against Israel. One is called the battle of Armageddon. It takes place just before and during the return of the Lord. In the middle of the battle of Armageddon, Jesus comes and destroys His enemies. He throws the beast and the false prophet into the lake of fire and casts Satan into the Abyss for one thousand years (see Revelation 19:11-21). Then the thousand-year millennial reign of Christ begins. There is no mention of any Muslim threat in that war. At that time, it is all the nations, not a specific group, who gather together to attack Jerusalem.

THE LAST WAR

The very last war mentioned in Revelation happens at the end of the Millennium. After the thousand years are completed, Satan is released from the Abyss to tempt the nations. Once again a huge army marches on Jerusalem where, at that time, Jesus rules as King of kings. Once again the army that assembles against Jerusalem is not comprised of Muslims, but of people from every nation. Before that battle is actually fought, the heavens open and God Almighty destroys the attacking army by sending fire down upon them. Then Satan is cast into the lake of fire where the beast and false prophet are. Like with the battle of Armageddon, the Muslim nations are not mentioned in the description of this last battle (see Revelation 20:7-10).

Now that we have some details of the last two battles and we see that the Muslims are not a threat in either of those battles, we ask, "What happened to them?"

It is logical to assume that the Muslim threat will be dealt with in the very first of the three major end-time wars that are mentioned in the book of Revelation.

WORLD WAR III

The first global apocalyptic war is recorded in Revelation 6:3-4. This war takes place just at the beginning of the Great Tribulation. This war is different from the other two wars because it does not focus on Israel; it takes place all over the globe. It will probably be World War III. Of course, if there are more global wars, it could be World War IV or V, but I think that time has run out on God's prophetic clock, so we do not have time for other global wars. So the war mentioned in Revelation 6 is likely World War III.

When World War III erupts, vast multitudes of people will die. More people will die in that war than in any previous war. As I write, influential voices in the United States are saying that World War III has already begun, but most in the West have not yet recognized it. They say it is a war against global terrorists and dictators.

Presently, the number-one military enemy of the free world is Muslim fanatics. Recently, I saw a documentary called *Obsession* that aired on national television here in the United States. It showed dozens of mullahs (Islamic Muslim Priests) giving public speeches in different nations, including European nations such as England. They were declaring war on the world. Many Mullahs repeated the message that Islam once ruled the world and will rule the world again. They unashamedly announced that it is Allah's will to kill all people who do not convert to Islam. They brazenly declared that they would overtake America and Europe and completely annihilate Israel.

More than one billion Muslims are on the earth today. If only one percent of them were fanatical suicide killers, they would number more than ten million committed warriors. Since September 11, 2001, when Muslim terrorists flew two airliners into the World Trade Center, the world went on alert. Many terrorist attacks have now taken place in dozens of nations around the globe. The fanatical Islamic threat is growing daily, and demonically inspired Muslim terrorists are emerging on the global stage with unprecedented frequency.

If not for the promise of Christ's victory in the Scriptures, my heart would sink into despair. Although Muslims will not be the only enemy of Israel and the free world during the first part of the Great Tribulation, they will be a major force. Fanatical Muslims will be the flash point group that will cause the nations to respond and be drawn into World War III.

THE MUSLIM THREAT DEFIED

As Muslim fanatics become more aggressive, the free world will react with a kind of spontaneous combustion. Non-Muslim nations will no longer stand by and allow their people to be pushed around and killed by these terrorists. They will go after them and their allies. They will do what President George W. Bush did after September 11, 2001. They will say, "We will hunt down these terrorists and all who side with them."

Other dictatorships will join with the Muslim nations. Some of those nations might include Venezuela, Cuba, North Korea and maybe even China and or Russia. If they become allies with the Muslim nations, then we will have a global war. Outwardly, the battle will consist of the free democracies fighting against the dictatorships of the world. The dictatorships will fall, and this battle will end the rule of the dictators, including the Muslims. This war, however, will claim an unprecedented number of lives. Perhaps as many as a billion people will die.

It is during this time that the threat of the Muslims will be broken. Within a year or two, at the very start of the Great Tribulation, the power of fanatical Islam will be finished. Major Arab cities will be totally destroyed, and although Islam will continue as a religion, their global manipulation and campaign of terror and fear mongering will be over.

At the end of this war, all the nations will embrace democracy. This is an essential move that will prepare the way for the political events of the last days, when the people of the nations willfully embrace the spirit of antichrist. When the world is a democracy, the people, by and large, will vote for the wrong leaders and the antichrist spirit, for a season, will rule the nations.

At first, the world will not be terrorized by this spirit. In fact, they will freely worship the image of the Antichrist. This is the spirit of humanism - man worshipping man and forsaking the true and living God.

THE FALL OF ISLAM

Let's get back to our focus on Islam. Here are some Scriptures which prophesy the end of major Islamic cities at the beginning of the Great Tribulation. No doubt, Israel and God Himself will be involved in their destruction.

"An Oracle concerning Damascus: "See, Damascus will no longer be a city but will become a heap of ruins" (Isa. 17:1).

"The word of the Lord is against ... Tyre and Sidon, though they are very skillful. Tyre has built herself a stronghold; she has heaped up silver like dust, and gold like the dirt of the streets. But the Lord will take away her possessions and destroy her power on the sea, and she will be consumed by fire" (Zech. 9:1-4).

Damascus is the capital of Syria, and Tyre and Sidon are two of the main port cities of Lebanon. Lebanon suffered heavy bombings from Israel in the summer of 2006. This was done in retaliation, because the Lebanese Hezbollah attacked Israel. The Scriptures prophesy that Damascus and the cities of Lebanon will be destroyed. This has never happened before, and it is logical to assume that it will take place during the first global battle mentioned in Revelation 6 at the beginning of the Great Tribulation.

When these cities in Syria and Lebanon are destroyed, the Palestinians in Gaza and Samaria will come unglued. The very next verse in Zechariah 9 prophesies the reaction of the Palestinians in Gaza. They are hoping that the Muslim nations will defeat Israel and allow them to possess the Holy Land. The Bible says that will not happen; rather the Palestinians will be in fear and writhe in agony when they see Lebanon and Damascus consumed by fire.

"Tyre ...will be consumed by fire. Ashkelon will see it and fear; Gaza will writhe in agony, and Ekron too, for her hope will wither. Gaza will lose her king and Ashkelon will be deserted. Foreigners will occupy Ashdod, and I will cut off the pride of the Philistines" (Zech. 9:5-6).

As the Muslim world is being reduced, Israel will receive her Promised Land. Israel will defend herself against the surrounding nations, and in so doing her land will be increased to the dimensions that God promised Abraham. Israel will extend from the Nile to the Euphrates in the early days of the Great Tribulation. This will happen because God will release supernatural military power to Israel; He will defend her. All who attack Israel, in those days, will injure themselves.

"On that day the Lord made a covenant with Abram and said, "To your descendants I give this land, from the river of Egypt to the great river, the Euphrates" (Gen. 15:18-19).

"I will make Jerusalem an immovable rock for all the nations. All who try to move it will injure themselves ... I will keep a watchful eye over Judah ... They will consume right and left all the surrounding peoples, but Jerusalem will remain intact in her place ... On that day I will set out to destroy all the nations that attack Jerusalem" (Zech. 12:3-4,6,9).

CHAPTER TWENTY-TWO

THE FOUR HORSES OF REVELATION

ISRAEL, THE CHURCH AND THE WORLD

IT will be helpful and fitting if we digress from our theme, for just this chapter, to look at the start of the Great Tribulation. Since Israel's national defense for the end times runs parallel to the beginnings of the book of Revelation, let us take a closer look at what will happen with the Church and the world at that time. I warn you that this chapter reveals a season of great pain that is coming upon the earth.

The war at the beginning of the book of Revelation will take such a heavy toll on the nations. War, however, is not the only aspect of God's wrath that will strike the world at that time; famines and plagues will also take a huge toll.

It all begins when Jesus breaks the seals off of the scroll that is in the right hand of God Almighty and the four apocalyptic horses are released from heaven.

"I watched as the Lamb opened the first of the seven seals. Then I heard one of the four living creatures say in a voice like thunder, 'Come!' I looked, and there before me was a white horse! Its rider held a bow and he was given a crown, and he rode out as a conqueror bent on conquest" (Rev. 6:1-2).

THE WHITE HORSE

John, the seer and writer of Revelation, watches as Jesus breaks the first seal. Immediately, one of the seraphim launches the first judgment. With a voice like thunder, his primal battle cry shakes the universe. The hosts of heaven have been waiting for eons to hear this upward call of God.

The seraphim cries, "Come!" and all of heaven responds. Immediately, the armies of heaven snap to attention. A stillness fills the air, as all the eyes look toward the throne. Suddenly, John sees a white spirit horse mounted by an angel. The rider holds a bow, as Jesus places a crown on his head. Once he is commissioned, he rides out to conquer. He is determined to achieve his mission. He is going to war against the devil and wickedness, and all the armies of heaven will go with him.

PURITY, PASSION AND POWER

This warhorse is white. He represents purity, passion and power. John feels the power and the passion with which he rides. He stares at the horse's brilliant coat; it points to the righteousness and purity of the One he represents. This is God's war, and it is the real holy war.

The horse does not release judgment like the other three horses that will soon follow. Instead, he gives the call to arms. His bow fires the flare to initiate heaven's charge, and all of heaven comes into agreement.

As all armies should, heaven declares war before attacking. The white charger is the chosen one who will release the declaration of war to the enemies of God. This horse comes as a prophetic sign. Like a banner unfurled in the wind, he rides out before the armies of God. His presence announces God's victory and Satan's defeat. He is bent on conquest because heaven cannot fail. He is a conqueror.

THE HORSES OF HEAVEN

The book of Revelation is not the only place in the Bible where we find the heavenly spirit horses. They are seen in 2 Kings 2:11, 2 Kings 6:17, Zechariah 1:8-11 and Zechariah 6:1-7. We are introduced to the same colored horses by Zechariah:

"During the night I had a vision – and there before me was a man riding a red horse! Behind him were red, brown and white horses. The angel... answered, 'They are the ones the Lord has sent to go throughout the earth'" (Zech. 1:8-10).

Again, Zechariah is shown the spirit horses of heaven.

"I looked again – and there before me were four chariots. The first chariot had red horses, the second black, the third white, and the fourth dappled – all of them powerful. I asked the angel... 'What are these?' The angel answered me, 'These are the four spirits of heaven, going out from standing in the presence of the Lord' ... so they went throughout the earth" (Zech. 6:1-7).

These horses have the same colors as the ones mentioned in the book of Revelation. They come from the throne room of God, and they are sent by Him. They are called the four spirits of heaven. They are not messengers from Satan, but holy ambassadors from God's kingdom. The white horse and its rider are servants of the Most High God.

Some suggest that the white horse is the Antihrist, but that cannot be true. These horses are four spirits of heaven that come from the presence of the Lord.

HORSES OF JUDGMENT

The next three horses come with devastating judgments which affect every person on the planet, and global catastrophes occur. Judgments from God have come throughout history, even in our own lifetime, but the ones that will come in the telling of Revelation are much more intense.

"They [the colored horses and their riders] were given power over a fourth of the earth to kill by sword, famine and plague, and by the wild beasts of the earth" (Rev. 6:8).

War, famine and plague will destroy a quarter of the earth's population. These horses are given power over one out of every four people, to kill them by war, famine and plague. These judgments will cover the entire planet, and it will likely happen within a one-year period. This takes place in just the first year of the Great Tribulation. As devastating as these are, the judgments that follow at a later time in the book of Revelation are much worse.

Today, more than six billion people inhabit the earth. A fourth of the earth will be killed during that first year of the Tribulation, and that is more than one-and-a-half billion people. Although there are other signs that tell us that the end of the age is near, when one-and-a-half billion people die within a year, we will know that the Great Tribulation has begun.

GRACE FOR SAINTS

This is a difficult picture to receive, but we must understand that we comprehend things from a limited perspective here on earth, but God sees from eternity. Whether we live on earth for a week or for ninety-five years, our time here is only a blip on the computer screen of eternity. The trials of this life are but a vapor, but the joys of eternity will last forever. Without that perspective, we can never understand the plans of God.

The people of God will have special grace during the Great Tribulation, and many will be protected; listen to what will be said of them:

"They overcame him [the devil] by the blood of the Lamb and by the word of their testimony; they did not love their lives so much as to shrink from death" (Rev. 12:11).

The saints who are present during the Tribulation will not shrink back, as do many today; rather they will stand as great warriors who overcome the devil and are not afraid to die.

ETERNAL JUDGMENTS

The righteous who die during this time will wake up in the presence of the Lord, as billions of people have done before them. The unsaved, however, will open their eyes in Hades after they die. We cannot determine who will go to heaven and who will go to Hades. That is God's business, but we know that every person who comes to God must come to Him through Christ. Keep this in mind: where sin abounds, God's grace abounds more (see Romans 5:20). I believe that many more will go to heaven than we think.

There is a difference between judgments that take place in heaven and those we receive while we are still on earth. In heaven, every individual will be judged by what he did in life. It does not matter what others from his family did; each will stand alone before God. That is not the case with judgments that fall at this time on the earth. Here, judgment is more of a package deal. Judgments come upon families, communities and nations. Many families and nations are under a curse because of their sin. Leaders who rule with evil intent bring judgment upon themselves, their families and their nations. If not for God's special protection when judgment falls on the nations, all would be affected, even the righteous.

THE RED HORSE

When Jesus removes the second seal, the second seraph cries, "Come."

"Then another horse came out, a fiery red one. Its rider was given power to take peace from the earth and to make men slay each other. To him was given a large sword" (Rev. 6:4).

A fiery red horse steps forward. The rider carries a sword and opens the floodgates of war on the earth. Nations attack nations, and civil war erupts in many countries. This is the first of the three global wars that are seen in the book of Revelation. Then hundreds of city gangs launch assaults on their neighbors. Violence rules the streets of major cities. Racial arrogance leads to ethnic cleansings and genocide. Entire people groups are decimated. Some nations will be completely obliterated, for not every nation will survive and make it to the new Millennium. God lifts his hand, and human restraint is cast aside. Greed, oppression and the pride that has simmered for centuries will suddenly have free course. The cup of pent-up malice and chaos will be unleashed. The apostle Peter explains the root cause of corruption in the world:

"Corruption in the world [is] caused by evil desires" (2 Peter 1:4).

Man's evil desires for selfish gain, his hatred of those different from himself, and his pride will rise up and undermine tolerance and kindness. A global bloodbath will erupt as peace is taken from the world.

THE BLACK HORSE

Jesus removes the third seal, and the third seraph says, "Come!"

"I looked and there before me was a black horse! Its rider was holding a pair of scales in his hand. Then I heard what sounded like a voice among the four living creatures, saying, 'A quart of wheat for a day's wages, and three quarts of barley for a day's wages, and do not damage the oil and the wine'" (Rev. 6:5-6).

A black horse charges from heaven, and famine covers the earth. Its rider holds a pair of scales for measuring weight in his hand. Strange weather patterns, drought, agricultural disease and natural disasters will cause crop failures around the world. Famine will not only affect third world countries, but the developed nations as well. Epidemics like hoof-and-mouth disease and Asian bird flu will devastate livestock, while new strains of plant diseases and mutant insects will destroy the fruit and vegetables of entire regions. Millions of people will die from starvation, and the price of food will sky-rocket out of control.

GROSS INFLATION

In 2005 a hurricane named Katrina slammed into the Gulf Coast of the United States. Momentarily, the oil refineries were shut down, and the price of gasoline rose. Before the hurricane, the average U.S. price of gas was $2.30 per gallon, but within a day it rose to more than $6.00 per gallon in some places.

When global famine hits, a loaf of bread will rise from $2.00 to $100.00. A quart of wheat will produce only one or two loaves of bread, but as the angel says, it will cost a day's wages. Conservatively, we can estimate a man's wages to be $100.00 per day. That will be the new price for a loaf of bread. Food will quickly rise beyond the reach of average people.

COMPASSION AND MERCY

When catastrophe takes hold of the world, the Church will take hold of God. Miracles and supernatural provisions will come to multitudes, and Christians will give generously to those in need. The angel prophesies it. He says, "A quart of wheat for a day's wages… and *do not damage the oil and the wine*" (Rev. 6:6; italics added).

Famine and lack will be everywhere, but the oil and wine will not be damaged. Oil and wine are the classic symbols of Christian care and compassion. They represent the work of the Holy Spirit and the blood of Christ. The pouring out of these elements represents the mercy ministry of the Church. Mission efforts will supply food, water, clothing, shelter and medical supplies to the poor and needy. Christian relief programs will be everywhere. Help will come from organized church groups as well as individual Christian families. They will have supplies because God will provide supernaturally. Testimonies of food coming from the hand of God and provisions being multiplied are common Bible stories. Many modern-day disciples have also seen these kinds of miracles. It is not strange to expect them during the Tribulation. The angel prophesied it when he said, "Do not damage the oil and the wine."

THE GOOD SAMARITAN

A Jewish politician asked Jesus, "'What must I do to inherit eternal life?' . . . he answered, 'Love the Lord your God with all your heart … and, Love your neighbor as yourself.' But . . . he asked, 'Who is my neighbor?'" (Luke 10:25-29).

In response, Jesus told the story of the Good Samaritan, who found a wounded traveler lying half dead on the side of the road. The man was a Jew, and normally the Samaritan would have no contact with him. Jesus taught us to express care beyond cultural and ethnic lines. Our neighbor is anyone in need. Jesus said that we are to love others as much as we love ourselves. In the story, the Samaritan cared for the wounded man.

Jesus said, "He went to him and bandaged his wounds, pouring on oil and wine" (Luke 10:34).

The oil and wine symbolize Christian compassion; we minister it to those in need. In the Great Tribulation, heaven's compassion will open the door for heaven's anointing. Believers will experience great joy as they serve the Lord and others. Unbelievers will realize that society can offer no solutions, and multitudes will turn to Christ as they witness His miraculous power and see His love coming from His people. This will produce the first of many revivals in the Great Tribulation.

Jesus unfolds the endtimes with the help of His servants. He enlists both angels and humans as He reaches out to a dying world. The angel tells John of this three-way partnership. He says, "Then the angel said to me, 'I am a fellow servant with you and with your brothers who hold to the testimony of Jesus'" (Rev. 19: 9-10).

Here we see it; Jesus, angels and people working together to accomplish the purposes of God Almighty.

THE PALE HORSE

When Jesus broke the fourth seal, the fourth living creature cried, "Come!"

"I looked and there before me was a pale horse! Its rider was named Death and Hades was following close behind him. They were given power over a forth of the earth to kill by sword, famine and plague, and by the wild beasts of the earth" (Rev. 6: 8).

Then the gray or dappled horse comes forward. This horse will bring the judgment of plagues and disease to the earth. Its rider will be named Death, and Hades follows close behind him. Diseases like the Asian bird flu, the bubonic plague, the Ebola virus and AIDS will kill whole communities. The medical experts of the world will not be able to stop the outbreaks, and the viruses will mutate at such a speed that yesterday's cures will be ineffective today. Huge numbers of people will die due to the plagues, so the rider on the gray horse is called Death.

I believe, although it is not stated, that these plagues will not affect believers because Hades follows close behind. Believers do not go to Hades. When they die they go to be with the Lord. That tells me that the believers will be protected from catching the plagues.

The combinations of war, famine, disease and wild beasts will kill a quarter of the people on the planet. The loss and mourning among the nations will be unrelenting. Everyone will know of a friend or family member who will die in the first year of the Great Tribulation and a deep pain will cover the earth. Without Christ, it will be unbearable.

BIRTH PAINS

Jesus spoke of these days. He said the following: "You will hear of wars and rumors of wars, but see to it that you are not alarmed. Such things must happen, but the end is still to come. Nation will rise against nation, and kingdom against kingdom. There will be famines and earthquakes in various places. All these are the beginning of birth pains" (Matt. 24:6-8; Mark 13; Luke 21).

It is only natural to be alarmed when we read about these things, but Jesus tells us not to be alarmed, for these things must happen. He says that they are just the beginning. He tells us that they are birth pains. But what is about to be born?

Further in the book of Revelation, we discover what will be born. It is the powerful end-time Church that will be born. The prophetic Church of the last days will emerge. This will include the Gentile Church and redeemed Israel, who together will make up the one new man. The world will step back and notice the glory of the Lord upon His people. Jesus will make His stand among the golden lampstands. His promise of miraculous power has not yet been fulfilled. He spoke of greater miracles working through His disciples in the days to come.

He said, "Anyone who has faith in me will do what I have been doing. He will do greater things than these, because I am going to my Father. You may ask for anything in my name, and I will do it" (John 14:12-14).

Scripture says that God's glory will come on His people when gross darkness covers the earth. We have not yet seen God's glory come to His people as described in Isaiah. We read: "Arise, shine, for your light has come, and the glory of the Lord rises upon you. See darkness covers the earth and thick darkness is over the peoples, but the Lord rises upon you and his glory appears over you. Nations will come to your light and kings to the brightness of your dawn" (Isa. 60:1-3).

This Scripture will apply to both the Gentile Church and to the Israelites who receive Jesus as Messiah. It will happen when gross darkness comes. God's glory brings revival to the earth as He shines through His people.

FOR YOU

If you are a Christian who has prayed and not yet seen God's power as much as you believe it should come, look with faith to the days that lie ahead. God's miraculous power will come to the Church during the first half of the Tribulation and will remain on them for all eternity.

Paul says, "He who did not spare his own Son, but freely gave him up for us all – how will he not... graciously give us all things" (Rom. 8:32).

We can see clearly what will happen in the Church and in the world at God's appointed moment when He releases Israel's national defense for the end times. The Tribulation will have started, and the world will suffer God's judgments. The Church will rise up and begin to partner with Israel, and together they will overcome the devil by the blood of the Lamb and the word of their testimony.

PART THREE

ISRAEL'S REVIVAL AND BEYOND

CHAPTER TWENTY-THREE

PREPARING FOR REVIVAL

CHAOS AND REVIVAL

WE now turn our study toward the theme of revival. In this chapter we will give an update on America's shifting political attitude toward Israel and the latest judgments that have come to her shores because of those new policies. More importantly, we will discover God's focus for the human race – a focus on revival. As we read Scripture, we discover that judgments and revival run together, at the same time, at the end of the age.

I am not happy to report that the United States is lining up for more judgments. The book of Revelation tells us that judgments such as earthquakes, famines and wars are inevitable at the end of the age, and with each passing day, it seems that America is making more wrong choices and that these decisions will yield terrible judgments. Many Christians are worried, and some are crying out in opposition to present U.S. policy on several fronts. The Tea Party movement, as it is called, is a coming together of people who are voicing their concerns about the direction our nation is moving in. Many Christians have lined up with this movement, and some are absolutely consumed with the troubles that they see brewing. Although I cannot agree with everything they are doing, in my opinion, they have strong reasons to be deeply concerned, and I am glad that they are speaking out.

One of the areas of policy change in America is this administration's negative attitude toward Israel. It seems that President Obama is so determined to see peace in the Middle East that he and his team are demanding that

Israel make unreasonable concessions. Over the last month (April 2010), the U.S. State Department has been insisting that Jerusalem be divided and that Eastern Jerusalem be given to the Palestinian Arab peoples. They are pushing for the establishment of a Palestinian state, with East Jerusalem as its capital. They are putting pressure on Israel to try to force her to retreat to the territory that she had before the Six Day War in 1967. That would mean that Israel would give away the land that the Bible says belongs to the Jews. So far, Israeli Prime Minister, Benjamin Netanyahu, has refused to comply with these outlandish demands. In response, President Obama has taken a very aggressive posture to increase pressure tactics against Israel. Here is a brief report from JNN News, Jerusalem-on-the-Line, given on May 2, 2010:

OBAMA TO CALL WORLD SUMMIT IF MIDEAST PEACE TALKS FAIL: US President Barack Obama has told several European leaders that if Israeli-Palestinian talks remain stalemated into September and October, he will convene an international summit on achieving Mideast peace, senior Israeli officials said on Thursday. The conference would be run by the Quartet Mideast peacemakers – the United States, European Union, United Nations and Russia – in a bid to forge a united global front for creating a Palestinian state.[44]

GULF COAST OIL CHAOS

During the same time period that these negative pressures have been launched against Israel from the U.S. State Department, a great tragedy has fallen on America. The facts regarding the date, volume of oil leaked, and the threat of devastation over this oil spill have been gathered from and article by Lee Ross from Fox News. [45]

On April 20, 2010, a BP oil well exploded in the Gulf of Mexico, just fifty miles off of the U.S. coast. The authorities have not determined how it happened, but it is a disaster, and less than two weeks later, as I write, the scenario darkens. It is reported that one mile below the water's surface, 500 barrels or 210,000 gallons of oil are spewing out of the well every day. Conservative estimates tell us that it will take at least three months to stop the leak. This will likely be the worst environmental disaster in U.S. history, to date.

As it comes ashore, it threatens the wildlife in the marshes and estuaries from Texas to Florida. It will do great damage to the seabirds and to the wildlife in the Gulf waters as well. It will have devastating consequences on fisheries, local industries, tourism and the entire economy of the South. This could ruin the Gulf waters and the shoreline for generations to come.

I do not think that the timing of this catastrophe is a coincidence, but rather a direct response to U.S. policy against Israel. It is a judgment. Every time America moves in a negative way toward Israel, something devastating happens. The negative pressure coming from the White House against Israel at this time is unprecedented, and I think this Gulf oil tragedy is unprecedented as well. Every good plan that America puts in play will be thwarted if she forces Israel to retreat from her God-given assignment.

1. I think it is no coincidence that the oil spill will hit the U.S. economy at a time when the nation is really struggling.
2. It is no coincidence that this trouble involves the oil industry, at a time when the United States wants to move away from their dependency on Mideast oil.
3. It is no coincidence that this happens just weeks after the U.S. government agrees to begin drilling for oil in the Gulf once again.
4. It is no coincidence that this happens when the U.S. administration wants to become more "green." They are aiming at making policies that are environmentally friendly, but this is the undoing of any "green" program that they make.

If we touch Israel, we touch the apple of God's eye. The terrible impact of this disaster will be far reaching.

SHIFTING OUR FOCUS

It is time for Christians to lose their fears. They must shift their focus from traumas to revivals. We must settle the matter in our hearts – judgments and devastating traumas are coming to America.

Calling upon God for mercy and doing all we can to alleviate pain and suffering are essential. The Lord will answer many prayers, and we will see God's mercy. While all of that is true, judgments are coming, and they cannot be completely avoided because too many people in America have turned away from the Lord. The book of Revelation does not give us a suggested end for the age; it gives us a clear description of the judgments that are coming.

It is so important that we understand that the primary goal of these judgments is not punitive, but redemptive. It is because of the great pain that they bring that multitudes will turn to the Lord and eventually be blessed. Too many believers are worried because of the traumas. They are wallowing in anxiety and stress instead of focusing on their partnership with God for revival and the harvest of the earth.

So what does the Lord want His people to do at this time in history? We are not called to fear, worry or anxiety, but we are called to stand in faith, to have confidence and to claim victory. We are not called to polish the brass on the *Titanic*, but to prepare the lifeboats and get as many people into them as possible. I am not suggesting that we forget about political policy, fighting for our freedoms or standing up for the Judeo-Christian ethics upon which this nation was founded. We must do that and do it well, but I am suggesting that our main focus needs to shift. I must begin to focus on the subject that the Lord is focusing on: the harvest.

GOD'S FOCUS IS REVIVAL

The traumas or judgments that are coming are designed by God to bring about two separate results; one is the destruction of the devil and all of his co-workers, and the other is world-wide revival.

From before time began, God Almighty has focused on the harvest of the earth. Starting with creation itself and God's involvement with humankind, He has looked to the purpose of bringing vast multitudes of people into fellowship with Himself. So many have turned away from Him, but in the end, He will still go after multitudes of souls. That is called the harvest of the earth; it is called revival. The harvest of the earth has always been God's theme, and as we near the end of the age, revival and the harvest will become the theme of all of God's people as well. There will be a specific Jewish revival and several revivals for the Gentile nations that will reach around the world.

A harvest comes when a crop is ripe and the workers gather to collect it. Last year I planted a blueberry bush in my yard. It is now yielding thousands of blueberries. This blueberry bush grew from the seed of a single blueberry. The seed was planted, and the bush started to grow. Branches, leaves, blooms and, finally, berries have come from that one blueberry seed. My blueberry bush is now experiencing revival; it is producing an amazing crop for the harvest.

That is what the Lord has done, and He is presently working on His revival program to bring it to its conclusion. As you know, His prize is not blueberries, but people, and by the end of the age, He will have the greatest harvest the world has ever seen.

So should the Church be consumed with fear because of the traumas of the nation, or should the Church partner with God during the time of traumas to be workers in the harvest?

Of course the answer is clear; the Church will work with God in the great revivals that are coming. It is time, therefore, to discover what the Church's God-given role is for this season and then make sure that we participate in it.

We must prepare ourselves for the harvest. We have a job to do, so here are some steps that will help us prepare ourselves to partner with God for the end-time harvest.

PREPARING FOR REVIVAL

Let me give you seven words, from the Bible, all starting with the letter "P," that will help you prepare for revival harvests: patience, pray, prophesy, preach, power, peace and praise.

 1. Patience

To start with we need patience. If we do not have patience, we will be full of fear, anxiety and worry as we see judgment after judgment coming upon the earth. Worry during this season is a distraction from the call of God on our lives, so we need patience. Every farmer looks to the future, and he needs patience because there is a proper time to collect the harvest. The crop must first be ripe before the harvest can be collected. God is the Great Farmer of Eternity, and He is patient, so we are called to follow His example and be patient as well. The apostle James explains this clearly: "Be patient, then, brothers, until the Lord's coming. See how the farmer waits for the land to yield its valuable crop and how patient he is for the autumn and spring rains. You too, be patient and stand firm, because the Lord's coming is near" (Jas. 5:7-8).

Ask yourself if you and your loved ones are becoming anxious in view of the troubles that are mounting in the nation. If so, ask the Lord to shift your perspective. Ask the Lord for patience.

"You have need of patience, that, after you have done the will of God, you might receive the promise" (Heb. 10:36 KJV).

If we are going to be faithful, we must have patience. Two times during the Great Tribulation we read about the need for patience. The following verse is repeated; note the Scripture references.

"This calls for patient endurance and faithfulness on the part of the saints" (Rev. 13:10; 14:12).

2. Pray
   The second word that will help us prepare for revival is *pray*. Read the following words, about the harvest. These are the words of Jesus to His disciples.

   "He told them, 'The harvest is plentiful but the workers are few. *Ask the Lord* of the harvest, therefore, to send out workers into the harvest field. Go! I am sending you as lambs among wolves'" (Luke 10:2-3; italis added).

Jesus taught many things about the harvest. If these truths applied back then, then they certainly apply today as we approach the greatest revivals in all of history. Jesus taught that the fields were ripe and ready for harvesting and that the harvest was plentiful. In other words, revival was just around the corner, and there were so many who were ripe and ready to be saved. Revival came to the early Church, starting with the day of Pentecost, and it is coming to the end-time Church as well.

He said that the laborers were few. There is nothing wrong with the harvest, but we have a worker shortage. The solution that Jesus gives is prayer. More specifically, we are to pray, or ask the Lord of the harvest to send forth workers. Then, in answer to our prayers, He says that He is sending us out as harvesters as lambs among wolves. So preparation for revival, step number two, is to pray.

3. Prophesy

The third word that will help us prepare for the harvest is *prophesy*. God does nothing on the earth without agreement from His people, so nothing happens without prayer and prophecy. Since the days of the patriarchs, prophecy has been God's way. We read the following in Scriputre: "Surely the Sovereign Lord does nothing without revealing his plan to his servants the prophets" (Amos 3:7).

We also read in Ezekiel 37 about the valley of dry bones. The dry bones represent an end-time picture of the people of Israel, dead in sin and far away from God. The prophet was told to prophesy over them, and in the vision, the bones came together, grew flesh and stood up like a mighty army. It represented the whole house of Israel coming to God at the end of the age.

Zechariah also prophecies of Israel's coming revival, as does Daniel, Micah, Joel, Zephaniah and most of the Old Testament prophets.

Jesus prophesied of Israel's coming revival, and so did Peter and Paul. Of course John prophesied; after all, he wrote the book of Revelation, where the great end-time revivals are mentioned. John was even told that he must personally prophesy. He said, "Then I was told, 'You must prophesy again about many people, nations, languages and kings'" (Rev. 10:11).

Before revival can come, God's people must prophesy. Even on the day of Pentecost, Peter prophesied, and the New Testament revivals were launched. He quoted the prophecies of the prophet Joel, and they came to pass, just as Joel said.

Soon the air will be filled with the prophetic words of the saints. Get ready – you also must take your place and prophesy.

4. Preach

    The fourth word that will help us prepare for revival is *preach*. Jesus continued to instruct His disciples about the harvest. While talking about reaching the harvest, He said this: "Go ... to the lost sheep of Israel. As you go preach" (Matt. 10:6-7).

The preaching of the cross is the most common way that God releases His power upon those who are being saved. We read, "The preaching of the cross is to them that perish foolishness; but unto us which are saved it is the power of God" (1 Cor. 1:18 KJV).

The Lord will call and equip many powerful preachers for the end-time harvest. Get ready to preach with authority, power and conviction. Wherever there are revivals, there is powerful preaching.

The greatest and most powerful preacher of the Old Testament was used by God to bring about an amazing revival to an almost impossible group of people who lived, in a so-called hard place. That preacher's name was Jonah, and the seemingly impossible place was the city of Nineveh.

You know the story; at first Jonah ran from the call of God on his life. Many Christians are in this situation today. God told him to go and preach in Nineveh, a city on the Tigris River, in the direction of India. Instead he got on a boat and headed for Tarshish, which is in Spain. He was going to a destination that was a thousand miles away, in the opposite direction from where God told him to go.

Then the Lord gave him his own personal tribulation experience. He was thrown overboard and swallowed by a great fish. Three days later he was vomited up on shore. After this powerful learning experience, God spoke to him again: "The word of the Lord came unto Jonah the second time, saying, Arise, go unto Nineveh, that great city, and *preach unto it the preaching that I bid thee.* ... So the people of Nineveh believed God, and proclaimed a fast, and put on sackcloth, from the greatest of them even to the least of them" (John 3:1-2 KJV; italics added).

Because of Jonah's preaching, the people of Nineveh repented and were saved. There were more than 120,000 inhabitants of the city, and revival came to everyone, from the least to the greatest among them. The mercy and grace of God fell on Nineveh, and they were spared and blessed because of it for more than one hundred years.

Preaching does not have to happen in a church building. You are called to preach God's Word. Don't be surprised if you find yourself moving in this direction. If God calls you to preach for the harvest, you may resist, but the Lord knows how to get His army ready. Remember Jonah's lesson in the belly of the great fish.

5. Power

When Jesus sent His disciples into the harvest field, He gave them more than words to preach. He sent them out to perform miracles. He gave the disciples these instructions:

"As you go, preach ... Heal the sick, raise the dead, cleanse those who have leprosy, drive out demons. Freely you have received, freely give" (Matt. 10:7-8).

Talk alone, will not be enough to produce the end-time revivals that have been prophesied and prayed over. God's power must be released to open the eyes of many unbelievers and sinners. Many church families do not see these kinds of miracles today. Some, however, especially those on the mission field in developing nations, see miracles. God answers prayer; He performs miracles of healings, the casting out of demons, and even the raising of the dead. My wife and I have witnessed the Lord at work through all of these types of miracles.

The early disciples ministered with supernatural power. The revivals that are before us require the partnership of God's people and the demonstration of miracles as well. Millions of Christians will become powerful prophetic intercessors, preachers and miracle workers. Pray and ask the Lord to give you His Holy Spirit gifts so that you may exercise miraculous signs and wonders for His glory.

6. Peace
   The sixth word that will help us prepare for revival is *peace*. Jesus has given supernatural peace to His children (see Philippians 4:7). He told the people, "My peace I give unto you" (John 14:27). Many, however, do not exercise enough faith to live in that peace. They do not enjoy the supernatural peace that the Lord has extended to them.

   Those who trust the Lord and walk in peace are instructed to share that peace with others. While teaching the disciples about the harvest, Jesus said the following:

   "The harvest is plentiful ... Go! I am sending you ... When you enter a house, first say, *'Peace to this house.' If a man of peace is there, your peace will rest on him*; if not, it will return to you" (Luke 10:2-3; 5-6; italics added).

People who lack faith, lack peace. Here is a short list of troubles that will steal peace away from people: hardships, sickness, hunger, strife, battles, war, poverty, lack of shelter, accidents, unfulfilled expectations, torment, fear, loneliness, rejection, curses, accidents, enemies, natural disasters, business failure and not knowing God, to name only a few.

The people of God have been given a supernatural gift of peace, and this peace passes human understanding. When we come into someone's house or, better still, when we come into someone's life, we should give him some of the peace that Jesus has given us. Giving peace includes helping the poor find water, food, clothes and shelter. In our day, giving peace also includes giving medical help, extending educational opportunities, freeing people from oppression and giving financial gifts. Those gifts are practical, and they can be easily seen, but other gifts that we should give may not be seen so easily. Giving peace also includes loving people, caring for them, praying for them, leading them to salvation, encouraging the weary, supporting the weak, breaking curses off of them, speaking a kind word, giving hope and being someone's friend.

Ministering to the wounded in body, soul and spirit is bringing God's peace to people. This is a very important part of reaping the harvest. When we care for people and bring peace to them, their hearts become open to receive the gospel. Once they believe, they are saved. They become part of the harvest, part of the revival, and part of the family of God.

7. Praise

    As we take steps to prepare for revival, we should remind ourselves to praise the Lord from start to finish. This is the seventh word that will help us prepare for revival. After Jesus teaches his disciples about the harvest, He warns them of persecution and tribulation. In Matthew 10, Jesus teaches His disciples to be partners in the harvest. This is also the chapter where He warns His disciples of the persecution and tribulation that they will have to endure. Praise is required for this part of the battle.

The Beatitudes, given in the Sermon on the Mount, teach us to praise the Lord even when we are persecuted for the sake of the gospel. Jesus tells us the following:

"Blessed are you when people insult you and persecute you and falsely say all kinds of evil against you because of me. Rejoice and be glad, because great is your reward in heaven, for in the same way they persecuted the prophets who were before you" (Matt. 5:11-12).

The Lord looks for the praises of His people. Faith is maintained and even increased as we praise the Lord. Praise allows our focus to remain on the Lord. It breaks the power of fear and distraction. Rejoice and be glad and praise the Lord, for He is great. He is the Lord of the Harvest.

REVIEW

It is important that God's people do more than learn about Israel's coming revival; they should do their part to partner with God in the harvest. They should pray and ask God how they can prepare themselves to be workers in the harvest. The following list gives us a review and an overview of the points we have studied in this chapter. These are the subjects we should focus on to prepare for revival.

1. Have Patience
2. Pray
3. Prophesy
4. Preach
5. Exercise Power
6. Extend Peace and Provisions
7. Praise Father, Son and Holy Spirit

CHAPTER TWENTY-FOUR

REVIVAL DURING WAR

ISRAEL'S SPIRITUAL DEFENSE

WE will now return to our study in Zechariah 12. We were looking at Israel's national defense, according to the prophet Zechariah. We discovered four powerful stages of Israel's military might that come to her as God blesses her in the last days:

1. God shields the Jewish people, and Jerusalem becomes an immovable rock.
2. The leaders of Israel react powerfully to any attack against their people. Like a firepot and a flaming torch, they send their armies out to consume their enemies.
3. The people of Israel receive supernatural power to defend themselves. The feeblest among them become strong warriors, and their mighty warriors become like God. Their army will be like the angel of the Lord.
4. The Lord God will personally go out to fight against and destroy Israel's enemies.

As we continue to study Zechariah 12, we find the focus shifting from Israel's national defense to Israel's spiritual revival:

"And I will pour out on the house of David and the inhabitants of Jerusalem a spirit of grace and supplication. They will look on me, the one they have pierced, and they will mourn for him as one mourns for an only child and grieve bitterly for him as one grieves for a firstborn son" (Zech. 12:10).

This power-packed verse reveals the start of Israel's coming revival. God will pour out a spirit of grace, which is for salvation, and a spirit of supplication, which is prayer, upon Jerusalem. Before we continue, let us take another look at revival, so that we are all on the same page.

WHAT IS REVIVAL?

When Christians talk about revival, they are referring to people coming to salvation through faith in Jesus Christ. The initial steps that people must take to be saved from hell and be brought into the blessings of eternal life with God are as follows:

1. They repent of their sins.
2. They believe that Jesus paid for their sins when He died on the cross.
3. They ask Jesus to remove their sins and to come into their lives.
4. They give their lives to Jesus and confess Him as their Lord and Savior.
5. As opportunity allows, they are baptized in water.

These steps will bring any person to salvation. For a Gentile person, this act of salvation makes him or her a Christian. A Jew must also follow the steps of believing in Jesus to be saved from hell and to have eternal life with God. The Jews, however, do not have to become Christians; they can remain Jews. Jesus is their Messiah, their Christ. If they believe on Him, they will be saved, and they can still be Jews. Jews who believe that Jesus is their Messiah are called *Messianic Jews*.

Whether Jew or Gentile, all are saved from the kingdom of darkness into the kingdom of God's dear Son in the same way. All must come through faith in Christ. This happens, one person at a time; however, *when multitudes get saved in a short period of time, we call it revival.* Many revivals have happened throughout history, but the greatest revivals, including the greatest Jewish revival, are still before us.

THE PEOPLE OF THE WAY

Here is a little more teaching on the subject of being a Messianic Jew. Do you know that, by and large, the first twenty thousand believers in Christ were all Jews? They were Messianic Jews. Look at the Apostle Paul's words when he stood before Governor Felix. He confessed that he was a Jew, that he followed the Law and the teachings of the prophets. He also acknowledged that the Jews who believed in Jesus were called a Jewish sect. They were called the "Followers of the Way." Read Paul's words.

> "I admit that I worship the *God of our fathers* as a *follower of the Way,* which they call *a sect. I believe everything that agrees with the Law and that is written in the Prophets,* and I have the same hope in God as these men, that there will be a resurrection" (Acts 24:14-15; italics added).

After Paul believed in Jesus as his Messiah, he continued to be a Jew, and he continued to believe in the Law and the words of the Jewish prophets. Paul and his fellow Jewish believers were referred to as a sect or a branch of Judaism called, "The Way."

They were called followers of the Way, because they had found a new and living way to become righteous and to come into the presence of God. It was through the body of Christ, not a curtain in the temple or through the keeping of the Law that they came into God's presence. Paul still believed in the Law, but not as a means to righteousness. It was, however, a continuing framework for religious life for the Jewish people. For example, they continued to keep kosher food and observe the feasts.

The new and living way was the way to righteousness. It was obtained through faith in Christ and that was now the only way to be righteous before God. The writer of Hebrews talks about this new and living way. He writes the following:

> *Therefore brothers, since we have confidence to enter* the Most Holy
> Place by the blood of Jesus, by a new and living way *opened for us*
> through the curtain, *that is,* his body, *and since we have a great priest*
> *over the house of God, let us draw near to God with a sincere heart in*
> *full assurance of faith, having our hearts sprinkled* to cleanse us from
> a guilty conscience and having our bodies washed *with pure water.*
> *(Heb. 10:19-22; emphasis added)*

The book of Hebrew tells the Jewish people how they must adjust their
thinking on many subjects as they come into the New Covenant. The way
into the presence of God, which was called the Most Holy Place, used to
be through the curtain in the temple. Only the High Priest could go to the
Most Holy Place, and that happened only once a year.

When Jesus died on the cross, however, the curtain in the temple was ripped
in two, opening the way for all to go into the presence of God at any time.
This became the main doctrine of the new Jewish believers, and that is why
they were called followers of the Way. They had found the new and living
way.

"Let us then approach the throne of grace with confidence, so that we may
receive mercy and find grace to help us in our time of need" (Heb. 4:16).

Both Jews and Gentiles are followers of the Way. All who have faith in Christ
can come boldly into God's presence to find help in time of need.

Later, as the Church grew, many disciples became known as Christians. The
term *Christian*, means "little Christ." The name *Christian* was first used in
Antioch while Barnabas and Paul were teaching there. *Christian* is now the
title that is given for all Gentiles who come to Christ. Some believing Jews
have also taken on this title, but many simply call themselves "Messianic
Jews"; they are Jews who receive Jesus as their Messiah.

"So for a whole year Barnabas and Saul met with the Church and taught great numbers of people. The disciples were called Christians first at Antioch" (Acts 11:26).

THE JEWISH REVIVAL

Now that we have defined the term *revival* and have noted that all Gentiles and Jews must be saved through faith in Christ, let us return to our Scripture of Israel's revival. Zechariah prophesied the following:

"And I will pour out on the house of David and the inhabitants of Jerusalem a spirit of grace and supplication. They will look on me, the one they have pierced, and they will mourn for him as one mourns for an only child and grieve bitterly for him as one grieves for a firstborn son" (Zech. 12:10).

If Zechariah 12 is presented in a chronological timeline, then revival will come to Israel when she is in the middle of a war. I think the amazing results of their military victories will soften their hearts toward the Lord. They will realize that their own skills, efforts and resources could not produce such amazing victories. When the supernatural stories of rescue and triumph start coming in and they hear, over and over again, about the extraordinary defeat of their enemies, they will know that the Lord God Almighty is watching over them.

NOT NEW TESTAMENT TIMES

At a chosen moment in history, when Israel is at war, God will pour His Holy Spirit upon the Jewish people. It will be like the day of Pentecost. The Lord is very specific; this verse says that the Holy Spirit will fall on the house of David and on the people who live in Jerusalem.

This does not refer, however, to Christ's first coming or to the time of the early apostles because the rest of the chapter does not fit that time period. Jerusalem was not an immoveable rock in Jesus' day, and Israel's national defense was not in play at that time. Many came against Israel in the time of Jesus; they scattered her people and injured them. No, the revival mentioned in Zechariah 12 happens when Israel is unmovable, when all who come against her will injure themselves, when her leaders are like a flaming torch, and when the house of David has supernatural power like the angel of the Lord. The only other place in the Bible where God's people have that kind of supernatural, military power is in the book of Revelation (see Revelation 11:5-6). The two end-time witnesses (redeemed Israel and the Gentile Church – the two olive branches) have supernatural power to kill the enemies of God. In Revelation 11, the plagues are described to be exactly like the ones that came during the time of Israel's exodus from Egypt. That is when the angel of the Lord moved through the streets, killing the firstborn of every Egyptian home (see Micah 7:15). This Jewish revival will come at the end of the age, and it will come to the house of David and the people of Jerusalem.

We will continue to study this and learn much more about the Jewish revival as foretold by Zechariah. In our next chapter, we will discover how deep this revival will go, how spiritually powerful it will be, and who in Israel will be a part of it.

CHAPTER TWENTY-FIVE

THE DEPTHS AND SCOPE
OF THE JEWISH REVIVAL

A SPIRIT OF GRACE AND SUPPLICATION

As we journey through Zechariah 12 we discover Israel's national defense. Then the chapter moves its focus to Israel's coming revival. The tenth verse starts to unveil a beautiful picture of the Spirit of the Lord moving upon the house of David and the people of Jerusalem. We will now pick up where we left off and continue our study of Israel's spiritual revival. Here is the verse once again.

"And I will pour out on the house of David and the inhabitants of Jerusalem a spirit of grace and supplication. They will look on me, the one they have pierced, and they will mourn for him as one mourns for an only child and grieve bitterly for him as one grieves for a firstborn son" (Zech. 12:10).

This verse tells us that the Holy Spirit will move upon Israel in two dynamic ways. One is a pouring out of grace, and the other is a pouring out of supplication.

Grace, like mercy, is God's undeserved favor toward humankind. It is different from mercy, however, because grace requires participation from the recipient. The Lord gives mercy to whom He will give mercy; He does not need a response from that person. He just blesses them. Grace is different; it always requires a response. Grace is an opportunity. Jesus died for everyone when He gave His life for us on the cross, but not everyone has received His grace. The cross is an opportunity to receive God's grace, but only those who respond with faith will receive it.

Soon a mighty outpouring of the Holy Spirit will come upon Israel, and the Jewish people will be given a fresh opportunity to receive God's grace. Like everyone who is offered grace, Israel does not deserve it. It is God's favor extended to the people of Jerusalem, for righteousness and salvation. Salvation is the most fundamental and essential aspect of God's grace for Jew or Gentile. Like on the day of Pentecost, this grace will literally be poured upon them. One aspect of this grace involves the opening of their spiritual eyes. They will look upon "the one they have pierced."

SUCH WEEPING

Suddenly, the people of Israel will understand that Jesus is their Messiah and that they participated in His death. This will happen to millions of Jewish people at the same time. They will begin to weep and mourn like one mourns over the death of a firstborn son or an only child.

"On that day the weeping in Jerusalem will be great, like the weeping of Hadad Rimmon in the plain of Megiddo" (Zech. 12:11).

Hadad Rimmon is a town in the valley of Megiddo where great weeping and lamentations were lifted up because of the death of King Josiah at the age of thirty-nine in a battle with Pharaoh Necoh of Egypt (see 2 Kings 23:25-29). It was a time of great weeping that was singled out as a national moment of enormous grief for Israel. King Josiah was the most upright and righteous of all of their kings. He is noted as Israel's most godly king, and when he was killed, the entire nation mourned (see Jeremiah 22:10).

For more details, see the article "Righteous King Josiah," by Fr. Josiah Trenham.[46]

That is what the weeping will be like when the eyes of the Jews are opened and they realize that Jesus died for them and that it was their collaboration that caused His piercings and His death. Bit by bit, the full revelation will come, and all of Israel will begin to mourn profusely. On one hand, they will realize what they have done, and, on the other hand, they will realize what they have missed by not receiving Jesus for all these centuries.

What mourning there will be! It will feel like the death of a firstborn son. Their grief will turn to repentance, and God's love will be poured out upon them with an enormous release of healing, forgiveness, and salvation. God's grace will provide the opportunity, and Israel will respond and experience her greatest revival.

SUPPLICATION

The other dynamic that will be poured out upon Israel is a spirit of supplication. Supplication is a desperate cry to God for a miracle in a time of tragedy or trauma. This is not a casual or half-hearted type of prayer, but a gut-wrenching, emotional cry to God. Supplication is when you take hold of the horns of the altar, and you refuse to let go until God blesses you. It is like Jacob wrestling all night with the angel of the Lord, until he receives God's favor. When Jacob did this, his hip was put out of joint, and his name was changed to "Israel," which means "one who has prevailed like a prince." Now, the people who bear his name will wrestle with the angel of the Lord, and they will supplicate in prayer. They will not let go until the Lord blesses them. Overnight, they will be changed to be a different people. They will limp as if their pride was broken, and they will receive a new name, as we all do when we have such an encounter with God.

If your child was involved in a terrible car accident and was in the hospital and the doctors said he was going to die, you would supplicate. You would cry out to God for a miracle in your hour of despair. That is what will happen to Israel when her revival comes. From deep within, the Jewish people will cry out to God, but this is more than human effort; God will pour out a Spirit of supplication upon them. The Holy Spirit will lead them in these prayers.

THOSE WHO SUPPLICATE

Jonah the prophet supplicated in the belly of the great fish and became the greatest revival preacher of the Old Testament. Hannah could not have children, and she supplicated. God answered her prayer and she gave birth to Samuel, the prophet of God. It is said that none of Samuel's words ever fell to the ground. Jesus supplicated in the Garden of Gethsemane and then stepped forward to bear the sins of the world.

The Jewish people will receive a spirit of supplication, and they will pray with amazing resolve. God will hear them and answer their prayers. Multitudes of Jews will be saved. They will find much more than national salvation; they will begin to go to the nations as evangelists. They will see the nations in despair and will send Jewish missionaries to the four corners of the earth. Their fervent supplication will bring forth the greatest preaching, release of miracles, and greatest revivals that the world has ever known will be witnessed by all.

A DOMESTIC, NOT A POLITICAL REVIVAL

We understand that Israel's coming revival will be as real and as powerful as any in history; it will be genuine to the core. All of Israel will consecrate and dedicate their lives back to the Lord. This will not be a political move but a grassroots phenomenon. The Jews will not just announce one day that their nation is becoming a Christian nation. No, they will always be Jews. This will not be a political experience, but a domestic one. Salvation will come to mothers and children, fathers and grandparents. The people of Israel will, one by one, receive the revelation that Jesus is Messiah, and they will repent and be saved.

I can picture a soldier in the plains of Megiddo, crawling out from the turret of his tank. Tears are streaming down his face as he repents and dedicates his life to Yeshua HaMashiach – Jesus the Messiah. I can picture women gathering for hot tea. They are unable to eat because they are overtaken with emotion. They are weeping, repenting and crying on each other's shoulders.

I see white-bearded men with ringlets hanging down from both sides of their broad-rimed hats, in prayer at the synagogue. Their faces are soaked with tears of repentance. I have seen fully grown men weep like this before. Their emotions are gushing forth with uncontrollable utterances. They are crying loudly, and no one would think of trying to stop them. Only God can understand them.

Zechariah 12:12-14 gives us a clear picture of the extent and the breadth of this revival.

"The land will mourn, each clan by itself, with their wives by themselves: the clan of the house of *David and their wives*, the clan of the house of *Nathan and their wives*, the clan of the house of *Levi and their wives*, the clan of *Shimei and their wives*, and all *the rest of the clans and their wives*" (Zech. 12:12-14; italics added).

REVIVAL FOR ALL OF ISRAEL

The mourning that leads to repentance will come upon Israel. It comes to all the tribes, and not just to the men – but the wives are specifically mentioned in every case. The scope and depth of this revival will reach every corner of Jewish society.

Repentance will come to *the house of David* and to their wives. David represents the kingly tribes.

Repentance will come to *the house of Nathan* and to their wives. Nathan represents the prophetic tribes.

Repentance will come to *the house of Levi* and their wives. Levi represents the priestly tribes.

Repentance will come to *the house of Shimei* and their wives. Shimei represents the house of Saul. He represents their repentance and redemption. Mordecai was a descendant of Shimei, and through him, Shimei rescued the Jews from genocide in the days of Queen Esther. He is in the list, for he represents a family that turned back to God from a place of great loss.

The Scripture tells us that revival will come to the house or family of David, Nathan, Levi and Shimei. Then it says that repentance will come to all the rest of the families of Israel and their wives; no one is left out. Salvation will come to every family, clan and tribe in Israel.

Salvation reaches every Jewish tribe, but another subtlety is given; it says that each clan will meet by themselves. Presently, there are fifty-two different sects of Orthodox Jews in Israel, not including the reformed, or secular Jewish groups. Each clan will meet by themselves. After personal salvation comes to individuals, they will meet in their family groups to mourn and repent and have prayer meetings. It will not be a hidden matter but a public one. This is not like Nicodemus, the priest who came to Jesus secretly at night; this is a time when the world will see household conversions and national dedications, where whole tribes will openly repent and commit themselves to the Lord.

THE FOUNTAIN OF SALVATION

This ends our study of Zechariah 12, but the revival story continues in the next chapter. In the original text, there are no chapter divisions, so Zechariah 13 is simply an unbroken continuation of Zechariah 12. Look at how the chapter begins:

"On that day a fountain will be opened to the house of David and the inhabitants of Jerusalem, to cleanse them from sin and iniquity" (Zech. 13:1).

On that day when Israel becomes an immovable rock among the nations, a fountain will be opened to the house of David and the people of Jerusalem. This fountain is the fountain of life that flows from Christ; there is no other fountain that can cleanse people from their sins.

A famous Christian hymn quotes this verse and gives us the details we need to understand what this verse is referring to. The song is called: "There is a Fountain Filled with Blood".

"There is a fountain filled with blood
Drawn from Immanuel's veins:
And sinners, plunged beneath that flood,
Lose all their guilty stains."[47]

Jesus is Immanuel, and from his veins flows His shed blood. Any sinner, Jew or Gentile, who receives the benefits of Christ's shed blood will have all of their sins removed. The fountain of salvation mentioned by the prophet Zechariah is the blood of Jesus. It was shed two thousand years ago, but many Jews rejected salvation through Christ back then. Now, in our time, God will open the fountain for them again. A spirit of grace and supplication will come upon them, and their eyes will be opened. Revival will come to Israel, and all of their sin and impurity will be washed away.

This is not the only place in the Bible that speaks of an end-time Jewish revival, and there are many more details to be shared about that revival. We will continue to study the Scriptures and discover more about Israel's coming revival in the next chapters.

CHAPTER TWENTY-SIX

JEWISH REVIVAL, PROPHESIED IN THE NEW TESTAMENT

IT HAS BEEN PROPHESIED

W E have studied Israel's coming revival from the book of Zechariah in the Old Testament. We will now look into the New Testament to see this revival from a different perspective. The following verses are found in the book of Revelation.

> *Do not harm the land or the sea or the trees until we put a seal on the foreheads of the servants of our God. Then I heard the number of those who were sealed: 144,000 from all the tribes of Israel. From the tribe of Judah 12,000 were sealed, from the tribe of Reuben 12,000, from the tribe of Gad 12,000, from the tribe of Asher 12,000, from the tribe of Naphtali 12,000, from the tribe of Manasseh 12,000, from the tribe of Simeon 12,000, from the tribe of Levi 12,000, from the tribe of Issachar 12,000, from the tribe of Zebulun 12,000, from the tribe of Joseph 12,000, from the tribe of Benjamin 12,000. (Rev. 7:3-8)*

This chapter covers the following points:

1. Revival will come to Israel at the beginning of the Great Tribulation.
2. Although some of the Jews were cut off in the past, they will be joined to Christ in the future.

3. Their cutting off was not permanent.
4. Many church fathers have preached about a coming Jewish revival.
5. The Jewish revival will come after Jerusalem becomes an immovable rock among the nations.
6. Most of the nation will be saved by receiving Jesus as Messiah, but not every single Jew will be saved.
7. Some Jews are saved at the end of the Great Tribulation

THE JOY OF REVIVAL

Many Christians fail to observe the joys and the hope that is given in the book of Revelation. The angels in heaven rejoice during the Great Tribulation because they see something that many Christians do not see. They see the blessings of God coming to the Church and to Israel, and they see the defeat of Satan. This will be the Church's finest hour prior to the new Millennium. The momentary chilling trials of the Great Tribulation will turn into extravagant expressions of evangelism and joy.

Revelation 7 reveals two great revivals. First we see 144,000 Jews who recognize Jesus as Messiah and become redeemed Israel. Immediately following that vision, we see a multitude of Gentile converts who cannot be numbered. In contrast to the first revival of Revelation 7 they are not Jews, but Christians. They come from every nation, tribe, language and people. Here are some interesting facts from Revelation 7.

1. There is a great Jewish revival in the Tribulation (symbolically 144,000 Jews are saved).
2. There is a massive revival of Gentiles during the Tribulation. They come from every nation on earth.
3. The number of Gentile Christians saved during the first part of the Tribulation is so large that no human can count them. Of course, God can.
4. Jews and Gentile saints are one in Christ, but the Jewish identity is preserved.

In this chapter we will discuss more details about the Jewish revival.

ONE HUNDRED AND FORTY-FOUR THOUSAND

Let me help you understand the meaning of the number *144,000*. God's mark of protection is put on the foreheads of the 144,000. Numerology is the study of numbers, and the Bible has God's numerology woven into it. One hundred and forty-four thousand is a number of importance in the book of Revelation because it symbolizes the great family of God. The number *twelve* stands for family or nation and twelve times twelve is one hundred forty-four. Jesus chose twelve disciples to be with him as His earthly family. God chose the twelve tribes of Israel to be His chosen nation.

The city of God in Revelation 21 is a picture of the bride of Christ, the family of God. Its dimensions are twelve thousand stadia, in each direction. It has twelve foundation stones and twelve gates. The leaves of its tree will bear twelve kinds of fruit for the healing of the nations. The number twelve seems to be everywhere. That is because it represents God's family or God's nation.

Twelve times twelve equals one hundred forty-four. Multiply that times 1000, and it gives us 144,000. That is the expanded number of the great family of God. The family is also known as the city of God. One hundred forty-four cubits is the measurement of the thickness of the walls of the city. The city of God is God's nation and God's family.

THE JEWISH FAMILY

The mention of 144,000 refers specifically to members of the Jewish family who are part of God's larger combined family of Jews and Gentiles. They are the two branches of the olive tree mentioned in Romans 11. The Jews are the natural branches, and the Gentiles are the wild olive branches.

Just in case we are predisposed to think that Israel, mentioned here in Revelation 7, is only symbolic, God clarifies the matter. Some believe that the reference to the 144,000 refers to a spiritual Israel made up of Gentile believers, but the Lord identifies each of the twelve tribes by name. It would be a gross mistreatment of Scripture to try to spiritualize these names and eradicate natural Israel from the pages of the book. It has been done throughout history, but I would not want to be guilty of mishandling any Scriptures. The fact that these are real Israelites is very important to God. He records their names emphatically. Indeed, these are Israelites indeed who have become followers of Jesus during the Great Tribulation.

THE TRIBE OF DAN

Twelve thousand Jews will be saved from each tribe, and each tribe is mentioned by name. It is reasonable to conclude that the number *twelve* is a symbolic number; it represents family. The fact remains that all the tribes are included in the list, except for the tribe of Dan.

As Judas was eliminated from the twelve disciples and replaced by another, perhaps Dan has been disqualified from the twelve tribes of Israel and replaced by Manasseh (see Revelation 7.) Some believe this happened because his tribe chose to remain in idolatry. We read of this in the book of Judges.

"The Danites rebuilt the city and settled there. They named it Dan after their forefather Dan, who was born to Israel. There the Danites set up for themselves idols. They continued to use the idols Micah had made all the time the house of the Lord was in Shiloh" (Judg. 18:30).

Some contend that all twelve tribes do not exist anymore, but only God knows for sure. For centuries, thousands of Jews have changed their names to escape persecution. Their lineage can now be traced by looking at DNA, but God does not need DNA tests to know who the Jewish people are. It is likely that many people in the world are Jews but are unaware of it. Like lost orphans who find their true parents later in life, many Jews will discover their identity in the end.

ISRAEL'S FOLLY IS NOT PERMANENT

Most of Israel has fallen from God's grace, but they will be restored. We have seen that the nation of Israel wandered from the ways of the Lord through unbelief and hardness of heart (see Romans 11:20). The Jews departed further from following the Lord when they rejected their Jewish Messiah. The Jews, as a whole, lost the kingdom of God for a season. We read this in the book of Matthew. Jesus said to the Jews, "The kingdom of God will be taken away from you and given to a people who will produce its fruit" (Matt. 21:43).

The kingdom of God was taken from the Jews and given to the Gentile Church, but that is not the end of the story. Israel will be reunited with her God.

Isaiah says this, concerning Israel:

"Can a mother forget the baby at her breast and have no compassion on the child she has borne? Though she may forget I will not forget you! 'See I have engraved you on the palms of my hands; your walls are ever before me'" (Isa. 49:15).

Romans says the following:

"Again I ask: Did they stumble so as to fall beyond recovery? Not at all!" (Rom. 11:11).

In the early days of the Tribulation, revival will come to the nation of Israel. A symbolic 144,000 will be saved just prior to the return of Christ. This is New Testament theology. Their revival is noted in Luke's Gospel. Here, Israel is pictured as a fig tree.

"At that time they will see the Son of man coming in a cloud with power and great glory. . . Look at the fig tree and all the trees. When they sprout leaves, you can see for yourselves and know that summer is near. Even so, when you see these things happening, you know that the kingdom of God is near" (Luke 21:27,29).

We remind you that the book of Romans speaks of Israel's coming revival.

I do not want you to be ignorant of this mystery, brothers, so that you may not be conceited: Israel has experienced a hardening in part until the full number of the Gentiles has come in. And so all Israel will be saved, as it is written: 'The deliverer will come from Zion; he will turn godlessness away from Jacob. And this is my covenant with them when I take away their sins.' For God's gifts and his call are irrevocable. (Rom. 11:25-29)

Here the Scriptures tell us there is a specific number of Gentiles that will be saved, and after that a great multitude of Jews will be converted. God has not forgotten his people. His gifts and call toward the Jewish people remain irrevocable.

CHURCH FATHERS SPEAK OF ISRAEL'S REVIVAL

Many of the Church fathers preached about a Jewish revival at the end of the age. Here are just a few of the many famous preachers who spoke of Israel's coming revival in their sermons.

Jonathan Edwards, a revivalist of the Great Awakening in America, wrote, "Nothing is more clearly foretold than this national conversion of the Jews in Romans eleven."[48]

Can you imagine what will happen to the Church around the world when multitudes of Israelites receive Jesus as their Messiah?

Romans 11:15 says, "If the casting away of them be the reconciling of the world, what shall the receiving of them be but life from the dead."

When revival comes to Israel, the Church will be invigorated to new life. The early Puritans believed this. They said, "The Scripture speaks of a double conversion of the Gentiles, the first before the conversion of the Jews, the second after the conversion of the Jews."[49]

Thomas Boston of The Church of Scotland also preached this message. A sermon recorded in 1716 declares the following: "Are you longing for a revival to the churches, then pray for the Jews. 'For if the casting away of them be the reconciling of the world; what shall the receiving of them be but life from the dead.' That will be a lively time, a time of great outpouring of the Spirit, that will carry reformation to a greater height than yet has been."[50]

In 1855, Charles Spurgeon preached the following:

I think we do not attach sufficient importance to the restoration of the Jews. We do not think enough of it. But certainly, if there is anything promised in the Bible it is this. The day shall yet come when the Jews, who were the first apostles to the Gentiles, the first missionaries to us who were afar off, shall be gathered in again. Until that shall be, the fullness of the church's glory can never come. Matchless benefits to the world are bound up with the restoration of Israel; their gathering in shall be as life from the dead. [51]

JEWISH REVIVAL COMES DURING CHAOS

The book of Revelation describes judgments, chaos and war. At the time when these things occur, Israel's revival will come.

1. Israel's Revival takes place when Israel has been brought back to her homeland.
2. At that time, she becomes an immoveable rock among the nations. That started in May of 1948 and continues today.
3. The nations will conspire against her, but her leaders rise up with new strength.
4. God protects Israel supernaturally, and all who attack her injure themselves.
5. During that time, when tanks are in motion and missiles are exploding, God will lift the veil from her eyes.
6. The people of Israel will begin to weep, repent and pray as the grace of God floods over them.
7. The Holy Spirit will bring repentance and salvation to all the families, including wives and children. They will have a revelation of Jesus as Messiah.

Not all Israel will be saved during this first revival, but God will be persistent with them.

CHAPTER TWENTY-SEVEN

ISRAEL DURING THE GREAT TRIBULATION

W E have studied Israel's national defense and her coming revival. Now let us look at her amazing rise to power and honor during the first half of the Great Tribulation. This position of power will not continue throughout the entire time of the Great Tribulation, but God has planned that both the Church and Israel will have a season of glory before Jesus returns.

In the next few chapters, we will study the significance and the role of God's two end-time witnesses. Understanding who they are and why they must shine, is necessary if we are to walk in partnership and faith with the Lord at the end of the age. We will begin this study in Revelation 11:

> I was given a reed like a measuring rod and was told, "Go and measure the temple of God and the altar, and count the worshippers there. But exclude the outer court; do not measure it, because it has been given to the Gentiles. They will trample on the holy city for 42 months. And I will give power to my two witnesses, and they will prophesy for 1,260 days, clothed in sackcloth". These are the two olive trees and the two lampstands that stand before the Lord of the earth. (Rev. 11:1-4)

THE NATURAL AND THE SPIRITUAL

The Holy City, called Jerusalem or Zion, has natural and spiritual counterparts. The natural city is the present capital of Israel; the spiritual one is

called the New Jerusalem. Both are referred to as Zion, the city of the Great
King. The New Jerusalem (the spiritual counterpart to Israel's capital) is
made up of all believers of Jesus, including Jews and Christians. Both natural
and spiritual Jerusalem will develop on parallel tracks as we approach the
second coming of Christ.

ALL KINDS OF JEWS

In the early days of the Great Tribulation, revival will come to Israel. Millions of Jews will receive Jesus as Messiah. That does not mean that they
become Gentile Christians. They continue to be Jewish in every sense of the
word, but they receive Jesus as Messiah. After receiving Jesus they will gain
a new understanding of the Law. They will also receive the Holy Spirit, and
an anointing of God's supernatural power will come upon them.

Like Nicodemus in Jesus' day, these born-again Jews will come into the New
Covenant. They will realize that most of the Jewish customs should still be
celebrated although some matters, such as animal sacrifices, are no longer
valid. They will understand that the Law is holy and good, but it can never,
and will never, make them righteous. They will keep the Law, but not as a
means to righteousness. They will know that the Law will not save them,
bring them into God's presence or make them holy. The Law is an illustra-
tive teaching, a living parable of man's fellowship with God. Each detail of
Jewish Law tells a story of God's involvement with, and His expectations for,
humanity. The Jews have been called to embrace this symbolic lifestyle, and
they will fly like a banner for all the nations to see.

Not all Jews, however, will come to Christ during the revival. In opposition
to undeniable evidence, many Jews will refuse to believe that Jesus is Messiah.
Some Orthodox and secular Jews will continue to resist the Lord. Because of
this, Jerusalem will be inhabited by a mixture of Messianic, Orthodox, and
non-religious Jews. It will be this way until the Lord returns.

When Jesus comes and His feet touch the Mount of Olives, there will still
be many unsaved Jews in Israel. In Zechariah 14, you will see that when the
Lord returns, some in Jerusalem do not receive glorified bodies. That means

they are not Christ's when He appears. They will run to the shelter that Messiah provides, and they will be rescued. War will be raging over Israel, and half of Jerusalem will be taken captive, when suddenly Jesus appears on the Mount of Olives. He destroys His enemies and rescues the Jews who are in the city (see Zechariah 14: 1-3). If they were Messianic Jews they would be caught up into the clouds and given immortality, but instead they are still vulnerable and must be sheltered from their enemies. Jesus splits the Mount of Olives in two, and the Jews rush into the crevice for protection.

JERUSALEM'S HISTORY IN BRIEF

Let us take the time to review a brief history of Jerusalem, a summary compiled from the Jerusalem Archaeological Park website.

It was the location to which God sent Abraham to sacrifice his son Isaac.

A millennium later, King David placed Israel's capital there.

Nebuchadnezzar captured it in 597 B.C. and subsequently razed it.

The city was conquered by the Persian King Cyrus. Alexander the Great then took control for the Greeks, after which it was briefly recaptured by the Jews, and then in A.D. 63, by the Romans.

In A.D. 635, Muslim armies captured Jerusalem, and set about Islami-cizing the Temple Mount, first by constructing the al-Aqsa mosque, then the dome of the rock on the Biblical site of Solomon's temple.

In 1099, Catholic Crusaders invaded, mercilessly expunging all Muslims and Jews.

Salah al-Din (Saladin), the Egyptian and Syrian sultan, recaptured the city in 1187. At the beginning of the 16ᵗʰ century, the Turks conquered and ruled the city until the disintegration of the Ottoman Empire in the early 20ᵗʰ century.

The British liberated it in World War 1.

The State of Israel was born in 1948, and, in the face of Arab attacks, overtook the whole of the city (Jerusalem) in 1967.

Christ will return to the city, cleanse it of its corruption, and establish the headquarters of His world-ruling kingdom in the city of God.[52]

JERUSALEM IS FAVORED

Bible prophecies tell us that a time is coming when Jerusalem will be favored by the Lord and will be rebuilt. The Psalms declare the following:

You will arise and have compassion on Zion, for it is time to show favor to her; the appointed time has come. For her stones are dear to your ser-vants ... The nations will fear the name of the Lord ... For the Lord will rebuild Zion and appear in his glory ... Let this be written for a future generation, that a people not yet created may praise the Lord ... So the name of the Lord will be declared in Zion and his praise in Jerusalem when the peoples and the kingdoms assemble to worship the Lord. (Ps. 102:13-22).

THEY GATHER TO JERUSALEM

During the first few years of the Tribulation, Israel will be restored physi-cally and spiritually. The Jews will experience an ebb and flow of victories and defeats, like the coming and going of the tides. She will be attacked, and then grow in size and strength, but eventually she will be trampled on just before the Lord returns.

As the end draws near, we will see the complete rebuilding of Israel, the expansion of her land and the full institution of all of her religious tradi-tions. At that time, there will be a mixture of religious activity in the city. Not all of those activities will be desired or set in place by the Lord. Some of them will be the carryover of Old Testament Jewish life, which should be adjusted or displaced by the New Covenant (see Hebrews 8:13). Some religious Jews, however, will still hold to the patterns of the Old Covenant. God will allow the Old Covenant, Orthodox Jews to do all that is in their hearts, even though they are misguided. As in the days of Paul, they will have great zeal toward God, but they will lack understanding (see Romans 10:1-4).

Christians from all nations will be excited as they see the prophecies for the Jews being fulfilled. Many will move to Jerusalem. They will want to receive the anointing of God that has fallen on Israel. They will support the Jews and witness to those who have not yet been born again.

Just prior to the midpoint of the Great Tribulation, God will bring deliverance and peace to Jerusalem and to the entire world. Here are some of Zechariah's prophetic words regarding Israel's wonderful disposition during the endtimes. These verses start with the scattering of the Jewish people, which has happened over the last 2500 years, but then we see them being blessed in the Promised Land.

"'When I called, they did not listen;' ... says the Lord Almighty. 'I scattered them with a whirlwind among the nations ... The land was left so desolate behind them'" (Zech. 7:13-14).

> This is what the Lord Almighty says: "I will return to Zion and dwell in Jerusalem. I will save my people from the countries of the east and the west. I will bring them back to live in Jerusalem ... You who now hear these words spoken by the prophets ... let your hands be strong so that the temple may be built ... As you have been an object of cursing among the nations, O Judah and Israel, so will I save you, and you will be a blessing ... Just as I had determined to bring disaster upon you, ... So now I have determined to do good ... Many people and the inhabitants of many cities will yet come ... And many peoples and powerful nations will come to Jerusalem to seek the Lord Almighty and to entreat him ... In those days ten men from all languages and nations will take firm hold of one Jew by the hem of his robe and say, 'Let us go with you, because we have heard that God is with you.'" (Zech. 8:2-23; emphasis added)

Christians of every language and nation will join themselves to a Jew and make their way to Jerusalem. They will live there and make their stand alongside of the Jewish people. After a brief time of miraculous grace and political success, the nations will turn against Israel and attack her. Before that happens, however, a majority of people around the world will be extremely excited about her renaissance. (For more details read my book, *Unexpected Fire*.)

REBUILDING THE TEMPLE

The temple of the Lord will be rebuilt by the Lord Himself. We have just read in Zechariah 8:9 that the Lord will encourage the building of His end-time temple.

He said, "Let your hands be strong so that the temple may be built" (Zech. 8:9).

Zechariah 6 also mentions the rebuilding of the temple:

> *This is what the Lord Almighty says: Here is the man whose name is Branch, and he will branch out from his place and* build the temple of the Lord. *It is he who will* rebuild the temple of the Lord, *and he will be clothed with majesty and will sit and rule on his throne. Those who are far away will come and help to* build the temple of the Lord, *and you will know that the Lord Almighty has sent me to you. This will happen if you diligently obey the Lord your God. (Zech. 6:12-15; emphasis added)*

The rebuilding of the Jewish temple will happen during, or just before, the Great Tribulation. There is much discussion as to whether this new temple is a physical one or just a spiritual one. Is it a physical building, or does it only represent the family of God, the one new man, the Church and redeemed Israel?

There is a spiritual and a physical temple that will be rebuilt in the last days.

The Lord mirrors everything that is spiritual and gives it a physical counterpart. The language in the verses mentioned point to a physical temple and not just a spiritual one.

"Those who are far away will come and help to build the temple," and "this will happen if you diligently obey the Lord your God" (Zech. 6:15).

I do not think those words would be spoken if the Lord was only building a spiritual house; after all, people are coming from far away to help, and it will only happen if people are diligent to obey the Lord. Orthodox Jews have already invested great sums of money to have the furniture of the temple crafted according to the exact pattern in the Scriptures. These furnishings are presently in storage in Jerusalem, waiting to furnish the temple of the Lord.

The Lord used non-religious Jews called Zionists to inspire the rebirth of Israel in 1948, but it was still an act of God. He can, in like manner, use non-Messianic Jews to build a temple. In the end, it happens because He sets the process in motion. He is able to perform His will through whomever He desires. The Lord himself is behind the building of His temple. He is the Branch that branches out, as Zechariah says. Those who do the work are working for Him.

ANIMAL SACRIFICES

One of the Old Covenant practices that will take place in the new temple will be the ill-advised animal sacrifices. Christ's death replaced the need for animal sacrifices. He did this on the cross two thousand years ago. No other sacrifice can remove sin and justify a man before God. Some Orthodox Jews, however, are stuck in the Old Covenant, and they will reinstate animal sacrifices.

They will continue offering these sacrifices until the midpoint of the Tribulation when their sacrifices will be stopped by the beast (the Antichrist). The beast will appear at that time, and God will allow him to break the power of the Church and Israel. We read, "When the power of the holy people has been fully broken, all these things will be complete" (Dan. 12:7).

The Jews will continue to rule over the Holy Land, and they will defend it until Jesus comes, but it will suffer devastating attacks in the last half of the Great Tribulation. The beast will defile God's temple and institute demonic sacrifices. This hideous counterfeit is an Antichrist sacrifice brought forth to mock and blaspheme the sacrifice of Christ. It is called the abomination of desolation. The Antichrist takeover will come at a time when the Jewish renaissance and the Church's glory are at their highest level. The beast will be allowed to squelch the power of God's people.

This will happen at the midpoint of the Great Tribulation. It will be another three-and-a-half years before the Lord returns and resurrection day finally arrives. It is described in the following Scriptures as a time (one year), times (two years), and half a time (half a year), totaling three-and-a-half years. We read about these things in the last chapter of the book of Daniel.

> *"At that time Michael, the great prince who protects your people will arise. There will be a time of distress such as has not happened from the beginning of nations until then. But at that time your people – everyone whose name is found written in the book – will be delivered. Multitudes who sleep in the dust of the earth will awake: some to everlasting life, others to shame and everlasting contempt. Those who are wise will shine like the brightness of the heavens, and those who lead many to righteousness, like the stars for ever and ever … close up and seal the words of this scroll until the time of the end"* … *"How long will it be before these astonishing things are fulfilled?"…* "It will be for a time, times and half a time. When the power of the holy people has been finally broken, all these things will be completed." *I asked, "My lord, what will the outcome of all this be?" He replied … "the words are closed up and sealed until the time of the end. Many will be purified, made spotless and refined, but the wicked will continue to be wicked. None of the wicked will understand, but those who are wise will understand.* From the time that the daily sacrifice is abolished and the abomination of desolation is set up, there will be 1,290 days … *As for you, go*

your way till the end. You will rest, and then at the end of the days you will rise to receive your allotted inheritance." (Dan. 12:1-13; emphasis added)

Some parts of Daniel, like its last chapter, are definitely in reference to the last days. These end-time Scriptures give such qualifying details as resurrection day, the coming of the Lord, the tell-tale three-and-a-half years, and a direct mention of the end of time.

ISRAEL RECEIVES HER INHERITANCE

Between 1948 and the midpoint of the Tribulation, Israel will receive her promised inheritance in incremental steps. All of the blessings will come before the Lord returns at the end of the Great Tribulation (see Revelation 19).

The Scripture tells of eight end-time promises that are extended specifically to the Jews. These promises are Israel's inheritance. Jerusalem is God's prophetic time clock. Only after seven of these eight promises are fulfilled for Israel will the Lord appear. The eighth blessing will be fulfilled at His coming. Here are Israel's eight end-time blessings.

1. Israel will be given the ownership and the full extension of her land (see Ezekiel 20:42; Genesis 15:18).
2. The Jewish people will be gathered to their land (see Isaiah 11:12; Zephaniah 3:20).
3. Israel's financial fortunes will be restored before her very eyes (see Zephaniah 2:7; 3:20; Joel 3:1).
4. Christian and Jewish intercessors around the world will stand on her spiritual walls and pray for Israel (see Isaiah 62:6).
5. A national revival will come to Israel as multitudes of Jews receive Jesus as their Messiah (see Isaiah 45:17; Zechariah 12:10; Romans 11:25-26).
6. God's glory and power will come upon Israel temporarily (see Romans 9:5; Isaiah 60:1-2).

7. The nations will give praise and honor to Israel temporarily (see Zephaniah 3:19; Isaiah 60:2).
8. God's judgment will come upon the nations for how they have treated Israel (see Joel 3:1-3).

After Christ returns, Israel will receive all of these blessings on a permanent basis. They will live in the Holy Land, and every promise that the Lord has made for them will be fulfilled.

CHAPTER TWENTY-EIGHT

IDENTIFYING THE
TWO WITNESSES

T HE Bible tells us about two prophetic witnesses who will shine for God at the end of the age. In this chapter we will study the Scriptures to discover who they are. To begin we look in the book of Revelation.

> *I was given a reed like a measuring rod and was told, "Go and measure the temple of God and the altar, and count the worshippers there. But exclude the outer court; do not measure it, because it has been given to the Gentiles. They will trample on the holy city for 42 months. And I will give power to my two witnesses, and they will prophesy for 1,260 days, clothed in sackcloth. These are the two olive trees and the two lampstands that stand before the Lord of the earth." (Rev. 11:1-4).*

In this chapter we will look at the following:

1. Recognizing the greatness of the Church
2. Identifying the false church
3. Identifying the two witnesses
4. Identifying the two olive branches at the end of the age
5. Identifying the two lampstands at the end of the age
6. Recognizing the one new man at the end of the age

THE PEOPLE OF GOD ARE MEASURED

In Revelation 11, John is asked to focus on Israel and the Church. He is to measure the temple and the altar and to count the worshippers there. In this case, the temple is a picture of God's people.

Ephesians reads, "Consequently, you are no longer foreigners and aliens, but fellow citizens with God's people and members of God's household, built on the foundation of the apostles and prophets, with Christ Jesus himself as the chief corner stone. In him the whole building is joined together and rises to become *a holy temple* in the Lord" Eph. 2:19-21; italics added).

John must measure the temple and the altar and count the worshippers. The altar is the spiritual place of sacrifice. Worshippers are to present their bodies as living sacrifices to the Lord on that altar. Obedience and devotion to Christ is our sacrifice and our reasonable service of worship (see Romans 12:1-2).

As John evaluates God's people in the vision, he discovers that they are ready to play their part in the Great Tribulation. God is showing His glorious Church to John. There will be multitudes of saints on fire for Christ, ready to partner with Him at the end of the age. Their numbers and passion will be greater than the world has ever seen. In the vision, the powerful end-time Church has arrived. It is as though God is saying, "John take notice of the worship of my people; count them and notice their devotion. They are ready, and I am about to use them as I said I would."

THE FALSE CHURCH

Like the Jewish temple, God's spiritual temple has an outer court. The Lord differentiates between His true Church and those in the outer court. Outer-court people are those who have a form of religion, even calling themselves Christians, but they are not God's people. They do not follow His directives or obey His will. Many false Christians are, in fact, enemies of God. They will trample on the people of God, the Holy City for forty-two months, or three-and-a-half years (see Revelation 21:2).

Throughout history the false church has hindered the work of Christ. They have resisted the mandate of the true Church, but they will experience a setback during the Tribulation. For a season, the Church will overcome and rise with awesome power.

During the first three-and-a-half years of the Tribulation, two kingdoms will engage in open conflict.

1. The people of God on one side will call the world to repentance and lift high the standards of biblical morality. They will minister compassion to the suffering and lead millions to salvation.

2. The false church, on the other hand, will be an ecumenical body of people, from all religions. They will try to undermine the message of Christ. They will mix witchcraft and humanism in their pluralistic religious soup. This will become the new world order. It is the inevitable outcome of societies merging together to make room for all. They will not, however, come under the Lordship of Christ. On the surface it sounds good to the secular mind, but there is only one true God, and He alone should be worshipped.

The governments of the world despise the claims of Christ and the narrow path that His devoted followers walk upon. The false church and secular societies will find themselves in an ideological dilemma as the Tribulation unfolds because the world will experience severe judgments, and multitudes will be turning to Christ.

THE TWO WITNESSES

The conflict between the two kingdoms will reach critical mass, as God releases supernatural power and authority to His two witnesses.

For centuries scholars have debated the identity the two witnesses. While I greatly respect many of these teachers, I must differ from them on some points of doctrine. I believe that the Scriptures tell us clearly who the two witnesses are. In Revelation 11, they are called prophets of the Lord. They are also called the two olive branches and the two lampstands that stand before the Lord of the earth. We read of them in Zechariah.

"I see a gold lampstand with a bowl at the top. Also there are two olive trees. I asked the angel, 'What are these two olive trees, what are these two olive branches beside the two golden pipes that pour out golden oil?' So he said, 'These are the two who are anointed to serve the Lord of all the earth'" (Zech. 4:2,11-12,14).

Notice, that the terms *olive trees* and *olive branches* are interchangeable. These are the two anointed ones chosen to serve the Lord of all the earth.

The book of Romans tells us the following:

> *If some of the* branches *have been broken off, and you, though* a wild olive shoot *have been grafted in among the others and now share in the nourishing sap from the olive root, do not boast over the* branches... *For if God did not spare* the natural branches, *he will not spare you either. And if they do not persist in unbelief, they will be grafted in, for God is able to graft them in again. After all* if you were cut out of an olive tree that is wild by nature *and contrary to nature were grafted into a cultivated olive tree, how much more readily will these,* the natural branches, *be grafted into their own olive tree! ...I do not want you to be ignorant of this mystery, brothers, so that you may not be conceited. Israel has experienced a hardening in part until the full number of the Gentiles has come in. And so all Israel will be saved. ...For God's gift and his call are irrevocable." (Rom. 11:17-29; emphasis added)*

We do not have to guess who the two olive branches are; Scripture identifies them for us. They are Israel and the Church: *the natural and the wild branches of the olive tree.* Some, but not all, of Israel's natural branches were broken off. They have experienced a hardening in part, until a specific time when the full number of the Gentiles will come in. Then revival will come to Israel and she will be grafted in again. This is the great mystery concerning Israel that we read of in Romans 11:25.

Israel and the Gentile Church are the two anointed witnesses who serve the Lord of the whole earth. Throughout history God has ordained these two groups to represent Him. They are the two who serve the Lord of all the earth. Both must embrace Jesus the Messiah before they can receive their full blessings. At the end of the age, they will come together to make one new man. They will partner with God in the great end-time battles of the Great Tribulation.

THE TWO PROPHETS

Within both groups, the Church and Israel, powerful prophetic people will emerge. We may call these great armies, "The Prophetic Church" and "Prophetic Israel". They are the ones who have received the small scroll (see Revelation 10). They have embraced the Word of God and the testimony of Jesus, and they will champion the cause of Christ like no other group in history.

We discovered the two groups in Revelation 7 as we looked at the two end-time revivals. The redeemed Jews were identified as the 144,000, and the Gentile Church was seen as the other multitude, the innumerable company of saints standing before the throne of God. Both groups are powerful during the first three-and-a-half years of the Tribulation.

They are intercessors, prophets, skillful evangelists, outspoken representatives of heaven and compassionate ministers of God's grace. They prophesy for 1,260 days, or just a little more than three-and-a-half years (see Revelation 11:4).

The Church (made up of saved Jews and Gentiles) is the body of Christ. It is the one new man. Calling the Church "a man" is not a new teaching. Here are two men of the Lord, the Gentile Church and redeemed Israel. They are the prophets of the Lord.

THE LAMPSTANDS

The two witnesses are the two lampstands that stand before the Lord of the earth. Revelation tells us what the lampstands represent.

"And when I turned I saw seven golden lampstands, and among the lampstands was someone like the son of man. ... The seven lampstands are the seven churches" (Rev. 1:12,20).

Lampstands in the book of Revelation represent churches. The two witnesses are Churches, not two individual people. Israel was the Old Covenant Church and, later, redeemed Gentiles joined them to form the New Covenant Church. The Church of the firstborn (Israel) is mentioned in Hebrews 12:23.

The book of Acts tells us of the Old Testament Church (Israel). Jesus was with the Israelites (in Spirit) in the church in the wilderness during the time of Moses.

We read, "This is he, that was in the church in the wilderness" (Acts 7:38).

The Church is not just a New Covenant entity. Before Jesus died on the cross, He taught His disciples to bring a believer before the Church if his moral conduct was in question.

He said, "And if he refuses to hear them, tell it to *the church*. But if he refuses even to hear the church, let him be to you like a heathen" (Matt. 18:17 NKJ; italics added).

The two lampstands mentioned in Revelation 11 are the two olive branches and the two witnesses of the Lord of the earth. They are the two Churches – reedeemed Israel and the Gentile Church. The Lord of all the earth is calling for the partnership of His two historical witnesses – the two will soon function as one new man.

It makes sense that the mighty signs and wonders that these witnesses are about to perform will be seen in every country around the world. Christians and redeemed Jews will infiltrate society, challenge the status quo and release the power of God upon the earth. The Church will shine exceedingly bright and, as promised, the glory of the Lord will come upon Israel before the return of the King (Isaiah 60:1-2).

Jesus did not die on the cross to produce an anemic Church. He promised that His followers would perform greater miracles than He did, and that promise has never been fulfilled. The Church and redeemed Israel will minister with a new level of anointing. Soon, spiritual darkness will cover the earth (see Isaiah 60:1-2), but the power of the Lord will rise upon his people, and many miracles will follow. Here are the words of Jesus:

"He who believes in me, the works that I do he will do also: and greater works than these will he do, because I go to my Father" (John 14:12 NKJ).

In the next chapter we will discover the miraculous power and anointing that is about to be displayed through Israel and the Gentile Church at the end of the age.

CHAPTER TWENTY-NINE

THE POWER OF THE
TWO WITNESSES

T HE book of Revelation describes the power of the two witnesses at the
end of the age. We read:

*If anyone tries to harm them, fire comes from their mouths and devours
their enemies. This is how anyone who wants to harm them must die.
These men have power to shut up the sky so that it will not rain during
the time they are prophesying; and they have power to turn the waters
into blood and to strike the earth with every kind of plague as often as
they want. Now when they have finished their testimony, the beast that
comes up from the Abyss will attack them, and overpower and kill them.
Their bodies will lie in the street of the great city, which is figuratively
called Sodom and Egypt, where also their Lord was crucified. For three
and a half days men from every people, tribe, language and nation will
gaze on their bodies and refuse them burial. The inhabitants of the
earth will gloat over them and will celebrate by sending each other gifts,
because these two prophets had tormented those who live on the earth.
But after three and a half days a breath of life from God entered them,
and they stood on their feet, and terror struck those who saw them. Then
they heard a loud voice from heaven saying to them, "Come up here."
And they went up to heaven in a cloud, while their enemies looked on.
At that very hour there was an earthquake and a tenth of the city col-
lapsed. Seven thousand people were killed in the earthquake, and the
survivors were terrified and gave glory to the God of heaven. The second
woe is passed; the third is coming soon. (Rev. 11:4-14)*

Here are the highlights that we can discover from this prophetic Scripture passage:

1. The humility of the Church
2. The world embracing democracy
3. The Bible ethic restored
4. The political and supernatural power of the saints
5. The rebel coup
6. The beast who comes from the Abyss
7. The death of the saints
8. Celebrations for the wicked
9. Resurrection and a rapture
10. Revival comes again

CLOTHED IN SACKCLOTH

God's prophetic Gentile Church and the prophetic people of Israel are the frontline ministers of the end-time Church. They are the two witnesses. They will minister the power of God at a level never before seen on earth. One all-important quality must be present – humility. This is demonstrated because the witnesses are clothed in sackcloth. I do not believe that they will literally wear sackcloth, although some might. Far more necessary is the sackcloth on their hearts; the attitude of repentance, humility and compassion. They will stand with a posture of humble piety and contrition. There can be no room for bravado or arrogance when one handles such enormous power. The fear of God is the only acceptable backdrop for this spiritual activity.

As the saints extend compassion and kindness to multitudes, but also demonstrate God's severity, they will rule responsibly and diligently.

A DEMOCRATIC WORLD

After the 9-11 terrorist attack on the World Trade Center in New York, the president of the United States, George W. Bush, called the entire world to embrace democracy. This is a very slow processs, and it is heavily resisted, but the Western nations are influencing and even overpowering the Eastern nations with the message of democracy. Democracy is an appealing lure for the educated people of the world, and it will eventually be irresistible. Even Muslim nations and North Korea will ultimately yield to the democratic form of government. Extensive warfare will ravage the earth during the first year of the Great Tribulation, and the dictatorships will topple.

After that, the vote of the masses will eventually rule the world. This is a God-ordained political format for the endtimes, and it is essential for the prophecies of Revelation to be fulfilled. It will be democracy, not dictator-ships, that will unite the world for the end-time war against Israel and the Church.

At first, when democracy unites the world, the Church will rise to her finest hour. A righteous phenomenon will surprise the world during the first three-and-a-half years of the Tribulation. As billions die because of God's judgments, multitudes around the globe will turn to Christ.

In a short space of time, the Christian and Jewish community will grow with unprecedented numbers. They will quickly outnumber the enemies of God. There will be much political conflict between the followers of Christ and the humanists of the world, but because there will be so many Christians, godly leaders will be voted to political power in every nation.

JUDEO-CHRISTIAN ETHIC RESTORED

For a short while, the disciples of Christ will lead the political systems of the world. They will be so popular that they will hold an overwhelming major-ity of governmental power. They will change the laws of nations and realign the morals of society to reflect a Judeo-Christian standard of civil practice and behavior.

Some of the changes will include outlawing abortion and declaring homosex-uality immoral. They will clamp down on drugs and stop the pornography trade from using the public market place. They will deal a deadly blow to organized crime and reinstate religious freedom. They will allow prayer, the teaching of creation and other expressions of faith in the public place. They will make open statements from political platforms declaring that Jesus is Lord. They will not force Christianity on people, but they will legally change the laws of the nations to uphold a Christian standard of morality.

REBEL RESISTANCE

Although they will come to power through legal democratic procedures, many will refuse to be governed by these disciples of Christ. They will form a rebel militia and muster a strong resistance against God's people. Guerrilla warfare will follow as they take up arms to overthrow the governments of the world.

Besides losing free access to many vices of the world, which the humanists believe is their right and privilege, the ungodly will lose billions of dollars because they cannot do business as usual. Their illegal or immoral trades will have been shut down. The abortion trade will lose billions of dollars, the pornography market will lose billions, the entertainment industry will be heavily censored and the homosexual community will be irate because they have lost the ground of popularity that they held for so long. The world will soon become a boiling pot of demonic anger, and uprisings will be common in every nation.

TORMENTING EVILDOERS

Ungodly merchants will feel tormented by the two witnesses because their evil business practices will be forced underground. Their industries will lose incredible amounts of money. Note the tell-tale words of verse ten:

"The inhabitants of the earth will gloat over them [after the saints are killed] and will celebrate by sending each other gifts, because these *two prophets had tormented those who live on the earth*" (Rev. 11:10; italics added).

The two witnesses will be seen as tormenting the people of the earth when they put an end to their wicked liberties. They will halt evil merchandising and curb outward expressions of immorality. That is why many will react and call Israel and the Church tormentors. Why else would the Church be called tormentors? There is no place in the doctrine of the Christian faith for saints to torture people.

SUPERNATURAL POWER

It will not be smooth political speeches alone that will give power to the two witnesses; they will have supernatural power from God. The rebel insurgence will be frustrated as they are held at bay by the miraculous power of Christian governments. Christian-led governments will defend their communities with supernatural power. As Christian leaders speak the word, their enemies, the rebels, will fall dead.

Revelation says, "If anyone tries to harm them, fire comes from their mouths. This is how anyone who wants to harm them must die" (Rev. 11:5).

This kind of power was demonstrated in the fifth chapter of Acts. Ananias and Sapphira fell on the floor dead when they resisted the word of the Lord spoken by the apostle Peter.

The Christian doctrine does not condone killing people except in war, in defense of a nation or for capital punishment. The two witnesses will not kill people because those people refuse the gospel or speak out against the government. Rebels will be killed when they rise up with violent terrorist acts against the government and the community.

It would be wrong for the two witnesses to go out and kill unless they are exercising civil or military protection over the people. They cannot be self-appointed, vigilante mercenaries. National and local governments have a God-given mandate to keep the peace and protect the people from any harm that comes from without or from within their borders. To kill without federal or local civil authority may be murder, and the prophets of the Lord would not commit murder. As governing rulers, however, they will function within God's laws and within the laws of their societies. In order for them to kill people as described in Revelation, they must have national authority, and that must be earned through democratic elections.

THIS WAS PROPHESIED FOR ISRAEL

Christian and Jewish leaders will have power to hold back the rain and to release plagues on the earth as often as they desire. This end-time power was prophesied over the Jewish people in the book of Micah:

"Do not gloat over me, my enemy! Though I have fallen, I will rise. Because I have sinned against him, I will bear the Lord's wrath, until he pleads my case and establishes my right. He will bring me into the light; I will see his righteousness. Then my enemy will see it and be covered with shame" (Mic. 7:8-10).

Then, in the next few verses, the Lord responds.

"As *in the days when you came out of Egypt, I will show them my wonders.* Nations will see and be ashamed deprived of all their power. They will come trembling out of their dens; they will turn in fear to the Lord our God and will be afraid of you" (Mic. 7:15-17; italics added).

Then Israel responds to the Lord.

"Who is a God like you, who pardons sin and forgives the transgression of the remnant of his inheritance? You do not stay angry forever … You will be true to Jacob [Israel] and show mercy to Abraham, as you pledged on oath to our fathers in days long ago" (Mic. 7:18-20).

God will show the people of Israel the same wonders that He showed them when they came out of Egypt. Revelation says, "They have power to turn the waters to blood and to strike the earth with every kind of plague as often as they want" (Rev. 11:6).

Just like Micah prophesied, the plagues of Egypt, such as waters turning to blood, the release of darkness and the spread of deadly diseases, will be repeated. They will come as Israel prophesies during the Tribulation. These prophecies about Israel, add further support to our understanding that the two witnesses are indeed the Gentile Church and Israel.

The saints will legally change the laws of nations and hold off violent uprisings with political responsibility and supernatural might. The saints will come into political power during the first couple of years of the Tribulation. Their reign among the nations will end at the midpoint of the Tribulation, at the three-and-a-half year mark. It will not extend beyond that season. Their reign of godly power may last for as long as two-and-a-half years, but no longer.

THE SECOND WOE

Then the Lord will release the beast (the antichrist spirit) that comes up from the Abyss. He will launch an offensive against the two witnesses and come to the aid of the rebels. He adds demons to their ranks and empowers them with supernatural ability. At the same time, God removes His power from the Christian rulers. They are overthrown and killed. This will be a massive uprising of evil. It will be a military coup against the saints, and the Lord will allow it to happen. God allowed His Son to be crucified in like manner, and, of course, He has good reason for the things He does.

This release is called the second woe (see Revelation 11:14) because it is the second major attack of demonic power upon the earth during the Tribulation. The third woe is still to come. This beast that comes up from the Abyss is called Apollyon or Abaddon (see Revelation 9). He is the angel of the Abyss, a king over the demons.

BARBARIC SLAUGHTER

Although many will not actually see the demons at work, it is the demonic power of Apollyon that enables the rebels to overpower the saints. This will be a worldwide coup. Suddenly a bloodbath will be perpetrated against the saints as humanists are allowed by God to seize the thrones of the world. Multitudes of prophetic Christians and prophetic Jews will be slaughtered, and their bodies will be left on the ground to rot for three days, an act that is so barbaric and so demonic. Even in ancient times, the bodies of enemies would be buried or burned immediately following a battle, for health reasons. This is especially true in tropical countries where dead bodies decompose quickly and disease follows.

DEMONIC CELEBRATIONS

Multitudes of vile men will sell their souls to the devil in order to obtain this victory. The demon spirits will gain enormous power, and they will be celebrating, and so will the perverted criminal element of humanity. By this time they will become fully demonized, yet many of them will be unaware of it. Evil people from every nation, tribe and language will insist that these dead bodies must not be buried. Thousands, if not millions, of bodies will be left out in the open, as a boastful show of evil hatred.

Wicked men will celebrate and gloat over the dead bodies. They will throw expensive parties and send gifts of congratulations to one another. The news media will show pictures of the dead bodies on TV, on the front covers of newspapers and internet sites.

Then the people of the world will be able to return to their public orgies, their drug trade and the craft of the abortion. Homosexuals will be bolder than ever. They will openly demonstrate every vile act in the streets and hard-core pornography will be displayed everywhere. The wicked of the world will revel in lust and chaos, and the godly who remain on the earth will hide in fear.

Not all Christians and Jews will be killed, but the prophetic leaders will be. The other saints who have not been on the front lines will escape death and go into hiding. At this time they will not be targeted for death, for they were not in the political forefront.

RESURRECTION AND A RAPTURE

Two thousand years ago, Jesus was resurrected from the grave. After three days, death could hold Him no more. Another three-day period of death will suddenly be disturbed by a powerful resurrection once again.

"After the three and a half days a breath of life from God entered them, and they stood on their feet, and terror struck those who saw them. Then they heard a loud voice from heaven saying to them, "Come up here," and they went up to heaven in a cloud while their enemies looked on" (Rev. 11:11-12).

This is a rapture of saints. Jesus does not come into the sky to take His Church to heaven, but on that day, the prophetic leaders will be resurrected from where they have lain. They will come back to life and stand for all to see. Then, as Jesus did on the Mount of Olives, they will rise through the clouds and ascend to the throne room in heaven. Thousands, if not millions, will be raised from the dead and go into the presence of God Almighty.

Orgies and vile parties will suddenly slam to a halt, as a rebellious world experiences a new terror. People will be jolted back to their senses. Many will cry out in fear, and others will run to get away from the crowds, repenting as best as they can as they go.

THE WORLD IS STUNNED

The media will cover the phenomena. The resurrections will be caught on tape, and the world will see it and be stunned. The demonized will not care, but other sinners will be shaken to the core. Within the hour an earthquake will hit a major city, killing seven thousand people. Even ungodly newscasters will make the connection. The two events are just too powerful and too well-timed to be coincidental. People who previously were enemies of God will fall on their faces in repentance.

THE HONOR OF REVIVAL

"The survivors were terrified and gave glory to the God of heaven" (Rev. 11:13).

God does not want so many people to go to hell. The powerful blood of Jesus will prevail, and even at this stage of the Tribulation, another revival will break forth. Multitudes of sinners will give glory to God when they see those who were slaughtered come to life and rise into the heavens. Some of them were guilty of murdering the saints, but the cross of Jesus will cover their sins just as Christ has covered ours.

It took the death of Christ to save a lost world, and it will take the death of the two witnesses (prophetic Gentiles and Jews) to turn so many hard-core sinners to Christ.

It will be such an honor to be a member of the two-witness Church.

It will be such an honor to help God reach the unreachable and bring them to salvation.

It will be such an honor to die for Christ, to be raised and raptured at such a time as this.

CHAPTER THIRTY

THE FIRST RESURRECTION

To talk about Israel's distant future is to talk about the resurrections. In this chapter we will look at the first resurrection from the dead. This applies to all Jews and Gentiles who have been born again through the blood of Christ. Here is a portion of Scripture from Revelation 20 that talks about it.

> *I saw thrones on which were seated those who had been given authority to judge. And I saw the souls of those who had been beheaded because of their testimony for Jesus and because of the word of God. They had not worshipped the beast or his image and had not received the mark on their foreheads or their hands. They came to life and reigned with Christ a thousand years. (The rest of the dead did not come to life until the thousand years were ended.) This is the first resurrection. Blessed and holy are those who have part in the first resurrection. The second death has no power over them, but they will be priests of God and of Christ and will reign with him for a thousand years. (Rev. 20:4-6)*

Here are some of the highlights that we will cover in this chapter:

1. Saints helping Christ to judge other saints
2. The judgment seat of Christ
3. Generous rewards given
4. Martyrs who end well
5. The first resurrection
6. The second death

WE WANT TO KNOW

Revelation 20 and 21 transition us from this world to a new heaven and a new earth. These chapters do the following:

1. Fill in information gaps about the future.
2. Enhance our understanding of the resurrections.
3. Include Christ's thousand-year reign.
4. Include rewards for saints.
5. Describe the judgment of sinners.
6. Show us Satan's final destination.

Almost everybody would like to know the details that are available to us about the afterlife. Although Revelation reveals little on the theme of eternity, other parts of the Bible give us more of a complete picture. We will look at several of these chapters to help us gain a better understanding. What we are told of eternity is absolutely fabulous.

SAINTS WILL HELP JUDGE

A select group of saints will help judge the rest of God's people after the return of Christ. This happens just before the new Millennium.

"I saw thrones on which were seated those who had been given authority to judge" (Rev. 20:4).

These people will become judges; they will sit on thrones and help to judge the saints. They will not judge sinners, nor will they determine the eternal destination of believers; only God has that right. They will, however, judge the behavior and the works of the believers. They will allocate to them roles of service and responsibility in Christ's millennial kingdom, according to what they did when they lived on the earth.

THE JUDGMENT SEAT OF CHRIST

This event is called, "the judgment seat of Christ". In the original Greek language, it is called the *bema*. It is different from the Great White Throne judgment. The Almighty alone presides over that. The Great White Throne judgment will be reserved for sinners and the mortals who are alive during the new Millennium. Many who stand before the Great White Throne judgment, will be sentenced to hell. The fact that Jesus will not raise unbelievers from the dead when He comes means that they have been judged already. That happens after the second resurrection. Let us now go back and study the first resurrection.

PERSONAL CONSIDERATION

Billions of saints will be judged at the judgment seat of Christ, the *bema*. Following the first resurrection, as it is called, each believer will be given personal consideration. Perhaps this is why the Lord delegates much of this responsibility to special disciples. They will help Him judge the nations. Many will be given special rewards to serve in the coming Millennium. The *bema* will reveal Christ's gracious assessment, not harsh judgments. It will be a time of wonderful restitution. The saints will receive all that was promised to them. Even the most failing saint will receive great rewards. Those who have served the Lord with distinction during their lifetime, however, will be given extra special blessings.

Paul says, "For we must all appear before the judgment seat of Christ, that each one may receive what is due him for the things done while in the body, weather good or bad" (2 Cor. 5:10).

In Jeremiah we read, "I the Lord search the heart and examine the mind, to reward a man according to his conduct, according to what his deeds deserve" (Jer. 17:10).

JESUS EXPLAINS THE REWARDS

Jesus told a parable of a man who went on a journey and returned to see how His servants behaved in His absence. The Lord has put us on the earth, and He will return to see how we have behaved in His absence. Here is the judgment the Lord gives to one of those servants:

"Well done, good and faithful servant! You have been faithful with a few things; I will put you in charge of many things. Come and share your master's happiness!" (Matt. 5:21).

Notice, the man served well and was given great authority, great responsibility and wonderful blessings.

MARTYRS WILL END WELL

John had a vision of the martyrs who will come to life and receive special honor to rule with Christ:

"And I saw the souls of those who had been beheaded because of their testimony for Jesus and because of the word of God. They had not worshipped the beast or his image and had not received the mark on their foreheads or their hands. They came to life and reigned with Christ a thousand years" (Rev. 20:4).

Special honor will be given to those who are martyred for Christ. During the Tribulation they will not receive the mark of the beast. They will refuse to worship the Antichrist. They will be killed because of their faith and loyalty to Christ, but they will be raised from the dead, and they will reign with Him for a thousand years.

THE FIRST RESURRECTION

The resurrection of the saints is called "the first resurrection" to distinguish it from the resurrection of sinners that takes place a thousand years later.

"This is the first resurrection. Blessed and holy are those who have part in the first resurrection" (Rev. 20:5-6).

Here, at the end of the Great Tribulation, the first resurrection takes place. The resurrection, or rapture as some call it, does not happen at the start of the Tribulation. Whoever is raised in the first resurrection will be blessed for all eternity. They will be given glorified bodies and will be holy unto the Lord. Paul gives us the following insights:

"But someone may ask, 'How are the dead raised? With what kind of body will they come?'" (1 Cor. 15:35).

"The body that is sown is perishable, it is raised imperishable; it is sown in dishonor, it is raised in glory; it is sown in weakness, it is raised in power; it is sown a natural body, it is raised a spiritual body" (1 Cor. 15:42-44).

"For the trumpet will sound, the dead will be raised imperishable, and we will be changed ... When the perishable has been clothed with the imperishable, and the mortal with immortality, then the saying that is written will come true: 'Death has been swallowed up in victory'" (1 Cor. 15:52-54).

The resurrected body will be like the new body that our Lord Jesus has.

"Dear friends, now we are the children of God, and what we will be has not yet been made known. But we know that when he appears, we shall be like him, for we shall see him as he is" (1 John 3:2).

The resurrected body is imperishable, incorruptible, glorious, immortal and mature. It will exist without getting older and without falling apart. It will be absolutely free from the process of decay. I am sure that each will be brought backward or forward to their prime fitness age before eternity begins. It would be no good to have a ninety-year-old body that is worn thin for one's final state. The ninety-year-old person will have his body as it was in his twenties, only perfected. A newborn will be fully mature, like a twenty-year-old, but his or her body will be upgraded and glorified.

Everyone's body is irregular or deficient, and some are deformed, crippled or in some way handicapped. The resurrected bodies of all who are part of the first resurrection will be perfect. They may have elements of dishonor now, but then they will be glorious (see 1 Corinthians 15:40).

THE SECOND DEATH

Those who are called to the first resurrection will never die again. They died once and will be raised back to life. They will never experience a second death because their bodies will be immortal. To understand this more fully, here is a simple bible definition of death:

"As *the body without the spirit is dead*, so faith without deeds is dead" (Jas. 2:26; italics added).

Physical death is the separation of the spirit from the body. When we die our spirit goes to Hades or heaven, and our body is buried in the ground or suffers decomposition in some other place. Resurrection happens when the body parts are gathered together again and the person's spirit comes back inside of it.

A second death is when the spirit leaves the body a second time and the body decomposes again. This will happen to sinners who are resurrected after the thousand-year period has passed. Their spirit will rise from Hades to join their re-gathered body parts. If they are sinners, however, the body is not raised imperishable, immortal or incorruptible. The person will be brought back to life in his old body. The Scripture does not say that unbelievers receive glorified bodies. After being judged at the Great White Throne, those people will be cast into the final hell. Their bodies will once again suffer decay and dishonor. This is the second death. Their spirits will be separated from their bodies a second time. From then on they will live in eternity without bodies, just like it was for them in Hades. As in Hades, they will still be recognizable, and they will still suffer pain, but they will not have bodies.

The second death has no power or place in the lives of believers. They will reign with Christ for a thousand years and then throughout eternity. They will be glorified and be supernatural in body, soul and spirit.

"The second death has no power over them, but they will be priests of God and of Christ and will reign with him for a thousand years" (Rev. 20:6).

CHAPTER THIRTY-ONE

THE NEW MILLENNIUM

AFTER the first resurrection, all who are alive will enter into a new age. It is called the thousand-year reign of Christ or the new millennium. Both Jews and Gentile believers will participate with Christ in this thousand-year reign. As we continue to read Revelation 20, we discover an introduction to the Millenium.

> *I saw thrones on which were seated those who had been given authority to judge. And I saw the souls of those who had been beheaded because of their testimony for Jesus and because of the word of God. They had not worshipped the beast or his image and had not received the mark on their foreheads or their hands. They came to life and reigned with Christ a thousand years. (The rest of the dead did not come to life until the thousand years were ended.) This is the first resurrection. Blessed and holy are those who have part in the first resurrection. The second death has no power over them, but they will be priests of God and of Christ and will reign with him for a thousand years. (Rev. 20:4-6)*

Here is an overview of what we will cover in this chapter:

1. The earth will be restored.
2. The environment will be refreshed.
3. People will help clean up.
4. Animals will become immortal.
4. Mortals and immortals will live together in the Millennium.
5. Children will be born in the Millennium.

AFTER THE SECOND COMING

Once Satan and his armies are removed, the thousand-year reign will begin. The process of the earth's restoration will be both natural and supernatural. Supernatural power will be released by the Lord into the air, sea and land, but the administration, clean up and management of the world will be a process that involves people.

A NEW GARDEN OF EDEN

During the Millennium, the earth will be like the Garden of Eden.

"This land that was laid waste has become like the Garden of Eden" (Eze. 36:35).

Jesus will not just speak the word to instantly renew the earth and give us a completed paradise. The earth will become a Garden of Eden; however, there will be an extended time of cleaning up the mess and developing the new world. There will be a time of transition and a time of building as the restoration of all things unfolds. Scripture speaks of the Tribulation and of the clean up that follows.

> *On the mountains of Israel you will fall, you* [unrepentant sinners] *and all your troops and the nations with you. I will give you as food to all kinds of carrion birds and to wild animals ... Israel will go out and use the weapons for fuel and burn them up ... For seven years they will use them for fuel ... On that day I will give Gog a burial place in Israel ... for seven months the house of Israel will be burying them in order to cleanse the land ... Men will be regularly employed to cleanse the land ... at the end of the seven months they will begin their search. As they go through the land and one of them sees a human bone, he will set up a marker beside it until the gravediggers have buried it. (Eze. 39:4-15)*

Jesus will be in charge of this Eden, and He will call forth many workers to assist Him in the work. The first Eden was left in Adam's charge, and he did not complete his task well. We will see what is possible when King Jesus rules.

The second Adam, Jesus, will cause the world to become all that it was intended to be from the beginning. At the end of the thousand-year reign, Jesus will finish His task well. Then He will release the entire kingdom back into the hands of His Father.

At the beginning of creation, Adam was immortal. He and Eve walked together in the Garden and the animals lived in harmony with them. Adam was commissioned to be fruitful; he was to have children, fill the earth, manage it and eventually rule the entire planet (see Genesis 1:28-30).

In those early days, before Adam fulfilled his mandate, the Lord God would come and fellowship with him in the Garden. They walked together in the cool evenings, and Adam was God's friend (see Genesis 3:8-9).

This will happen again; peace and righteousness will be the order of the day. We will enjoy harmony and fellowship with God and with one another, and all things will become new. Our joy will be complete when we worship and serve the Lord in Spirit and in truth.

THE ENVIRONMENT

When the Lord returns to earth at the end of the Great Tribulation, the planet will be uninhabitable. The environment will be totally devastated. Man's pollutants and the judgments from heaven will have flattened most cities, burned up most of the vegetation and killed everything in the seas. Groundwater will be undrinkable, and most animals will have died. The planet will be in a complete mess.

All of creation has an eager expectation. It is waiting for the return of Jesus and the resurrection of the saints. Paul wrote the following:

The creation waits in eager expectation for the sons of God to be revealed. For the creation was subjected to frustration, not by its own choice, but by the will of the one who subjected it, in hope that the creation itself will be liberated from its bondage to decay and be brought into the glorious freedom of the children of God … We know that the whole creation has been groaning as in the pains of childbirth right up to this present time. Not only so, but we ourselves, who have the firstfruits of the Spirit, groan inwardly as we wait eagerly for our adoption as sons, the redemption of our bodies." (Rom. 8:19-23)

FIRSTFRUITS OF THE SPIRIT

Today believers receive the firstfruits of their inheritance. They receive the Holy Spirit after they receive Christ as Savior. This has happened to men and women since the day Jesus rose into heaven following His death on the cross. At that time He released the Holy Spirit to the earth, and now God's Spirit lives inside of His people. This is the firstfruit of the Spirit, the down payment of our inheritance. Our adoption process has begun, but it is not yet complete. Our souls are redeemed, but not our bodies. When Jesus returns and His people are resurrected, they will experience the redemption of the body as well as the soul.

That is the moment creation is waiting for. The curse that came upon creation at the fall of Adam will begin to lift. The environment will start a process of renewal. It will be replenished in quick order. We have never seen plants grow so fast or be as beautiful as they will then.

Jesus will supernaturally clean up the water and the air, and all pollution will vanish. The Lord will heal the cracks in the earth due to the massive earthquakes. He will recreate animals and plants, even some that have become extinct. Maybe we will see dinosaurs, although I do not recognize them in the original Garden of Eden story. The details are yet to be discovered. Soon the oceans will team with life and the wild places of the world will once again be filled with all manner of living creatures.

"Behold, I will create new heavens and a new earth. The former things will not be remembered, nor will they come to mind" (Isa. 65:17).

THE ANIMALS

During the transition between the Tribulation and the new Millennium, animals will feast on flesh and remain wild, but once the *bema* (the judgment seat of Christ) is complete and the sons of God are revealed, then a transformation will occur in the animal kingdom. During the thousand-year reign, all people and animals will be vegetarians. There will be no killing of animals anymore.

We know that fisheries will exist, for the Dead Sea will team with fish, and we are told that fishermen will be catching them (see Ezekiel 47:9-10). Even today, Jews do not consider fish to be the same as other animals. Their flesh is not considered meat like that of land animals.

When God destroyed the world in the flood during the days of Noah, He said that every living thing that moved on the ground and every bird would be destroyed. The fish in the sea, however, were not destroyed. Genesis describes it this way:

"Everything on the dry land *that had the breath of life* in its nostrils died. *Every living thing* on the face of the earth was wiped out: men and animals and the creatures that move along the ground and the birds of the air were wiped from the earth. Only Noah was left and those with him in the ark" (Gen. 7:22-23; italics added).

The fish were not considered as living things because they did not have the breath of life in them. That is the Jewish understanding and it fits the picture we are given of the new Millennium.

With pollutants gone, the plant life re-energized and fish available, no one will lack the nutrition that has been supplemented through the consumption of land animals. Before Noah and his family entered the ark, they were all vegetarians. Only after they departed from the ark did God invite them to eat meat (see Genesis 9:2-3).

FRIENDLY ANIMALS

In the new Millennium, the world will return not only to life as it was before the flood, but to life as it was before the fall. That was a time when all animals were friendly. In the Millennium, massive grizzly bears, killer whales, Siberian tigers and king cobras will be as gentle and sociable as the most loving pet. Read the prophetic words of Isaiah.

The wolf will live with the lamb, the leopard will lie down with the goat, the calf and the lion and the yearling together; and a little child will lead them. The cow will feed with the bear, their young will lie down together and the lion will eat straw like the ox. The infant will play near the hole of the cobra and the young child will put his hand in the viper's nest. They will neither harm nor destroy on all my holy mountain, for the earth will be full of the knowledge of the Lord as the waters cover the sea. In that day the root of Jesse will stand as a banner for the peoples; the nations will rally to him, and his rest will be glorious. In that day the Lord will reach out his hand a second time to reclaim the remnant of his people. (Isa. 11:6-11)

At that time, animals will not suffer decay. Romans 8:21 says that they will be liberated from the bondage of decay. They will not have the wisdom, the higher intelligence or the level of understanding that man has; they are not made in God's image. They will be more like pets that roam freely throughout the earth. Little children will lead them.

It will be a wonderful sight to see a little boy or girl lead a black panther or a wolf through the streets of a city. The animals will have babies, and their young will get along together. No animal will be carnivorous; in fact, lions will eat straw like an ox. Nothing and no one will destroy an animal or a person in God's new world. There will be a new understanding in the world, for the knowledge of the Lord will be everywhere.

MORTALS AND IMMORTALS ARE THERE

There will be different kinds of people living on earth as well. Mortals and immortals will live together, side-by-side. Different races and nationalities will retain their identities. The Jewish nation will especially be identifiable and honored.

We know that billions of people will be immortal and possess glorified bodies. They include all believers who died and went to heaven throughout history. Some already had new bodies while in heaven, but most in heaven will be waiting for resurrection day when their spirits will be reunited with their bodies.

Also included in this number are those believers who will be alive at His coming. They will be caught up into the air and, in a flash, receive new bodies and return to earth with the Lord. The Scripture says they will forever be with the Lord.

These glorified, resurrected people are not the only ones who will be alive on earth during the Millennium; mortals will be there as well. We know this is true because at the end of the Millennium, Satan is released to tempt the nations once again. A great multitude of mortals join his army, and the Lord Almighty kills them (see Revelation 20:9). If they can be killed, they are not immortal.

SURVIVORS

The mortals are made up of different groups of people. Some are survivors of the battle of Armageddon.

"Then the survivors from all the nations that have attacked Jerusalem will go up year after year to worship the King, the Lord Almighty, and to celebrate the Feast of Tabernacles" (Zech. 14:16).

The survivors are some of those who attacked Jerusalem. For reasons unknown, the Lord does not destroy every individual who fights against Him at His coming. Perhaps He extends grace to those who might have been dragged or forced to follow the beast. We do not know, but there are survivors among Christ's enemies. The Lord is giving them another chance to escape eternal damnation. He is gracious.

There will be babies and unborn children who will be alive at His coming. God does not send children to hell.

NON-MESSIANIC JEWS

There are two different groups of Jews in Jerusalem when Christ returns. The Messianic Jews believe that Jesus is Messiah. They will instantly receive glorified bodies at the Second Coming of Christ.

There will also be a group of Jews in Jerusalem who do not believe that Jesus is their Messiah. The Lord will still rescue them when He returns, but they will not receive glorified bodies (see Zechariah 14:1-2). I am sure that these Jews will believe on Him when they see Him, but they will not gain their glorified bodies until after the Millennium is over. These Jews will live as mortals and even have babies in the new Millennium.

For reasons only known to God, He will give many people another chance to believe on Him. He welcomes them into the Millennium with His holy ones, but they are mortal. In the next chapters, we will look more closely at the life of the Jewish people and the life of the Gentiles during the thousand-year reign of Christ on earth.

MORTALS IN THE MILLENNIUM

Whether you have a glorified body or a mortal one, it will be absolutely amazing to live under the rule of King Jesus in the new Millennium. Mortals will be married and have children during this time. We are told that people will bear children during these days, for children of various ages are mentioned playing with the animals (see Isaiah 65:23). It is reasonable to think that mortals will continue procreating as they have always done. We cannot say that for the immortals during the Millennium.

While debating with the Sadducees, Jesus said, "Are you not in error because you do not know the scriptures or the power of God? When the dead rise, they will neither marry nor be given in marriage; they will be like the angels in heaven" (Mark 12:25).

It may seem to be a great loss for immortals that they cannot procreate. In keeping with this, however, Jesus said to the Sadducees that they did not understand the power of God. It therefore remains certain that an area of understanding and supernatural power will come to immortals, and I am sure that they will be surprised and grateful for the new arrangement.

The fact that mortals will still give birth to children means that over the span of the thousand-year period, millions of babies will be born, and each will have a free will to choose or reject the Lord Jesus.

Some of the mortals will die during the Millennium, although it will be rare. As it was before and during the days of Noah, people will live for centuries. Speaking of the new Millennium, Isaiah says the following:

"Never again will there be in it an infant who lives but a few days, or an old man who does not live out his years; he who dies at a hundred will be a mere youth; he who fails to reach a hundred will be considered accursed ... They will not toil in vain or bear children doomed to misfortune; for they will be a people blessed by the Lord, they and their descendants with them" (Isa. 65:20-23).

In the new Millennium, even mortals will live long, wonderful lives. Many, especially the newborns, will no doubt live for the entire length of the thousand-year reign.

CHAPTER THIRTY-TWO

THE NATIONS IN THE MILLENNIUM

IN this chapter we will discover what the nations will be like in the new Millennium. Then in the next chapter we will specifically focus on Israel. The book of Revelation says this:

"They came to life and reigned with Christ a thousand years. [The new millennium] (The rest of the dead did not come to life until the thousand years were ended.) This is the first resurrection. Blessed and holy are those who have part in the first resurrection. The second death has no power over them, but they will be priests of God and of Christ and will reign with him for a thousand years" (Rev. 20:4-6).

This chapter focuses on the following themes:

1. Judging the nations
2. The saints in hiding
3. Unsaved survivors in the Millennium
4. Children in the Millennium
5. The nations of the saved
6. The blessings of the nations
7. Mortals and immortals
8. A population explosion
9. Growing contempt among the mortals

THE NATIONS

Throughout history, God has formed the nations and given them their allotted time (see Acts 17:26). On the whole, the nations have fallen prey to the lies of the devil. By the time the Great Tribulation arrives, many among the nations will be evil. They will be diametrically opposed to God's standards, which we know as the Judeo-Christian ethic. Worse than that, the majority of people who are still alive at the end of the Tribulation will be sold-out servants of Satan. They will gladly receive the mark of the beast and follow his religious philosophy. The nations will be an abomination to the Lord; that is, all of the nations except Israel.

Before the last half of the Tribulation, the Lord will rescue and redeem most people on the earth, but many who are alive at the end will hate Him. The Lord will judge them for how they have treated Israel and for the many sins committed against His Anointed One. Their crimes against each other and especially against the innocent will be far beyond recovery. In the end, the Lord will destroy them and cast them into Hades, where they will wait in bondage for one thousand years. After that, they will be brought forth to stand before the Great White Throne for final judgment and sentencing.

SOME UNBELIEVERS ARE SPARED

With all of the shaking and sifting that takes place during the Tribulation, by the end of it, the vast majority of people will stand firmly in either the camp of the holy ones or the wicked. Some, however, will be caught in the middle. They will not serve the devil, but neither will they follow the Lord, and God will not destroy them. When the Lord comes to judge the nations, some fence-sitters will be allowed to live. This may seem to be contrary to popular theology, but the Bible speaks of this reality. These people are called survivors, and they live beyond the Second Coming, and, strangely enough, they enter the Millennium along with the redeemed. Because of God's surprising grace, they will be given another opportunity to be saved.

"The earth is defiled by its people; they have destroyed the laws, violated the statutes and broken the everlasting covenant. Therefore a curse consumes the earth; its people must bear their guilt. Therefore earth's inhabitants are burned up and *very few are left*" (Isa. 24:5-6; italics added).

Notice that very few are left. That means that some, although not many, are spared. Look at this next verse.

"*Then the survivors* from all the nations *that have attacked Jerusalem* will go up year after year to worship the King, the Lord Almighty, and to celebrate the Feast of Tabernacles" (Zech. 14:16; italics added).

In this verse we discover that there are survivors, and these survivors come from among the group that attacked Jerusalem.

"For with fire and with his sword the Lord will execute judgment upon all men, and *many* will be those slain by the Lord" (Isa. 66:16; italics added).

Here we find the word many and many is not necessarily the same as all.

"They will neither harm nor destroy on all my holy mountain … *In that day the Lord will reach out his hand a second time to reclaim the remnant of his people*" (Isa. 11:9,11; italics added).

Isaiah 11:9 tells us that this is a description of the new Millennium, for that is the only time in history when there is no harm on all of God's holy mountain. Then we are told that during the Millennium, God will reach out a second time to reclaim some of His people. Some people will be saved even during the Millennium. Even Jesus taught us about this possibility. He said the following:

"The wedding banquet is ready, but those I invited did not deserve to come. Go to the street corners and invite to the banquet anyone you find." So the servant went out into the streets and gathered all the people they could find, both good and bad, and the wedding hall was filled with guests. But when the king came in to see the guests, he noticed a man there who was not wearing wedding clothes… Then the king told the attendants, "Tie him hand and foot and throw him outside, into

the darkness where there will be weeping and gnashing of teeth." (Matt. 22:8-13)

Jesus allows some survivors to enter the Millennium. They will be given a second chance. Many undeserving will come to the Great Marriage Supper of the Lamb. We read that both the good and the bad are brought in so that the hall will be filled. Some refuse to wear the robes of righteousness and will eventually go to hell after the Millennium is over and the Great White Throne judgment is complete.

CHILDREN ARE WELCOME

The ambiguous survivors from among those who attacked Jerusalem during the battle of Armageddon are not the only ones who will enter the Millennium as mortals. Unborn children and many young people will also enter without glorified bodies. They, as with adult survivors, are mortal during the thousand-year reign of Christ. They will not know the Lord or receive the forgiveness of sins or eternal salvation before His Second Coming. They will not be caught up into the clouds to meet the Lord in the air when He appears, so they will not receive glorified bodies.

This will happen because some will be in the womb of an unbelieving woman when Jesus comes. Some will be unsaved teens who the Lord will not send to hell. Many more children will be born to these survivors during the Millennium. Jesus loves children. In all of the synoptic Gospels, Jesus says, "Let the little children come to me, and do not hinder them, for the kingdom of heaven belongs to such as these" (Matt. 19:14; Mark 10:14; Luke 18:16).

If we try to put God in our own theological box, we will be surprised to discover that He does not fit. He will not be restrained to our understanding of His grace. All of us will be surprised at the extent of God's designs at the end of the age.

HIDDEN BELIEVERS

Many undercover believers will be alive when the Lord returns. These saints will be incognito in the nations, watching and waiting for the Second Coming. By the end of the Tribulation, Israel will be the only place on earth where believers will be open about their faith. Israel will have many enemies, and the world will be at war with them. The Holy Land will be inhabited with Messianic Jews, Old Covenant Jews, secular Jews and Christian Gentiles. When the Lord comes to Jerusalem, He will rescue the people who live there. Many will be saved from wrath even though they did not previously accept Jesus as Messiah.

"After that, we who *are still alive and are left* will be caught up together with them in the clouds" (1 Thes. 4:17; italics added).

Notice that some believers are still alive and remain until the end of the Tribulation, when the Lord comes.

"I will gather all nations to Jerusalem to fight against it … Then the Lord will go out and fight against those nations … On that day His feet will stand on the Mount of Olives" (Zech. 14:2-4).

God fights for and protects the people of Jerusalem when He comes and stands on the Mount of Olives. After that battle the new Millennium begins.

BELIEVERS WILL RULE THE NATIONS

In the Millennium, those who previously served the Lord will be given special blessings. They will become kings and priests and rule over the nations. The nations will look to Israel as the people who host the government of God's kingdom. Jerusalem will be the capital city of the world. Jesus will live and rule from there, and the nations will worship Him. The nations will be rebuilt and will live in righteousness and peace.

THE NATIONS REFORMED

All countries during the Millennium will be called the nations of the saved. Each nation that is chosen to be there will be rescued from annihilation to be ruled by the sons and daughters of God.

Speaking of the temple in Jerusalem, Scripture says the following: "The *nations of those who are saved* shall walk in its light, and the kings of the earth bring their glory and honor into it." "And they shall bring the glory and the honor of the nations into it" (Rev. 21:24,26 NKJ; italics added).

Every nation has a special and distinct destiny given to it by God. Some are peacemakers; others are inventors. Some nations are rich in the arts, and others reflect amazing gifts of service, worship, leadership, athletics, hospitality, farming or business administration. During the Millennium, all countries will have experts in different areas of life. Each will excel with some distinction, a skill that is superior to that of other nations. Each nation will be known for their own excellence, and they will offer their most excellent achievements in service to the Lord.

Like individual people, each nation will reflect a beautiful aspect of the glory and character of God. No individual person has the full measure of God shining through him; people must partner with other saints to see a display of glory that even approaches God's. The nations, likewise, will partner with other nations to demonstrate God's glory. The heavens declare the glory of God – so do individual people, and so do nations.

The glory of each nation will be brought to Jerusalem to be presented to the Lord. We are not told that every nation will be in the Millennium, but I believe that most will be resurrected to be part of the new world. We know that people from every nation and language are in heaven. Jesus purchased them with His blood, and their nationality and ethnicity will be recognizable as they stand around God's throne (see Revelation 7:9).

On this mountain the Lord Almighty will prepare a feast of rich food for all peoples, a banquet of aged wine – the best of meats [foods] *and the finest of wines.* On this mountain he will destroy the shroud that enfolds all peoples, the sheet that covers all nations; *he will swallow up death forever. The Sovereign Lord will wipe away the tears from all faces; he will remove the disgrace of his people from all the earth. The Lord has spoken.* (Isa. 25:6-8; emphasis added)

The Lord will take away the shroud that covers the nations. This shroud hides the inherent talents and gifts of the nations. Presently, people and nations are being robbed of their identity, their destiny and their godly heritage. All of that will change in the Millennium. At that time, they will shine as they should with God's glory. The nations will be reformed, and the shroud that covers them will be removed. They will bring their special grace, honor, talent, distinction and glory to Jerusalem and offer it to the Lord.

THE GLORY OF THE SAVED

The saved will be immortal, and their bodies will be incorruptible. They will be supernatural and spiritual. In many ways, they will be like Jesus; they are His family. They will take hold of the mandate given to the first Adam, to subdue the world, steward it and manage it in righteousness. Adam failed, but they will not.

Billions of animals will be there, living in peace, and all of creation will flourish to its optimum potential. Mankind will fully enjoy the pleasures of creativity, invention, work, recreation and prosperity. The human race will be blessed with adventure, fun, and glorious fellowship. People will be thrilled with the wealth of friends that they have because there will be no place for inferiority or rejection. Most of all they will experience rich fellowship with the Lord. The kingdom of God will have come to earth in answer to the Lord's Prayer.

Jesus prayed, "Your kingdom come, your will be done on earth as it is in heaven" (Matt. 6:10).

The people of God will enjoy their reward. Non-believers among the nations will live in the glory of God's people. They will be blessed because of the blessing that rests on the saints and on the land, but some will be unthankful.

EVEN MORTALS ARE BLESSED

In many ways, immortals and mortals will live differently during the

Millennium. One obvious difference will be childbirth and population growth. As the years pass, more and more babies will be born to the mortals, but none to the immortals. The mortals are the survivors of Armageddon, and many will come into the Millennium without making Christ their Lord and Savior.

In just twenty years, children become adults, marry and begin to have children of their own. In the Millennium, they will have grandchildren and great-grandchildren and so on, and this will be multiplied exponentially, for many generations. Because very few die, billions of unsaved mortals will soon inhabit the earth. Many of those will become followers of Christ, but a vast multitude will not bow the knee to the Lord Jesus willfully.

MORTALS BREED CONTEMPT

As the Millennium endures and moves toward its end, a growing disquiet will begin to surface. It will not come from the immortals. They will remember the old life when they had frail bodies. In the Millennium, they will be sons of God and will not trade that glory for anything. They will know the fullness of God's fellowship and live like angels. They could not and will not turn away from the Lord. They will be totally one with Him for all eternity.

Some mortals, on the other hand, will drift away from the Lord. Presently, we know what the Scriptures tell us about waywardness:

"We all, like sheep, have gone astray, each of us has turned to his own way" (Isa. 53:6).

Some mortals in the Millennium will take their blessings for granted and their hearts will fall from gratitude and grace. Most of these people will be born during the new Millennium. They will not have experienced the ravages of sin or the temptations of the devil. They will have lived, only in the millennial kingdom. All they will have known is the rule of Jesus and His holy ones.

Many will earn positions of authority and responsibility and will begin to influence their community in a direction away from Jerusalem. Some will want to skip out on the feast celebrations.

The Lord says that all who refuse to come up to Zion for the Feast of Tabernacles, for example, will find that the rains will not fall on their nation and their national productivity will begin to fall. Zechariah says,

"Then the survivors from all the nations will go up year after year to worship the King, the Lord Almighty, and to celebrate the Feast of Tabernacles. If any of the people of the earth do not go up to Jerusalem to worship the King, the Lord Almighty, they will have no rain" (Zech. 14:17-19).

Some of the mortals among the nations will begin to show signs of rebellion against the Lord. Soon, after that, Satan will appear from the Abyss for his final campaign. He will tempt the nations and seal the awful judgment that is already hanging over the lives of many people.

CHAPTER THIRTY-THREE

ISRAEL IN THE MILLENNIUM

MOST of the nations will be present in the new millennium, and Israel will have a very special position among them. Revelation tells us the following:

"They came to life and reigned with Christ a thousand years. (The rest of the dead did not come to life until the thousand years were ended.) This is the first resurrection. Blessed and holy are those who have part in the first resurrection. The second death has no power over them, but they will be priests of God and of Christ and will reign with him for a thousand years" (Rev. 20:4-6).

In this chapter we will focus on the following.

1. The chosen people for all eternity
2. Jesus' rule from Zion
3. Ruling with a rod of iron
4. Israel's amazing blessings
5. Miraculous water
6. The feasts of Israel
7. The nations celebrating with Israel
8. Israel's second chance at finding salvation

GOD'S CHOSEN PEOPLE

The Jews are and will be a distinct people before God for all eternity. They will enjoy the blessings of a very special inheritance. They will lead the world in global worship and in the international celebration of the holy feasts of the Lord. They will live in close proximity to Christ's throne in the land of Israel. Jerusalem will be the most honoured city on the planet, and her people will be revered. Redeemed Jews will be a distinct group of people in the Millennium, and while all people will be blessed beyond their imagination, the Jews will have specific responsibilities.

JESUS RULES FROM ZION

Jesus will live in and rule from Jerusalem. From there, He will give the Jewish people and the nations of the world everything that was ever promised to them through the prophets. Micah tells us, "The Lord will rule over them in Mount Zion from that day and forever" (Mic. 4:7).

Although He is the most compassionate and gracious of kings, Jesus will rule with a rod of iron. The iron scepter will be operational from the moment He returns to earth. Revelation says,

"Out of his mouth comes a sharp sword with which to strike down the nations. 'He will rule them with an iron scepter'" (Rev. 19:15).

Jesus will rule, but He will not rule the planet alone. He will enlist many believers to rule alongside of Him, and each will have his delegated responsibilities and the authority of the iron scepter. Christian leaders will rule over the nations, and Jews will rule alongside of Jesus in the land of Israel. Besides being the King of the whole world, Jesus will continue to be the King of the Jews.

"To him who overcomes and does my will to the end, I will give authority over the nations. 'He will rule them with an iron scepter'" (Rev. 2:26-27).

Notice that everyone who rules at that time, rules with a rod of iron. Jesus will rule, and the Scriptures say that His name will be the only name (see Zechariah 14:9). This means some matters are not negotiable; He rules supreme. This will be the way of the new kingdom.

1. Jesus will demand righteousness in His kingdom.
2. There will be no hurt or destruction in all of His holy mountain.
3. He will not tolerate wickedness.
4. No other religions will be accepted on the earth. All religion that originates outside of God's throne room is of the devil. No other religion will be permitted during the Millennium.
5. No crime will be tolerated.
6. No abuse of innocent people, extortion or killing will be tolerated. The entire world will be safe, joyful and righteous.

The nations will experience the productivity and the joys of Eden, plus the glories of heaven on earth. God's blessings will cover the entire planet, but Israel will be given a special place of honor.

ISRAEL WILL BE BLESSED FOREVER

The nation of Israel will be blessed in an unusual way. God will fix that which is broken and will bless her with all that was ever promised to her. Amos says, "In that day I will restore David's fallen tent. I will repair its broken places, restore its ruins and build it as it used to be" (Amos 9:11).

Jesus will live in Jerusalem. That is why it is, and will continue to be called, the Holy Land. The Jewish people will live around Him, and He will give them their full inheritance. Isaiah says, "Rejoice with Jerusalem and be glad for her, all you who love her ... For this is what the Lord says: 'I will extend peace to her like a river and the wealth of nations like a flooding stream'" (Isa. 66:10, 12).

The Holy Land will be established to her mandated borders. The Promised Land will extend from the Nile to the Euphrates and will forever be Israel (see Genesis 15:18). It will overflow with temple worship, industry, agricultural productivity, amazing beauty and the global seat of government. At that time, the Jews will say this:

> *Lord you established peace for us; all that we have accomplished, you have done for us. O Lord, our God, other lords besides you have ruled*

over us, but your name alone do we honor. They are now dead, they
live no more; those departed spirits do not rise. You punished them and
brought them to ruin; you wiped out all memory of them. You enlarged
the nation, O Lord; you have enlarged the nation. You have gained
glory for yourself' you have extended all the borders of the land. (Isa.
26:12-15)

A JEWISH POPULATION EXPLOSION

Israel's population will also increase extensively. It seems that the Lord wants
more people to be part of this special nation. Perhaps this is one of the
reasons why many Jews will still be mortal during the Millennium – so that
they can have many more children.

We read in Isaiah, "Then will all your people be righteous and will posses
the land forever. They are the shoot I have planted, the work of my hands,
for the display of my splendor. The least will become a thousand, the small-
est a mighty nation. I am the Lord; in its time I will do this swiftly" (Isa.
60:21-22).

"As the new heavens and the new earth that I make will endure before me,"
declares the Lord, "so will your name and descendants endure" (Isa. 66:22).

MIRACULOUS WATER

Water, at present, must be carefully managed in Israel because, like the
surrounding nations, its natural water supply is very limited. In the Millennium, it will flow freely from springs and gush forth in powerful rivers.
This is God's water, and it will have special healing qualities. Even the desert
between Jerusalem and the Dead Sea will enjoy an extravagant flow of living
water. The new water will bring renewal and restoration to the entire nation:

"Water will gush forth in the wilderness and streams in the desert. The
burning sand will become a pool, the thirsty ground bubbling springs. In the
haunts where jackals once lay, grass and reeds and papyrus will grow. And
a highway will be there; it will be called the way of holiness" (Isa. 35:6-8).

The Dead Sea will receive so much of this unique water that it will experience a new identity. People will no longer be able to call it the Dead Sea. Now, at this time, it is totally dead. No fish or creature of any kind lives in the Dead Sea. The oceans are 3 percent salt; the Dead Sea is 35 percent salt. Nothing can live there. In the Millennium, the Dead Sea will change; it will abound with aquatic life.

> *This water flows toward the eastern region and goes down into Arabah, where it enters the Sea. When it empties into the Sea, the water there becomes fresh. Swarms of living creatures will live wherever the river flows. There will be large numbers of fish, because this water flows there and makes the salt water fresh; so where the river flows everything will live. Fishermen will stand along the shore; from En Gedi to En Eglaim there will be places for spreading nets. The fish will be of many kinds — like the fish of the great sea. (Eze. 47:8-10)*

Wealth, joy and peace will fill the land of Israel, and nations all around the world will see the glory of God that rests on her. The wealth of the nations will stream into the Holy Land, and many people will desire to go up to Israel and serve the people and the land of the Jews because it will be the city of the Great King, and they are His chosen people.

Many details are given in Scripture to specifically describe Israel's glory and wealth during the Millennium. There are too many verses to record them all. For those who want a more detailed picture of Israel's national prosperity during the thousand-year reign, I encourage you to read Isaiah 60 – 66. There, you will find more than one hundred verses that focus on the theme of Israel's coming glory. In short, Israel will become the praise of the whole earth.

Concerning Israel, the scripture says:

"Arise, shine, for your light has come, and the glory of the Lord rises upon you ... but the Lord rises upon you and his glory appears over you. Nations will come to your light, and kings to the brightness of your dawn ...The wealth of the seas will be brought to you, *to you the riches of the nations will come ... Foreigners will rebuild your walls, and their kings will serve you*" (Isa. 60:1,2,10; italics added).

Scriputre also tells us, "You who call on the Lord, give yourselves no rest, and give him no rest till *he establishes Jerusalem and makes her the praise of the earth*" (Isa. 62:6-7; italics added).

THE FEASTS OF ISRAEL

The feasts of Israel are God's solemn, appointed holy days. They are not man-made, but God-made. They highlight specific times when God's people must gather for worship, dedication, consecration and celebration. They focus on seasons of remembrance, thanksgiving and honor. They are memorials, and the Lord will insist that these feasts continue during His thousand-year reign. In the Millennium, He commands that all of the nations celebrate the feasts along with Israel.

The Jews have been chosen by God to organize, administrate and lead the world in the celebration of the feasts. Earlier in the book, we studied the eight blessings of Israel's inheritance. In a list of eight things, this privilege, called the temple worship, specifically belongs to the Jews. In Romans 9:3-5, Paul mentions the eight things that are part of Israel's inheritance. Notice that the temple worship belongs to them. It is their place of spiritual leadership.

Paul says, "My brothers, those of my own race, the people of Israel. Theirs is the adoption of sons; theirs the divine glory, the covenants, the receiving of the law, the *temple worship* and the promises. Theirs are the patriarchs, and from them is traced the human linage of Christ" (Rom. 9:3-5; italics added).

This is not an Old Testament verse, but a New Testament verse. The leadership of the temple worship during the Millennium has been allocated to the Jews. The most memorable feast during that time will be the Feast of Tabernacles.

"Then the survivors from all the nations that have attacked Jerusalem will go up year after year to worship the King, the Lord Almighty, and to celebrate the Feast of Tabernacles. If any of the peoples of earth do not go up to Jerusalem to worship the King, the Lord Almighty, they will have no rain" (Zech. 14:16-18).

The Feast of Tabernacles is called *Sukkot*. It has special significance.

Sid Roth further explains this feast: "Sukkot commemorates the forty-year period during which the children of Israel wandered in the desert, living in temporary shelters. Sukkot is the feast that we also celebrate the birth of Yeshua, who is the Son of the living God and who is our Salvation and our Provision, our Shelter, and our Provider." [53]

During the Millennium, the Lord insists on the nations coming to Jerusalem to celebrate the Feast of Tabernacles. The whole world must recognize that God alone is their shelter. They must remember that man's time on earth has been a journey through a barren wilderness, and God alone has brought mankind through it. Like the children of Israel, in ancient days, the nations in the Millennium will have come to their Promised Land. They must come through the wilderness and walk into the eternal promises of God. The Feast of Tabernacles is a joyous, yet solemn reminder of man's humility, frailty and his total dependence on God.

THE NATIONS GO UP TO ZION

Representatives from every nation will go up to Jerusalem to celebrate the Lord and participate in all of His glorious events. The gatherings will be rich in fellowship, and worship charged with the Holy Spirit will fill the city of Jerusalem.

In the last days the mountain of the Lord's temple will be established as chief among the mountains; it will be raised above the hills, and all nations will stream to it. Many peoples will come and say, "Come, let us go up to the mountain of the Lord, to the house of the God of Jacob. He will teach us his ways, so that we may walk in his paths. The law will

go out from Zion, the word of the Lord from Jerusalem. He will judge
between the nations and will settle disputes for many peoples. They will
beat their swords into plowshares and their spears into pruning hooks.
Nation will not take up sword against nation, nor will they train for
war anymore. Come, O house of Jacob, let us walk in the light of the
Lord. (Isa. 2:2-5).

SALVATION EXTENDED AGAIN

At that time, Jesus will become the obvious choice for all Jews; even for those
who once would not accept Him as Messiah. Now they will worship Him as
Lord and Messiah. Orthodox zealots have always believed in the coming of
Messiah, but they just did not want to believe that Jesus was the One. That
delusion will instantly pass when He appears on the Mount of Olives. They
will become believers, but they will have to wait for the Great White Throne
judgment, at the end of the Millennium, to receive glorified bodies. They
will wait with enthusiasm for the second resurrection.

"The calf and the lion and the yearling together; and a little child will lead
them ... In that day the Lord will reach out his hand a *second* time to
reclaim the remnant of his people" (Isa. 11:6,11; italics added).

God will reach out to the Jews a second time. These late blooming Jews will
be grafted into their own olive tree during the Millennium. Notice from this
verse, it will happen when the calf and the lion and the yearling are together.
At that time a second opportunity for salvation will come to God's chosen
people.

I wonder if the Lord is so gracious to them because it was His Church who
caused many Jews to suffer persecution over the past two thousand years.
It has been difficult for them to believe that the very religion that has hurt
their people so excessively could be right about the Messiah. Jesus will make
it up to them and much more besides. Paul says, "How much more readily
will these, the natural branches, be grafted into their own olive tree?" (Rom.
11:24).

This eternal salvation offer, will no doubt be extended to all mortals during the Millennium. It seems strange to think that many will refuse, even though they are living in the kingdom of God. When Satan appears, many people will rally to his evil call. The hearts of those who are wicked will be exposed, and their secret malaise of defiance and rebellion will be uncovered for all to see.

JERUSALEM OUR CHIEF JOY

There are many things to get excited about, but the Lord is telling us to get excited for the Jews and for the city of Jerusalem. That is because the return of the Lord and the blessings due His people are tied together with the fulfillment of His promises for Jerusalem. This city and her nation is God's prophetic time clock. When Jerusalem comes into her own, then the Church will also blossom. At that time, the Lord Himself will also be blessed, for He will receive His inheritance. At that time, God Almighty will receive the harvest of the earth.

Jesus will not return, and the Ancient of Days will not receive His reward unless Jerusalem obtains her blessings. That is the promise of the Lord. Prophetically speaking, the psalmist writes a word that will posture our hearts correctly concerning Jerusalem. May this prayer be our prayer!

"If I forget you, O Jerusalem, may my right hand forget its skill. May my tongue cling to the roof of my mouth if I do not remember you, if I do not consider Jerusalem my highest joy" (Ps. 137:5-6).

Let us focus on Israel. Let us be strong alongside of her, to defend and protect her as we approach the final battles. Let us encourage her people and support the reclaiming of all of her Bible-promised lands. Let us pray for the quick release of her coming revival. Let us pray for her financial prosperity and for her well-being. Let us defend her verbally and speak the blessings of God over her. Let us prophesy the words of the Lord over her, for they have great power.

Let us watch in faith as we behold the glory of the Lord that will come upon her. Finally, let us get ready to partner with Israel for world-wide revival and the end-time purposes of the Lord to be fulfilled.

Pray this with me: *Lord God of Abraham, Isaac and Jacob we call upon You to fulfill Your promises to Israel. We come into agreement with You so that Israel may be blessed, and ultimately You will be blessed, through the completion of Your sovereign will concerning her. As You promised, let all the people of the earth be blessed a second time, because of Israel's coming revival.*

CHAPTER THIRTY-FOUR

UNTO THE KING ETERNAL

WINDING DOWN OR GEARING UP

As the millennial reign of Christ draws to an end, eternity begins. At that time, the Bible narrative launches us into a world without end, ruled by God Almighty and the Lamb. Several monumental things happen as time draws to a close. It is not that things will be drawn to a close; in fact, they will just be warming up. Things are not winding down in the purposes of God; they are gearing up. Finally, at the end of the Millennium, the plans of God that were initiated at Creation will be complete, and things will be as they were meant to be for all eternity. Before that happens, several maneuvers must fall into place.

Here are some of the details that Bible prophecy fortells for the end of the Millennium and beyond.

1. The devil is released to tempt the nations.
2. Those who are enemies of Christ are routed.
3. Satan is cast into hell.
4. The Great White Thone judgment begins.
5. The wicked are cast into hell.
6. God Almighty comes to Jerusalem.
7. Heaven has a new headquarters.
7. We shall reign with the Almighty and the Lamb forever.

THE DEVIL IS RELEASED

The thought of the devil's being released to tempt the nations at the end of the Millennium has caused fear and concern for many ill-informed saints. This fear is not necessary. No believer will be affected by the devil's evil schemes. Let us explore the facts. To start with, Revelation states, "When the thousand years are over, Satan will be released from his prison and will go out to deceive the nations" (Rev. 20:7).

God will use the devil to serve the purposes of heaven, one last time. Like with the Crucifixion of Christ, the devil does not understand that his wicked plotting will be used by God. Satan's collaboration in the death of Christ actually opened the gates of salvation and freed the world from his grasp. At the end of the Millennium, Satan, unknowingly, will be released from prison to fulfill the plans of God once again.

THE ENEMIES OF CHRIST

At the end of the thousand-year reign of Christ, the world will be full of people who have never made a public confession of faith in Jesus. They have never been tested, and God is determined to give every person a choice. He maintains that all people have the right to express their free will and choose. At that time, many will not be born again; in fact, some will be secretly rebellious. They will be unable to stop or even resist the political rule of Christ openly, for He rules with a rod of iron, but in their hearts, they refuse to give their allegiance to Him. In the Garden of Eden, Satan tempted Adam and Eve, and they rebelled against God and fell from grace. This will happen again, to many people, at the end of the Millennium.

Belivers do not need to worry about the temptation of the devil. They are already immortal because they were Christ's when He came. They received new bodies in the first resurrection. They will have no interest in the temptations of the devil because they have already been perfected in body, soul and spirit.

Those, however, who will be born during the Millennium, never will have been tested. Many of them will be filled with arrogant pride, and they are looking for an opportunity to rebel against the government and rule of Christ. You may ask how it is possible; but think for a moment – if it happened once in the original Garden of Eden, can it not happen again?

When Satan comes, he will present himself as an angel of light. He will communicate to the masses that following him will result in freedom. In fact, all who follow him will be promised immortality and to become like God. Together with the devil, they will announce war on the Lamb and march on Jeusalem. We read,

"They marched across the breadth of the earth and surrounded the camp of God's people, the city he loves. But fire came down from heaven and devoured them. And the devil, who deceived them, was thrown into the lake of burning sulfur" (Rev. 20:9-10).

Multitudes of mortal people, who have evil in their hearts, will rally around the devil and begin their attack on Jerusalem. Before a weapon is fired, God Almighty will destroy all of them. The heavens will open, and fire will come and consume them. The multitudes who are left on the earth will be called the people of God. Satan will be cast into hell, never to be released again.

THE GREAT WHITE THRONE

The final judgment is called the Great White Throne judgment. It will be a sobering sight. We read,

"Then I saw the great white throne and him who was seated on it. ... And I saw the dead, great and small, standing before the throne, and the books were opened. Another book was opened which is the book of life. The dead where judged according to what they had done as recorded in the books ... If anyone's name was not found written in the book of life, he was thrown into the lake of fire" (Rev. 20:11,12,15).

The souls that have been waiting in Hades will be resurrected (given back their old bodies), and they will stand before the throne of God. That is called the second resurrection. All of those who are not immortal, from the Millennium, will stand before God as well. The books will be opened. The books include those writings that have our behavior recorded in them and also the famous book of life, which contains the list of people who have believed on Jesus Christ for salvation.

The people who already have immortal bodies and have reigned with Christ in the Millennium will not stand before this throne. They already stood before the throne of Christ when He came. They were judged already, and, at that time, they were found to be justified and sanctified, and so they were glorified.

The judgment will begin, and those from the Millennium who trusted in Christ will become immortal with the other believers. They will have perfected bodies.

Those from Hades, however, and those who sided with the devil at the end of the Millennium will be cast into the lake of fire with the devil and his angels. This is called the second death because their bodies will die a second time. These people are wicked people. They did not make a mistake, miss a sermon or slip a bit along the way. No, they are people who had clear opportunity to accept Christ and to walk in the ways of righteousness. They arrogantly refused the life of God and gave themselves over to wickedness and evil. They will live in torment for all eternity. In the end, more people will be with the Lord than will go to hell (for an explaination of this statement, see my book, *Unexpected Fire*).

GOD ALMIGHTY COMES TO JERUSALEM

Finally, the eternal purposes of God will be revealed. All this time, God was looking for and preparing a new headquarters for heaven. Did Jesus not teach His disciples to pray a prayer about this phenomenon?

"Our Father in heaven, hallowed be your name, *your kingdom come*, your will be done *on earth as it is in heaven*" (Matt 6:9-10; italics added).

The Lord's kingdom will come to earth. Jesus will be already ruling in Jerusalem, but at that time something far more monumental will take place. God Almighty will come and set up His throne in Jerusalem as well. We read the following in Revelation:

"No longer will there be any curse. *The throne of God* and of the Lamb *will be in the city*, and his servants will serve him. *They will see his face*, and his name will be on their foreheads" (Rev. 22:3-4; italics added).

For the first time since Adam and Eve, people will be able to see the face of God Almighty and live. Before this time, no person could see God and live because of Adam's sin and the curse it brought. Finally, that curse will be totally removed, and we will see God Almighty. To see God's face will be so amazing; it will be the greatest moment in the history of humanity.

God will come and set up His throne alongside of Jesus in the earthly city of Jerusalem. He will put His name on the foreheads of all of His people, and we will serve Him forever. Once again the focus is placed on the city of the Jews. They will serve the Almighty and Jesus at close range, but all of the people on the earth will serve God and the Lamb from that time and forevermore.

THE GLORY OF ALL HIS SAINTS

The earth will be filled with the glory of the Lord as the waters cover the sea. There will be no pain or crying, and the former things will pass away. Every person will become like Jesus, having supernatural ability and godly character.

People will change even more than that. They will move to be in line with the nature and character of God. He is Eternal, He is Love, and He is the Creator. In that regard we will be like Him. That means we will live forever, in unity and harmony with the Lord and with His people. We will also become extremely creative. Humans have always been explorers, inventors and even creators, but these attributes will move to a new and improved level in eternity. Soon, the world will be too small, and I imagine the Lord Almighty and the Lamb will send us on assignments to the farthest reaches of the universe. We will explore, discover, conquer and manage many worlds beyond our own. I am sure we will always return to this planet we call Earth, because this will be our homebase. The Almighty and the Lamb have chosen this planet, and the throne of God and of the Lamb will be in Jerusalem.

I trust that after reading this book you will look at Jerusalem and the Holy Land with different eyes. Now you understand more of the untold story. Now you know why Jerusalem is so precious to God and why He chose this ragtag group of people that we call the Jews. Now you know why the devil wants to annihilate them and why he will never be able to do it. With this understanding, the following Scripture is all the more meaningful:

"If I forget you, O Jerusalem, may my right hand forget its skill. May my tongue cling to the roof of my mouth if I do not remember you, if I do not consider Jerusalem my highest joy" (Ps. 137:5-6).

MORE REVELATION IS COMING

Much more revelation about the last days is coming to the Church. This knowledge has been sealed by God until the end. The last days are approaching, so get ready for the Scriptures to open and revelation on this subject to increase more than ever before. The Lord told the following to Daniel:

> *Multitudes who sleep in the dust of the earth will awake: some to everlasting life ... Those who are wise will shine like the brightness of the heavens, and those who lead many to righteousness, like the stars for ever and ever ... close up and seal the words of this scroll* until the time of the end ... None of the wicked will understand, but those who are wise will understand ... *"As for you, go your way till the end. ... you will rise to receive your allotted inheritance. (Dan. 12:1-13; emphasis added)*

At the time of the end, the seal of knowledge will be opened, and we will understand what the wicked cannot see. We will discover the glories of the Lord and His end-time plans. Do not get stuck in past revelation about the last days. If you do, you will be left behind, intellectually and spiritually speaking. Open your heart, for the Lord is releasing new revelation. Get ready for the miracles, the prophecies, the prayers and the revelations. These are great days, and you have been chosen by God to be included in them. Lift up your heads, oh ye gates, and the King of glory will come in. Look to Israel for the signs of the end. Bless her and you will blessed.

ENDNOTES

1   Richard Attenborough, Shadowlands, Film, a Sovoy Pictures
    Release, HBO Video, New York.
2   Peter Wyns, Unexpected Fire, Great Reward Publishing, Rock Hill,
    SC, Copyright 2007, ISBN: 13: 978-0-9793394-1-7.
3   Peter Wyns, Great Reward Publishing, Rock Hill, SC, copyright
    2008, ISBN: 13:978-0-9771633-2-8.
4   John P. McTernan, As America Has Done To Israel, pg. 83.
    Whitaker House, New Kensington, PA, 2006 -2008 - ISBN:
    978-1-60374-038-8
5   John P. McTernan, As America Has Done To Israel, pg. 83.
    Whitaker House, New Kensington, PA, 2006 - 2008 - ISBN:
    978-1-60374-038-8
6   John P. McTernan, As America Has Done To Israel, pg. 87.
    Whitaker House, New Kensington, PA, 2006 - 2008 - ISBN:
    978-1-60374-038-8
7   John P. McTernan, As America Has Done To Israel, pg. 88.
    Whitaker House, New Kensington, PA, 2006, 2008 - ISBN:
    978-1-60374-038-8
8   John P. McTernan, As America Has Done To Israel, pg. 98.
    Whitaker House, New Kensington, PA, 2006 - 2008 - ISBN:
    978-1-60374-038-8
9   John P. McTernan, As America Has Done To Israel, pg. 99.
    Whitaker House, New Kensington, PA, 2006 - 2008 - ISBN:
    978-1-60374-038-8
10 John P. McTernan, As America Has Done To Israel, pg. 99.
    Whitaker House, New Kensington, PA, 2006 - 2008 - ISBN:
    978-1-60374-038-8
11 Barbara Yaffe, Vancouver Sun Article – Tiny Country Scores a Big

Coup, Monday May 17, 2010, filed under Israel, OECD, Canada Israel Committee

12 List of Jewish Nobel laureates, From Wikipedia, the free encyclopedia –on-line

13 (As America Has Done to Israel, by John P. Mc Ternan, 2008, Whitaker House, PA, USA. ISBN: 978-1-60374-038-8, pg 116)

14 (The Letter of Barnabas, 4:6-7; FCCH, Apostolic Fathers, p. 195, as cited by Edward H. Flannery, The Anguish of the Jews: Twenty-Three Centuries of Antisemitism, Paulist Press, New York/Mahwah, 1985, p. 34)

15 (Augustine 354-430) (Transcript of a talk by Olga Marshall (Lydia Research Advisor), Swanwick, England, May 1997, p. 7)

16 (Olga Marshall p.7)

17 (Quoted in Malcolm Hay, The Roots of Christian Anti-Semitism, Liberty Press, New York, 1981, p.27, as cited by Michael L. Brown, Our Hands are Stained With Blood: The Tragic Story of the Church and the Jewish People, Destiny Image Publishers, Shippensburg, 1992, p.11.)

18 (Ibid., pp.68-69; also Dr. William James Broadway, Has the Church Fallen Under a Curse? Broadway Ministries, Edmonton, Alberta, Canada, p. 16)

19 (also Ibid., as mentioned above, p.70)

20 (Ibid., as above, p. 93)

21 (David Rausch, A Legacy of Hatred; Why Christians Must Not Forget the Holocaust, Baker, Grand Rapids, 1990, p. 27, and Robert Payne, The Dream and the Tomb: A History of the Crusades, Dorset Press, New York, 1984, pp. 102-103, as cited by Brown, pp.206-207)

22 (Flannery as above p. 95)

23 (Flannery, as prior, p. 98, 119)

24 (Ibid., as previous p.119)

25 (Petrus aberardus, Dialogus inter Philosophum, Judaeum, et Christianum (PL, 178:1617-18), as cited by Flannery, pp. 142-143.)

26 (Hans Kuhner, Der Antisemitism der Kirche, Verlag Die Waage, Zurich, 1976, p.108)

27 (Flannery, as prior, p.109, 111)

28 (Flannery, as prior, p.107)

29 (Ibid., as prior, p.112)

30 (Ibid., as prior, p.135)

31 (Flannery, as prior, p.137)

32 (Brown, as prior, p.78)

33 (Ibid., as prior, p.139-140)

34 (John Hagee, Should Christians Support Israel?, Dominion Pub-
    lishers, San Antonio, 1987, p.167, cited by Broadway, p. 35)

35 (Martin Luther, Concerning the Jews and Their Lies, reprinted in
    Talmage, Disputation and Dialogue, pp.34-36, as cited by Brown,
    pp.14-15)

36 (Ibid., as prior, p.157)

37 (Werner Keller, Und Wurden Zerstreut Unter Alle Volker: Die
    Nachbiblische Geschichite Des Judischen Volkes, Evangelische
    Buchgemeinde Stuttgart, Droemersche Verlagsanstalt Th. Knaur
    Nachf., Munich/Zurich, 1966, pp. 330-331)

38 (Ibid., as prior, p.158)

39 (Ibid, as prior, p.172)

40 (Ibid., as prior, p.189-190)

41 (Ibid., as prior, p.191, 272)

42 (Prophecy Today, The Park, Moggerhanger, Beds., MK44 3RW,
    England, Vol.5, No.1, Jan./Feb. 1989, pp.12-13. See also None is
    Too Many, p.32, and Martin Gilbert 9author of The Holocaust:
    A History of the Jews of Europe During the Second World War,
    Henry Holt, New York, 1985, in Final journey: The Fate of the
    Jews in Nazi Europe, Mayflower Books, New York, and George
    Allen & Unwin, London, 1979, pp. 1-9)

43 (Flannery, as prior, p.295)

44 JNN News – JERUSALEM-ON-THE-LINE, News Update, May
    2nd 2010, 1:34 AM, - contact address, PO Box 7411, Jerusalem
    91073, Israel

45 www.Foxnews.com, May 3, 2010 – website, news article by Lee
    Ross

46 "Righteous King Josiah," by Fr. Josiah Trenham at St Andrew
    Orthodox Church, Riverside CA.

47 Hymns of Glorious Praise, By William Cowper, 1731-1800, Gospel Publishing House, Springfield, Missouri, USA, 1969, pg 95

48 Iain H. Murray, *The Puritan Hope; Revival and Interpretation of Prophecy*, (publishers, 3 Murrayfield Rd. Edinburgh, UK), 113.

49 Iain H. Murray, *The Puritan Hope; Revival and Interpretation of Prophecy*, (publishers, 3 Murrayfield Rd. Edinburgh, UK), 113.

50 Iain H. Murray, *The Puritan Hope; Revival and Interpretation of Prophecy*, (publishers, 3 Murrayfield Rd. Edinburgh, UK), 113.

51 Iain H. Murray, *The Puritan Hope; Revival and Interpretation of Prophecy*, (publishers, 3 Murrayfield Rd. Edinburgh, UK), 256.

52 Archpark, website, www.archpark.org.il, February, 10, 2007

53 Sid Roth, The Race To Save The World, (Lake Mary, Charisma House Publishers 2004) 129, 130

Fighting Death

Dr. Peter Wyns

If you are facing a dark battle for life or staring at hopeless impossibilities, this story is for you. From a certain death tragedy comes unbelievable recovery. From hopeless diagnosis comes a report so incredible that everyone fighting for life should read it. Too many give up without fighting, often because they lack the knowledge of how to win. Against all odds, Clarice Holden, armed with faith, fought a battle and saved the life of her husband. She would not go into the night quietly. Neither should you.

Great Reward Publishing
PO Box 36324
Rock Hill, SC 29732

Great Reward Publishing

Christians for Messiah Ministries
www.peterwyns.org
www.unexpectedfire.com
e-mail: ReachUs@peterwyns.com

Blessings or Curses

Dr. Peter Wyns

All around the world, people recognize the trauma of curses on their families. From Genesis to Revelation, the Bible speaks of blessings and curses. Many Christians are living with unreasonable pain and turmoil; families are plagued with troubles and catastrophic problems, and to them, it does not make sense! This book brings to light the truths about blessings and curses. It will teach you how to bless your children, how to break curses, and how to minister to people's deeper problems.

Great Reward Publishing
PO Box 36324
Rock Hill, SC 29732

Great Reward Publishing

Christians for Messiah Ministries
www.peterwyns.org
www.unexpectedfire.com
e-mail: ReachUs@peterwyns.com

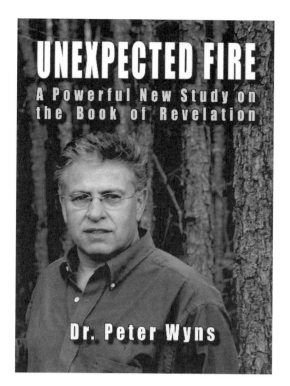

Unexpected Fire

Dr. Peter Wyns

Finally it is here, a teaching on the book of Revelation that makes sense from start to finish. For students of end-time studies, this book will bring a truck load of new understanding. It challenges popular beliefs with amazing details backed up by hundreds of scriptures. This thrilling study will inspire and embolden every believer who is longing to see the church's finest hour. You will not want to put this book down until you pass it on as a precious treasure to someone else.

Great Reward Publishing
PO Box 36324
Rock Hill, SC 29732

Great Reward Publishing

Christians for Messiah Ministries
www.peterwyns.org
www.unexpectedfire.com
e-mail: ReachUs@peterwyns.com

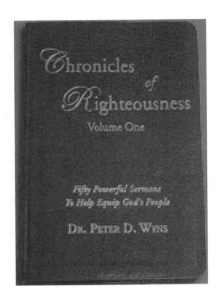

Chronicles of Righteousness Vol. 1

Dr. Peter Wyns

In 2005, Dr. Peter Wyns began producing a new series of special teaching letters called Instructions in Righteousness. Right from the very start, reports and testimonies came to us with words of thanksgiving and gratitude. We have compiled the first 50 teachings of Instructions in Righteousness in this beautiful special edition book. This book is designed with a genuine bonded leather cover and gold edging. It is a Special Limited Edition with only 500 copies printed.

Great Reward Publishing
PO Box 36324
Rock Hill, SC 29732

Great Reward Publishing

Christians for Messiah Ministries
www.peterwyns.org
www.unexpectedfire.com
e-mail: ReachUs@peterwyns.com